Study Guide
for use with

Understanding

Second Edition
Economics
A Contemporary Perspective

Prepared by

Mark Lovewell
Ryerson University

Brenda Gayle-Anyiwe
Seneca College

McGraw-Hill Ryerson

Toronto   Montréal   Boston   Burr Ridge, IL   Dubuque, IA   Madison, WI   New York
San Francisco   St. Louis   Bangkok   Bogotá   Caracas   Kuala Lumpur   Lisbon   London
Madrid   Mexico City   Milan   New Delhi   Santiago   Seoul   Singapore   Sydney   Taipei

McGraw-Hill
Ryerson Limited
A Subsidiary of The **McGraw·Hill** Companies

STUDY GUIDE
for use with
Understanding Economics
Second Edition

ISBN: 0-07-089150-8

1 2 3 4 5 6 7 8 9 10 JFM 0 9 8 7 6 5 4 3 2

Printed and bound in Canada

Vice President and Editorial Director: Pat Ferrier
Senior Sponsoring Editor: Lynn Fisher
Developmental Editor: Maria Chu
Marketing Manager: Kelly Smyth
Supervising Editor: Carrie Withers
Production Coordinator: Madeleine Harrington
Printer: J. F. Moore Lithographers, Inc.

Table of Contents

Preface

This study guide, for students using the 2nd edition of *Understanding Economics*, has a range of features to enhance your understanding of text material. An introductory section, 'Working with Graphs', extends the quantitative parts of the text's Skills Resource, outlining mathematical concepts you'll apply in your economics course. Subsequent sections in the guide accompany each text chapter, containing summaries of learning objectives and chapter highlights, along with helpful hints and practice questions and answers. Questions are of various types. Fill-in-the-blank and true-and-false questions review basic chapter content. Multiple choice questions deal with important topics in more detail. Finally, short-answer questions provide in-depth focus on challenging material. At the end of the sections accompanying the first eight chapters and after the sections accompanying the remaining nine chapters, supplementary tests give added practice in working with key topics. The guide closes with ten basic economic principles you can take away from your economics course.

This guide will be a valuable tool throughout your economics course. It is meant to improve your academic performance and your enjoyment of economics as well.

Brenda Gayle-Anyiwe
Mark Lovewell

Working with Graphs

This section reviews how to draw and interpret graphs, extending the discussion found in the text's introductory Skills Resource. A picture, it is often said, is worth a thousand words. A graph pictures the way two or more variables are associated. Graphs are important in economics because its models are often expressed in numerical terms. In particular, graphs portray mathematical relationships in a readily recognizable format.

Understanding and Creating Graphs

Dimension and Scale

All graphs start with a single dimension, represented by a line. This line may be thought of as going from minus infinity to plus infinity – out to the stars and beyond. The arrowheads placed on either end of the line imply that it continues in either direction. We draw only a segment of the line, and as a useful reference, this segment customarily includes the point where the line passes through a value of zero (point *a* in Figure A). For point *a*, as well as every other point on the line, there corresponds one, and only one, number, which is the coordinate of that specific point. For example, point *b* in Figure A has a coordinate of 1, which means the point is one unit to the right of 0 along the line. Point *c* has a coordinate of -2, so it is two units to the left of 0 along the line. When plotting a line, use a ruler to ensure the appropriate scale is maintained.

Figure A: A Line

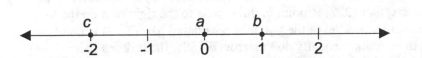

A second dimension on any graph is represented by another line, perpendicular to the first. The result, as shown in Figure B, is a two-dimensional plane, whose horizontal and vertical reference lines are called the x-axis and y-axis. Let these two lines intersect at zero. This point (point *a* in Figure B) is known as the origin. Notice that the plane is divided into four quadrants, which can be labeled counterclockwise as quadrant I, quadrant II, quadrant III and quadrant IV.

Many graphs in economics are represented solely in quadrant 1, since often economic variables can have only positive values. But when an economic variable can be negative, other quadrants are also used. For example, the use of quadrant IV is found in the text on pages 142, 149 and 172 (where negative portions of marginal revenue curves are shown); pages 308 and 309 (where negative saving is shown); and pages 242, 303 and 397 (where deflation, budget deficits, and negative net foreign assets are shown).

Figure B: A Two-Dimensional Graph

Points and Ordered Pairs

Each point on the two-dimensional graph in Figure B can be represented by an ordered pair of numbers (x, y) identifying the point's horizontal (x) and vertical (y) coordinates. For example, the origin (0,0) at point *a*, where both coordinates have a zero value, is always included. When plotting any other point, the two coordinates are used to identify the point's position relative to the origin. For example, the ordered pair (3, 2) is point *b*, three units to the right of *a* on the x-axis, and two units vertically upwards, parallel to the y-axis. The ordered pair (2, -3) is point *c*, two units to the right of *a*, and three units vertically downwards. Finally, the ordered pair (-1, -3) is point *d*, one unit to the left of *a*, and three units vertically downwards.

If a point's coordinates are too far from the origin to be presented on a page, then a break (—∿—) is included on the relevant axis. There are quite a few broken axes in the text. Look for examples on pages 70 and 272.

Functions and Curves

Most graphs portray relationships with an independent variable (the cause) and a dependent variable (the effect). A relationship is known as a function when, for each value of the independent variable, there is a unique value for the dependent variable. The demand curve D in Figure C, from page 39 of the text, is an example of a function. For each price on this curve, there is a unique quantity demanded. In other words, we can say "if price has a certain value, then quantity demanded has a certain value." Likewise, the supply curve, S, in the same graph is a function. For each price, there is a unique quantity supplied, so again we can say "if price has a certain value, then quantity supplied has a certain value."

Unlike mathematicians, economists do not always put the independent variable on the horizontal axis and the dependent variable on the vertical axis. For example, when drawing demand and supply curves, as in Figure C, price (the independent variable) is on the vertical axis, and quantity (the dependent variable) is on the horizontal axis. Similarly, when drawing aggregate demand and aggregate supply curves (as in Figure 11.9 on page 272 of the text), the price level (the independent variable) is on the vertical axis and real output (the dependent variable) is on the horizontal axis. But, other than these two important cases, the conventional mathematical practice is followed.

Figure C: Demand and Supply Curves

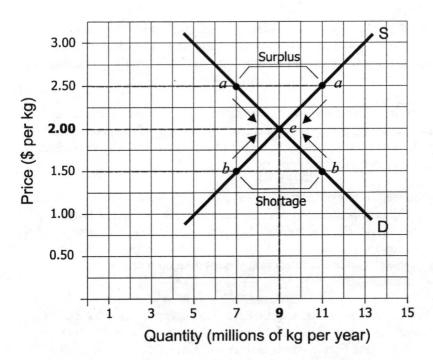

Not all graphs show functions. Time series graphs, where time is on the horizontal axis (such as Figure 10.5 on page 242 of the text), and bar graphs (such as the Figure B on page 397 of the text) are not functions showing causal relationships. But these are exceptions.

Once they are graphed, functions appear as curves, with lines defined as straight curves. A curve may decline as it moves from left to right, in which case it is downward sloping. This represents an inverse relationship between two variables, as illustrated by the demand curve in Figure C. As we move to the right along this demand curve, the decrease in the price of strawberries causes their quantity demanded to increase. In contrast, if a curve rises as it moves from left to right, it is upward sloping. This represents a direct relationship, as illustrated by the supply curve in Figure C. With a rightward move along this curve, the price of strawberries increases, which causes their quantity supplied to increase as well.

Slopes and Marginal Analysis

Calculating Slopes
When isolating two points on a curve, the vertical change between the two points is known as the "rise", while the horizontal change is the "run". The ratio of the rise over the run gives the numerical value of the curve's slope in this range.

This can be expressed in mathematical terms for any two points – (x_1, y_1) and (x_2, y_2) – on the curve. The curve's average slope between these points is found by dividing the change in the y-variable $(y_2 - y_1)$ by the change in the x variable $(x_2 - x_1)$. If a curve is downward sloping, the formula gives a negative number. For example, along Figure C's demand curve D, an increase in the vertical variable (price) from 2.00 to 2.50 causes the horizontal variable (quantity demanded) to decrease from 9 million to 7 million. This gives a negative slope, since $(y_2 - y_1)$ is positive (.50) and $(x_2 - x_1)$ is negative (-2 million). With an upward sloping curve, such as the supply curve S in Figure C, slope is positive. For example, a price increase in from 2.00 to 2.50 causes quantity demanded to increase from 7 million to 9 million, with both $(y_2 - y_1)$ and $(x_2 - x_1)$ being positive (.50 and 2 million).

For a straight line, the rise over the run is always the same, so the slope is constant. Any horizontal line, meanwhile, has a zero slope, because the slope formula's numerator (the rise) is always zero. Likewise, any vertical line has an infinite slope, because the formula's denominator (the run) is always zero.

Curves that are not straight lines are called curvilinear. The slope of these curves continually changes, as illustrated by Figure D from page 8 of the text. This is a graph of the production possibilities curve that a hypothetical economy faces in a given year when choosing to produce a combination of two products, hamburgers and computers.

The number of hamburgers produced in this economy is measured on the vertical axis (from zero to 1000 possible hamburgers), while the production of computers is measured on the horizontal axis (from zero to 3 possible computers). Each of the four highlighted points on the curve – a, b, c and d – represents a possible production combination of hamburgers and computers. When moving along the curve from point a to point d, the economy must give up more and more hamburgers to gain an additional computer.

The number of hamburgers that must be sacrificed to gain each extra computer is the absolute value of the average slope between each pair of points. For example, between a and b, 100 hamburgers must be sacrificed to gain the first computer, since the average slope is -100 (the vertical change of -100 divided by the horizontal change of 1). Meanwhile, between b and c, 300 hamburgers must be sacrificed to gain the second computer, since the average slope is -300 (the vertical change of -300 divided by the horizontal change of 1).

Figure D: A Production Possibilities Curve

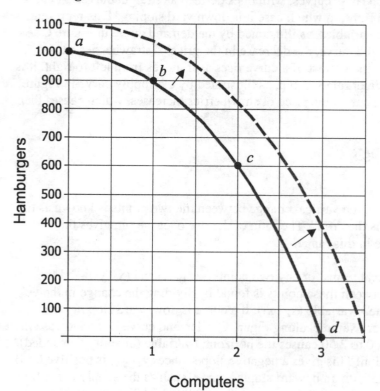

Marginal Analysis

As we have just seen, the ratio of the changes on one axis in relation to the other is useful for measuring tradeoffs along the production possibilities curve. This is an example of analysis at the margin, which focuses on changes caused by an additional unit of some variable – in this case the production of one more computer. As we will see, marginal analysis is very common in economics. In this case, we asked how many units of hamburgers were sacrificed for an extra computer. In other possible applications, we may ask how many units of output will be created by an additional unit of labour, or what will be the effect of a change in income on domestic consumption or on saving. In each of these examples, as you'll see in later chapters of the text, the marginal value is related to the slope of a particular curve.

When Curves Shift

Intercepts and Ceteris Paribus

The points where a curve meets the horizontal and vertical axes are called intercepts – the vertical y-intercept and the horizontal x-intercept. For example, in Figure D, point *a* is the y-intercept and point *d* is the x-intercept. In economics, intercepts stay constant as long as "all other things remain the same." This is based on the *ceteris paribus* assumption discussed in the text's introductory chapter. For example, for the production possibilities curve in Figure D, the curve stays in the same position (and therefore has the same intercepts) as long as resources and technology are both fixed.

Shifting Curves

Shifts occur as soon as the *ceteris paribus* assumption is loosened. For example, the economy whose production possibilities curve is portrayed in Figure D may gain more resources or experience improvements in technology in the production of both hamburgers and computers. The entire curve then shifts out and to the right, as portrayed by the dashed curve in the graph. Accompanying this shift is a change in the curve's intercepts, with the y-intercept (point *a*) moving vertically upwards, and the x intercept (point d) moving horizontally rightwards. Similarly, if the curve in Figure D were to shift down and to the left, both the intercepts would decline.

Shifting curves makes it possible to employ graphs to identify the impact of variables other than those shown on the graph's two axes. This is just one of many ways that graphs allow you to gain a fuller understanding of economic theories. The techniques reviewed in this section are all basic mathematical concepts, but they have a wide range of applications.

Fill in the Blank and True False Questions

1. A graph is a _____-dimensional representation showing the relationship between _____ variables.

2. A single dimension is represented by _____ line(s).

3. The _____ axis is the x-axis, and the _____ axis is the y-axis.

    Place the following terms in the correct order in the blanks above.

    vertical   horizontal

4. The x-axis and the y-axis intersect at the _____ which is represented by the ordered pair _____.

5. **T F** The quadrants created by the intersection of the two axes are labelled in a clockwise direction from I to IV.

6. **T F** A downward sloping curve indicates a direct relationship between two variables.

7. When a relationship is inverse, the changes in the variables are in _____ directions; when a relationship is direct the changes in the variables are in the _____ direction.

    Place the following terms in the correct order in the blanks above.

    opposite   same

8. **T F** In any ordered pair, the first number indicates the distance along the x-axis, and the second number represents the distance along the y-axis.

9. **T F** The value of the slope of a curve between two points is determined by the ratio of the run over the rise.

10. A horizontal curve has a slope of _____, while a vertical curve has a slope that is _____.

    Place the following terms in the correct order in the blanks above.

    infinite   zero

Figure 1 Use this graph to answer questions 11, 12 and 13.

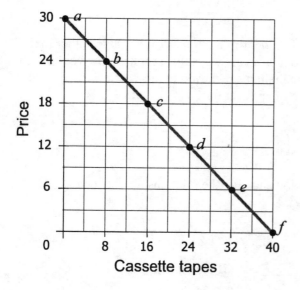

11. Figure 1 shows the relationship between the price of cassette tapes and the number of cassette tapes that a consumer buys each year. In this relationship, the price of CDs is the _____ variable and the number of cassette tapes purchased by the consumer is the _____variable.

Place the following terms in the correct order in the blanks above.

dependent   independent

12. In order to draw Figure 1, the consumer's income must be kept constant using the assumption of _____ _____.

13. The slope of the line in Figure 1 is _____.

Multiple Choice Questions

1. Which of the following is not true? A line may be:
    A. horizontal
    B. vertical
    C. downward-sloped
    D. curvilinear
    E. upward-sloped

2. Analysis that focuses on changes caused by an additional unit of some variable is known as:
    A. marginal analysis
    B. total analysis
    C. mathematical analysis
    D. average analysis
    E. economic analysis

Figure 2 Use this graph to answer questions 3 to 5.

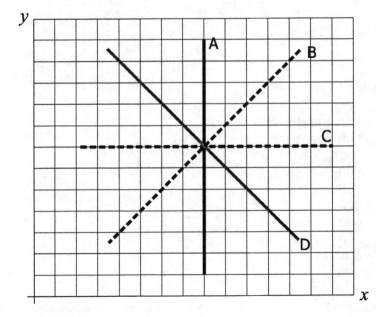

3. The slope of A is:
   A. positive
   B. negative
   C. zero
   D. infinite
   E. unknown

4. The slope of B is:
   A. positive
   B. negative
   C. zero
   D. infinite
   E. unknown

5. The slope of C is:
   A. positive
   B. negative
   C. zero
   D. infinite
   E. unknown

6. The slope of D is:
   A. positive
   B. negative
   C. zero
   D. infinite
   E. unknown

7. A straight line has a slope that is:
   A. equal to 1
   B. greater than 1
   C. less than 1
   D. less than zero
   E. always constant

Short Answer Question

Figure 3 Use this table to answer question 1.

Financing Rate (% per year)	Automobile Purchases (thousands per year)
0.6	900
0.8	800
1.0	700
1.2	600
1.4	500
1.6	400
1.8	300

1. Figure 3 shows the relationship between two variables: the financing rate and the number of automobile purchases.

a. In this relationship, which is the independent variable? the dependent variable?
b. Draw a graph portraying this relationship. Consider which variable you would place on the vertical axis. Decide on an appropriate scale. Give the graph a heading. Label the axes and add the units of measurement.
c. Is this relationship direct or inverse? Explain your answer.
d. What is the slope of this curve?
e. Does the curve you have drawn in part b shift if the rate of financing changes? Explain using the *ceteris paribus* assumption.
f. If the incomes of consumers increase, explain what will happen in the graph.

Solutions to Questions for Working with Graphs

Fill in the Blank and True False Questions
1. **two, two** The number of dimensions is the same as the number of variables.
2. **one** Again, the number of dimensions is the same as the number of variables.
3. **horizontal, vertical** This terminology is the same as found in mathematics.
4. **origin, (0,0)** This is the reference point used in plotting all other points on a two-dimensional plane
5. **F** The quadrants are labelled in a counterclockwise direction, starting from the northeast quadrant.
6. **F** A downward sloping curve indicates an inverse relationship.
7. **opposite, same**
8. **T** This is because the x-axis represents the horizontal dimension and the y-axis the vertical dimension.
9. **F** The value of slope is the ratio of the rise over the run.
10. **zero, infinite** This is because, for a horizontal line, the rise in the numerator of the slope formula is zero. In contrast, for a vertical line, the run in the denominator of the slope formula is zero.
11. **independent, dependent** Because the consumer's purchases of cassette tapes depend on their price, price is the independent variable and the number of cassette tapes purchased is the dependent variable.
12. **ceteris paribus** According to this assumption, "all other things remain the same."
13. **-0.75** Taking the line's y-intercept and x-intercept as our two points on the line, its slope is found by dividing the rise (30 - 0) by the run (0 - 40), which gives -0.75.

Multiple Choice Questions
1. **D** Lines are straight, not curvilinear.
2. **A** This is known as marginal analysis.
3. **D** This is a vertical line and therefore has an infinite slope, since the denominator of the slope formula (the run) is zero.
4. **A** This is an upward-sloping line and therefore has a positive slope, since the rise and the run both have the same sign.
5. **C** This is a horizontal line and therefore has a zero slope, since the numerator of the slope formula (the rise) is zero.
6. **B** This is a downward-sloping line and therefore has a negative slope, since the rise and the run have the opposite sign.
7. **E** The slope on a straight line may be of any value. However, it does not change.

Short Answer Question
1. a. The independent variable is the financing rate, and the dependent variable is the number of automobiles purchased.
   b.

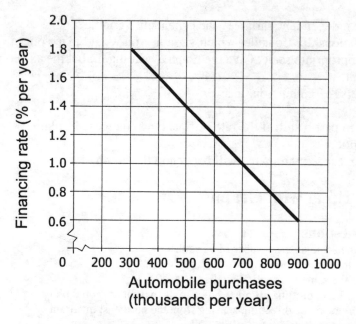

In mathematics, it is customary to place the independent variable on the horizontal axis. However, when dealing with prices and quantities, economists break with this custom and place the price variable (in this case, the financing rate) on the vertical axis and the quantity variable (in this case, the number of automobiles purchased) on the horizontal axis.

c. The relationship is inverse. As the financing rate increases, the quantity of automobiles purchased falls.

d. The slope is the rise over the run, which equals the change in the rate of financing divided by the change in automobile purchases, or -0.000002 (0.2/-100 000)

e. No. If the financing rate changes, then there will be a movement along the curve rather than a shift in the curve. This is because there is no loosening of the *ceteris paribus* assumption, what states that all other things, besides the two variables on the axis, are being held constant.

f. As incomes increase, consumers will purchase more automobiles at each price. Therefore the curve will shift up and outward.

Chapter 1

The Economic Problem

Learning Objectives

In this chapter, you will:
- consider the economic problem – the problem of having unlimited wants, but limited resources – that underlies the definition of economics
- learn about the way economists specify economic choice
- examine the production choices an entire economy faces, as demonstrated by the production possibilities model
- analyze the three basic economic questions and how various economic systems answer them

Chapter Highlights

- What Economists Do
  1. Humans have unlimited wants for products. Products are made with limited economic resources. Therefore the economic problem of scarcity is caused by the relationship between unlimited wants and limited economic resources.
  2. Economic resources are classified in three groups: natural resources, capital resources, and human resources. Natural resources include land, raw materials, and the processes of nature. Capital resources include processed materials, tools, equipment and buildings. Human resources are classified as labour or entrepreneurship. Labour is the physical and mental effort of humans. Entrepreneurship is initiative, risk-taking, and innovation.
  4. Economics is the study of how limited resources are used to satisfy unlimited human wants in the best possible way.
  5. Two main areas of economics are microeconomics and macroeconomics. Microeconomics is the study of the behaviour of individual economic units: the consumer and the firm. Macroeconomics is the study of the entire economy and its sectors: households, businesses, government, and foreign markets. Macroeconomics investigates variables such as unemployment, inflation, and total output.
  6. In the study of economics, we use models to simulate economic reality. An economic model is a simplification of economic reality. To simplify, we select the important economic features. In an economic model we use variables that can be measured, and investigate the relationships between these variables. When relationships are causal, changes in the independent variables cause changes in the dependent variables.
  7. When a dependent variable changes in the same direction as the change in an independent variable, the relationship is direct. When a dependent variable changes in the opposite direction to the change in an independent variable, the relationship is inverse.
  8. When certain variables are being investigated, economists assume all other variables remain unchanged. This is known as the *ceteris paribus* assumption.
  9. There are two types of economic inquiry: positive economics and normative economics. Positive economics investigates 'what is', while normative economics investigates 'what ought to be'.

◆ Economic Choice

1. Given scarcity, choices must be made. Choices are based on the maximization of utility and the minimization of opportunity cost. Utility measures the satisfaction gained by consumers who are acting in their self-interest. Opportunity cost is the utility lost from sacrificing the next-best alternative action in order to pursue the desired action.

2. The production possibilities model is designed to represent the basic economic concepts of scarcity, choice and opportunity cost It is based on three simplifying assumptions: two products are being produced, resources and technology are unchanged, and full production is attainable.

3. The production possibilities schedule is a table showing the combinations of the two products that may be chosen. There is an inverse relationship between the quantities of the two products. The production possibilities curve is negatively sloped and concave to the origin. The negative slope reflects opportunity cost. The concavity to the origin represents increasing opportunity cost.

4. A product's opportunity cost increases as more of the product is supplied, because resources are not fully transferable between one product and another. If one product replaces another, the more malleable resources are transferred first, while the more committed resources are used later, at greater opportunity cost.

5. All the points on the production possibilities curve are attainable and imply full production. All points inside the curve are attainable, but imply under-production or unemployment of resources. All points beyond the curve are unattainable if resources and technology remain unchanged.

6. Economic growth takes place when an improvement in technology or an increase in resources permits the curve to shift outwards, so that more of both products can be produced.

◆ Economic Systems

1. Three basic questions that must be answered by any economic system are: what to produce, how to produce, and for whom to produce.

2. An economic system represents the interaction of social customs, political institutions, and economic practices. There are three main classifications of economic systems: the traditional economy, the market economy, and the command economy. Most real-world economies are mixed economies.

3. In traditional economies, decisions are based on custom. These economies resist change and provide stability.

4. In market economies, resources are privately owned, and buyers and sellers are free to act, each in their own self-interest. A market is a set of organized trading arrangements between buyers and sellers. The operation of the market system is described by the circular flow diagram. In the circular flow diagram two types of markets are represented: product markets and resource markets. In product markets, consumer goods and services are traded, while in resource markets, economic resources are traded Product markets have households as buyers and businesses as sellers. Resource markets have households as sellers and businesses as buyers. There are two counterpoised flows in each market: spending and product flows in product markets, and income and resource flows in resource markets.

5. Market economies benefit from consumer sovereignty, price signals, and incentives to innovate. They suffer from an inequitable distribution of income; market inefficiencies; and variations in the price level, employment and output.

6. In a command economy, the government holds the resources and government planners make economic decisions. Planners can distribute income more equally and focus on

economic growth. However, planning errors cause surpluses and shortages, permit waste and inefficiency, and constrain freedoms.

7. Modern mixed economies combine features of market and command systems. The boundary between the private and public sectors is blurred as government often intervenes in the private sector. Traditional mixed economies combine a traditional sector with a private and/or public sector.

8. Economic goals reflect normative issues and require value judgements. The main economic goals of Canada are economic growth, full employment, price stability, income equity, a viable balance of payments, economic efficiency, and environmental sustainability. Some of these goals are conflicting, while others are complementary.

Helpful Hints

♦ What Economists Do
1. The premise of scarcity is fundamental to the study of economics. Scarcity arises when unlimited wants for products confront limited resources for providing these products. (See the counterargument that greed, the unrestrained desire for products, creates scarcity in "Thinking About Economics" on page 3 of the text.) Without scarcity there would be abundance, all products would be free, and we would not need to study economics!

2. An illustration of scarcity, arising from limited resources, is provided by the labour force of a country. Consider Canada. A labour force of approximately 16 million permits approximately 32 billion labour hours in a year. Therefore, with a given technology, there is a limit to the amount of products that may be produced.

3. It is most important to remember the special definition of capital in economics. Capital is fabricated or processed by human hands and is used to produce a product. Sometimes capital is called 'real capital' to ensure it is not confused with financial capital (i.e., money, stocks or bonds) which is not of itself productive.

4. The prefixes 'micro' and 'macro' are derived from Greek words – micro means small, and macro means large. The individual consumer and the firm are the small units in microeconomics; the entire economy and its sectors are the large units in macroeconomics.

5. Economic reality is complex. To comprehend this reality, we create simplifications by extracting the most essential variables and their relationships. A simple model can be used to explain many situations, so we refer to these simple models as generalizations. We 'play' with these models, much as a child plays with a toy, in order to understand reality. See the text sideline "Economics as an Art" to understand why economic models act as reference points for economists.

6. *Ceteris paribus* (meaning all other things being constant) is a logical device for making models work. If more than two variables are changing at the same time it would be difficult to determine which variable caused what response. It is easy to remember the term *ceteris paribus* because we use similar words when we say et cetera and when we use parity, meaning the same or equivalent. Notice the hard k sound of the first syllable of *ceteris paribus*, as explained on page 5 of the text.

7. Relationships are causal and can be expressed as functions. But some associations between variables, which appear to be causal relationships, are not. Remember that correlation – two variables acting in association with each other – does not always imply causation.

♦ Economic Choice

1. Economists like to reflect on the fact that opportunity cost permits the measurement of cost without referring to money. Opportunity cost is usually expressed in terms of another product. In doing this we feel that we have expressed the true nature of cost and that the production possibilities model may be applied generally to barter economies as well as economies that use money. Remember that opportunity cost is not measured by contemplating all alternative products, but by only one product – the next best.

2. The production possibilities model is the first model presented to students of economics. Its simplicity is beguiling. Notice how few assumptions are used to represent the basic, yet profound, concepts of scarcity, choice and opportunity cost.

3. It is important to remember that the production possibilities curve is a boundary representing the best that can be done. This fact is essential to understanding the model. This curve will not move unless the assumption of fixed resources and technology is released. Other names for the production possibilities curve are: production possibilities boundary, production possibilities frontier, or trade-off curve.

4. Unless increasing opportunity cost is specified, the production possibilities curve may assume either of three possible shapes: convexity to the origin, a straight line, or concavity to the origin. Convexity to the origin reflects decreasing opportunity cost, a straight line reflects constant opportunity cost, while concavity to the origin reflects increasing opportunity cost. With concavity to the origin, opportunity cost will increase, whether the direction of the movement along the curve is down or up. Most real world situations reflect increasing opportunity cost. However, decreasing opportunity cost does exist and its implications for long-run decreasing-cost industries are discussed in Chapter 3 on page 67. Constant cost is a simplifying assumption that is often used to make models more general.

5. The options at the extremes of the production possibilities curve, where all of one product and none of the other product is being produced, are as fully productive as any other option. This is so even if only hamburgers are produced – so that the entire product is consumed, or if only computers are produced – so that there is nothing to eat. Economic growth takes place whether the curve shifts outwards on one axis or on both axes. In each case, more of both products can be produced.

♦ Economic Systems

1. The production possibilities model covered in the previous section is sufficiently general to be useful for dealing with scarcity, choice and opportunity cost in any economic system, whether the system is traditional, market, command or mixed.

2. Economists have observed that while the market system emphasizes freedom, the command system provides security, and the traditional system perpetuates stability. In the market system, initiative is rewarded by incentives. Command economies disregard incentives, and traditional economies uphold customs at the expense of initiative. Mixed economies strive for an optimal blend of more than one system.

3. The circular flow diagram is designed to represent the operation of the market system. It reflects private ownership, with products and resources each owned by households, and with households and businesses pursuing their individual self-interest. A household is an economic unit of one or more people, usually living in the same dwelling. Economic decision-making is reflected in both resource and product markets.

4. We must be careful with the terms equity and equality when used to refer to income distribution. Equality means everyone receives the same income, while equity means that incomes are distributed in a fair way. To have equal incomes may be equitable – again it may not be. So the question arises: How much inequality is equitable? These

considerations surround the role of incentives in the market system and the extent to which incentives can be permitted to determine the distribution of income.

5. Efficiency is a word that is much abused. Like democracy, it is one of our "hurrah" words. It is applauded, but we seldom stop to ask exactly what it means. To be meaningful, economists must say, as do engineers, how efficiency is being measured. In the production possibilities model, efficiency means full employment and full production. Full employment means that all resources are being used. Full production means that resources are employed appropriately. Each of these conditions, by themselves, are necessary but not sufficient for economic efficiency, which is attained at any point of the production possibilities curve.

Key Concepts

economic problem
economic resources
natural resources
capital resources
labour
entrepreneurship
economics
microeconomics
macroeconomics
economic models
variables
independent variables
dependent variables
inverse relationship
direct relationship
ceteris paribus
positive economics
normative economics
utility
self-interest motive
opportunity cost

production possibilities schedule
production possibilities curve
law of increasing opportunity costs
economic growth
economic system
traditional economy
market economy
market
product markets
resource markets
consumer sovereignty
command economy
modern mixed economy
traditional mixed economies
economic efficiency
inflation
unemployment rate
balance-of-payments accounts

Fill in the Blank and True False Questions

1. The fact that human wants are virtually unlimited while economic resources are limited is known as the economic _____.

2. **T F** The shares issued by a software development company are included in capital resources, as defined in economics.

3. **T F** The number of pairs of skates sold in a given year is an example of a question studied in macroeconomics.

4. The human resource that brings together natural resources, capital resources, and labour to make products is _____.

5. A reduction in speed limits that leads to fewer highway accidents is an example of a(n) _____ relationship. A rise in the use of sunscreen products that results in fewer cases of skin cancer is an example of a(n) _____ relationship.

   Place the following terms in the correct order in the blanks above.

   inverse   direct

6. **T F** "If average incomes rise, purchases of new homes increase," is an example of a positive statement.

7. **T F** Pedro enjoys action movies over romantic movies. For Pedro, the opportunity cost of seeing an action movie is lower than for a romantic movie.

8. In product markets, _____ are buyers and _____ are sellers.

   Place the following terms in the correct order in the blanks above.

   households   businesses

9. The market for business accounting computer software is a _____ market, while the market for computer games is a _____ market.

   Place the following terms in the correct order in the blanks above.

   product   resource

10. The notion that competition transform selfish actions into socially beneficial results is known as the operation of the _____ _____, while the principle that governments should interfere as little as possible in private markets is known as _____ _____.

   Place the following terms in the correct order in the blanks above.

   laissez faire   invisible hand

Multiple Choice Questions

1. The economic problem of scarcity arises when:
   A. limited resources are used to try to satisfy limited wants
   B. unlimited resources are used to try to satisfy unlimited wants
   C. unlimited resources are used to try to satisfy limited wants
   D. limited resources are used to try to satisfy unlimited wants
   E. limited resources are used to increase the costs of wants

2. Which of the following is not an economic resource?
   A. natural resources
   B. real capital
   C. financial capital
   D. labour
   E. entrepreneurship

3. Which of the following is studied in microeconomics?
   A. the growth of an economy's total output
   B. the rate of inflation
   C. the general unemployment rate
   D. the wage paid to construction workers
   E. the consumer price index

4. Economic models are:
   A. exact replications of economic reality.
   B. used to measure economic reality.
   C. used to create a virtual economic reality.
   D. falsifications of economic reality.
   E. simplifications of economic reality.

5. Which of the following is an assumption commonly made by economists, in order to analyze a relationship between two variables?
   A. self-interest motive
   B. *ceteris paribus*
   C. utility maximization
   D. maximization of opportunity cost
   E. two products are being produced

6. Economic models are used to:
   A. explain the relationships between independent and dependent economic variables.
   B. identify the purpose of the *ceteris paribus* assumption in economics.
   C. facilitate the compilation of data by economists at Statistics Canada.
   D. predict unusual economic phenomena.
   E. present a detailed analysis of the operation of global economic markets.

7. Which of the following is a positive economic statement?
   A. The interest rate should be reduced by 1 percent to stimulate business activity.
   B. When the interest rate was decreased by 1 percent, bank loans increased by 5 percent.
   C. Interest rates on bank loans ought not to rise above 6 percent.
   D. Interest rates on bank loans should be increased by 2 percent so that banks can make a healthier profit.
   E. Interest rates should not be reduced to stimulate the economy, since a rise in government spending would be more effective.

Figure 1 Use this table to answer questions 8 to 10.

Production Scenario	Champagne (bottles)	Caviar (jars)
a	16	0
b	15	1
c	12	2
d	7	3
e	0	4

8. Figure 1 shows the production possibilities schedule for Luxuria, a country that produces only champagne and caviar. Given this schedule, which choice below represents a feasible output combination?
   A. 14 bottles of champagne and 2 jars of caviar
   B. 6 bottles of champagne and 3 jars of caviar
   C. 16 bottles of champagne and 1 jar of caviar
   D. 4 bottles of champagne and 4 jars of caviar
   E. 16 bottles of champagne and 4 jars of caviar

9. Based on Luxuria's production possibilities schedule in Figure 1 the opportunity cost for the third jar of caviar is:
   A. 3 bottles of champagne
   B. 7 bottles of champagne
   C. 1 bottle of champagne
   D. 12 bottles of champagne
   A. 5 bottles of champagne

10. In Figure 1, if Luxuria wishes to move from combination *d* to *c* it:
    A. will require more resources
    B. must improve its technology
    C. will sacrifice champagne
    D. will be less efficient
    E. will sacrifice caviar

11. The specific assumption required to draw the production possibilities frontier concave to the origin is:
    A. two products are being produced
    B. resources are fixed
    C. technology is fixed
    D. full production is attained
    E. opportunity costs are increasing

12. The opportunity cost of transferring resources from health care to education is:
    A. the resulting improvement in education
    B. the extra cost of maintaining health care
    C. the resulting decrease in health care services
    D. the extra cost of employing more teachers
    E. the resulting overtime payments to hospital staff

13. The production possibilities model can be applied to:
    A. traditional economies
    B. market economies
    C. command economies
    D. mixed economies
    E. any economy

14. Which of the following is not a feature of a pure market economy?
    A. self-interest
    B. freedom to produce and purchase products
    C. private property
    D. incentives to innovate
    E. government-maintained prices

15. Which of the following is not a major economic goal for Canadians?
    A. full employment
    B. economic efficiency
    C. a constant level of economic activity
    D. a viable balance of payments
    E. environmental sustainability

Short Answer Questions

Figure 2 Use this figure to answer question 1.

Production Scenario	Milk (litres)	Missiles
a	600 000	0
b	560 000	10
c	500 000	20
d	400 000	30
e	260 000	40
f	0	50

1. Figure 2 shows the production possibilities schedule for Defencia, a country where milk represents food and missiles represent armaments.
   a. Graph and correctly label the production possibilities curve, placing milk on the vertical axis and missiles on the horizontal axis
   b. Calculate the opportunity cost of missiles as production moves from scenarios a to *b*, *b* to *c*, *c* to *d*, *d* to *e*, and *e* to *f*. What do you observe about the opportunity cost of missiles as the production of missiles increases?
   c. Calculate the opportunity cost of milk as production moves from scenarios *f* to *e*, *e* to *d*, *d* to *c*, *c* to *b*, and *b* to *a*. What do you observe about the opportunity cost of milk as the production of milk increases?
   d. How are your observations about changes in the opportunity cost of missiles and milk reflected in the shape of the production possibilities curve?
   e. Are scenarios *a* and *f* as efficient as scenarios *b*, *c*, *d*, and *e*?
   f. With the production of 20 missiles and 300 000 litres of milk, has Defencia attained full production? If not, how can full production be attained without a reduction in the output of either good?
   g. Can Defencia produce 40 missiles and 400 000 litres of milk? Explain

h. What changes may be made in the assumptions of this model if Defencia is to produce 500 000 litres of milk and 50 missiles?

i. Suppose that foot and mouth disease decimates the cow population of Defencia and reduces by half the production of milk. What will happen to the production possibilities curve?

j. Is it possible to determine which combination of milk and missiles Defencia ought to produce?

2. Specify whether the following relationships are direct or inverse.
    a. An increase in the price of a high speed connection to the internet reduces the amount of time students spend online.
    b. A rise in the price of tomatoes raises the quantity supplied
    c. A reduction in the price of DVD players raises DVD sales.
    d. A fall in Canadians' disposable incomes reduces their consumption expenditures
    e. A decrease in Canada's inflation rate raises the international value of the Canadian dollar.

Figure 3 Use this figure to answer question 3.

Number of Workers in Factory	Output per Worker (pins per day)
1	1
10	271

3. Figure 3 shows the relationship between the number of workers in a pin factory and the daily output per worker.
    a. Using the theories of Adam Smith, explain why this relationship exists.
    b. What would be the total daily output of this factory with 1 worker? with 10 workers?
    c. Give an approximate estimate of the daily output per worker if 5 workers were employed, based on the assumption that the relationship between the number of workers in the factory and output per worker is linear. Given your estimate, what would be the total output of the factory be? Explain how you derived your estimate.

Solutions to Questions for Chapter 1

Fill in the Blank and True False Questions

1. **problem**
2. **F** In economics, capital resources are real assets such as equipment and buildings.
3. **F** This question is studied in microeconomics.
4. **entrepreneurship** This is the only economic resource not explicitly mentioned in the question.
5. **direct, inverse** The first is a direct relationship, since the two variables move in the same direction. The second is an inverse relationship, since the two variables move in opposite directions.
6. **T** This is a statement of fact that can be tested against reality.
7. **T** The utility Pedro sacrifices by missing the romantic movie is lower than the utility he sacrifices by missing the action movie.
8. **households, businesses**
9. **resource, product** Because accounting software is an input for businesses, it is traded in a resource market. In contrast, computer games are a consumer good traded in a product market.
10. **invisible hand, laissez faire** The invisible hand refers to the benefits of competitive markets, while laissez faire refers to what government should do to reap these benefits.

Multiple Choice Questions

1. **D** The use of limited resources to try to satisfy unlimited wants creates the economic problem.
2. **C** Financial capital (stocks or bonds) is not an economic resource, since it is not of itself productive.
3. **D** All of the other answers are studied in macroeconomics.
4. **E** Economic models are simplifications or generalizations of economic reality.
5. **B** *Ceteris paribus* means "all other things remaining the same."
6. **A** Economic models explain the relationships between independent and dependent economic variables. They are used to study economic behaviour.
7. **B** Positive economics is based on fact, not opinions or value judgements.
8. **B** This is a feasible combination, since it is possible to produce up to 7 bottles of champagne along with 3 jars of caviar.
9. **E** To get the third jar of caviar, the sacrifice is 5 (=12 - 7) bottles of champagne.
10. **E** In moving from points *d* to *c*, Luxuria will sacrifice 1 jar of caviar to gain 6 bottles of champagne.
11. **E** With increasing opportunity costs, each new unit of the product on the horizontal axis requires a greater sacrifice of the product on the vertical axis, giving a concave curve.
12. **C** The opportunity cost is the resulting decrease in health care services.
13. **E** The production possibilities model can be applied to any economy.
14. **E** In the pure market economy the principle of laissez faire excludes government control of prices.
15. **C** Economic growth, rather than a constant level of economic activity, is an economic goal for Canada.

Short Answer Questions

1. a.

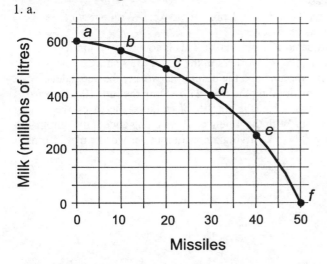

b. From *a* to *b*, 10 new missiles cost 40 000 litres of milk, which means each missile costs 4 000 (40 000/10) litres. From *b* to *c*, the corresponding cost is 6 000 (60 000/10) litres; from *c* to *d*, 10 000 (100 000/10) litres; from *d* to *e* 14 000 (140 000/10) litres, from *e* to *f* 26 000 (260 000/10) litres. Therefore, the opportunity cost of missiles rises as missile production increases.

c. From *f* to *e*, 260 000 litres of milk cost 10 missiles, which means each litre of milk costs .00004 (10/260 000) missiles. From *e* to *d*, the corresponding cost is .00007 (10/140 000) missiles; from *d* to *e*, .00010 (10/100 000) missiles; from *c* to *b* .00017 (10/60 000) missiles, from *b* to *a* .00025 (10/40 000) missiles. Therefore, the opportunity cost of milk rises as milk production increases.

d. Increasing opportunity costs are represented by a production possibilities curve that is concave to the origin. In terms of the opportunity cost of missiles, each new unit on the horizontal axis requires a greater sacrifice of milk on the vertical axis, making the curve steeper as missile production rises. In terms of the the opportunity cost of milk, each new unit on the vertical axis requires a greater sacrifice of missiles on the horizontal axis, making the curve flatter as milk production rises. Both cases can be used explain the concavity of the curve.

e. All scenarios on the curve, including *a* and *f*, are efficient, even though at *a* the country has no missiles for defence, and at *f* there is no milk for sustaining life.

f. With 20 missiles and 300 000 litres of milk Defencia is operating below its production possibilities curve and has not attained full production. Full production can be attained, without a reduction in the output of either good, by moving to 20 missiles and 500 000 litres of milk, or to 40 missiles and 300 000 litres of milk, or to any combination of milk and missiles that lies on the arc of the curve that is bounded by those options.

g. No. 40 missiles and 400 000 litres of milk lie beyond the existing production possibilities curve.

h. The changes are an increase in resources, or an improvement in technology. An improvement in technology for either or both products would result in an outward shift of the production possibilities curve and the production of more milk and/or more missiles.

i. If half the cow population were to die because of disease, the curve would shift inward along the milk axis, but not the missiles axis. The economy would produce less of both goods, unless only missiles were being produced.

j. Positive economics subscribing to the positive approach cannot determine which combination of milk and missiles to produce. The decision would involve a normative approach, with the expression of value judgements.

2a. inverse

b. direct

c. inverse

d. direct

e. inverse

3a. As the number of workers at this factory increases, tasks can be specialized through the division of labour. The result is that output per worker is increased.

b. With one worker, the factory's daily output is 1 pin (1 worker x 1 pin per worker). With ten workers, daily output rises to 2710 pins (10 workers x 271 pins per worker).

c. With 5 workers, each worker will produce an estimated 121 pins daily. This is found by assuming that the relationship between output per worker and the number of workers in the factory is a straight line, with the number of workers in the factory the independent variable and the output per worker the dependent variable. The slope of this line is 30, which is found by dividing the rise (271 - 1) by the run (10 - 1), or 270/9. This means that for every unit the independent variable (the number of workers) increases, the dependent variable (output per worker) increases by 30. With the 4 new workers being added, the output per worker should therefore rise by approximately 120 (4 x 3), giving a new output per worker of 121 pins and a new total output of 605 pins (5 x 121).

Chapter 2

Demand and Supply

Learning Objectives

In this chapter, you will:
- consider the nature of demand, changes in quantity demanded, changes in demand, and factors that affect demand
- examine the nature of supply, changes in quantity supplied, changes in supply, and the factors that affect supply
- see how markets reach equilibrium—the point at which demand and supply meet

Chapter Highlights

- The Role of Demand
    1. A product market exists when households and businesses demand and supply products.
    2. Demand is the relationship between the prices of a product and the quantity consumers will purchase at these prices. While the demand schedule specifies the combinations of prices and quantities demanded in a table, the demand curve shows these combinations in a graph. Market demand is the sum of the quantities demanded for all consumers at various prices.
    3. The law of demand states that there is an inverse relationship between price and quantity demanded. The negative slope of the demand curve reflects the law of demand.
    4. A change in the price of a product causes a change in quantity demanded. This change is shown by a movement along the existing demand curve. All other factors affecting the amount demanded are assumed to remain the same, i.e., the ceteris paribus assumption is invoked.
    5. When other factors known as demand determinants change, these cause a change in demand. This change is shown by a shift of the entire demand curve. A rightward shift is an increase in demand, while a leftward shift is a decrease in demand. The five main demand determinants are the number of buyers in the market, the average income of buyers, the prices of other products, consumer preferences, and consumer expectations about prices and incomes.
    6. There are two cases related to changes in average income: normal products and inferior products. A normal product is one whose demand changes directly with the change in income. An inferior product is one whose demand changes inversely with the change in income. There are two cases related to changes in the price of other products: substitute products and complementary products. Two products are substitutes when demand for one changes directly with the change in the price of the other. Two products are complements when demand for one changes inversely with the change in the price of the other.

- The Role of Supply
    1. Supply is the relationship between the prices of a product and the quantity businesses supply at these prices. While the supply schedule specifies the combinations of prices and quantities supplied in a table, the supply curve shows these combinations on a graph. The

law of supply states that there is a direct relationship between price and quantity supplied. The positive slope of the supply curve reflects the law of supply

2. A change in the price of a product causes a change in quantity supplied. This change is shown by a movement along the existing supply curve. All other factors affecting the amount supplied are assumed to remain the same, i.e., the ceteris paribus assumption is used.

3. When other factors known as supply determinants change, these changes cause a shift of the supply curve. A rightward shift is an increase in supply, while a leftward shift is a decrease in supply.

4. The six main supply determinants are the number of producers, resource prices, the state of technology, changes in nature, the prices of related products, and producer expectations.

♦ How Competitive Markets Operate
1. In a competitive market, buyers and sellers interact. Interaction is resolved at market equilibrium. Market equilibrium is the price at which quantity demanded equals quantity supplied. This equilibrium price is found where the demand and supply curves intersect.

2. At a price above equilibrium, quantity supplied is greater than quantity demanded, resulting in a surplus. At a price below equilibrium, quantity supplied is less than quantity demanded, resulting in a shortage.

3. Surpluses cause equilibrium price to fall. Shortages cause equilibrium price to rise. Adjustments in price continue until equilibrium is attained.

4. An increase in demand (i.e., a rightward shift of the demand curve) will cause a shortage. As a result, equilibrium price and quantity will increase as buyers and sellers respond to this shortage. A decrease in demand (i.e., a leftward shift of the demand curve) will cause a surplus. As a result, equilibrium price and quantity will decrease as buyers and seller respond to this surplus.

5. An increase in supply (i.e., a rightward shift of the supply curve) will cause a surplus. Equilibrium price will decrease and equilibrium quantity will increase as buyers and sellers respond to this surplus. A decrease in supply (i.e., a leftward shift of the supply curve) will cause a shortage. Equilibrium price will increase and equilibrium quantity will decrease as buyers and sellers respond to this shortage.

Helpful Hints

♦ The Role of Demand
1. Terminology is important. Understand, and use appropriately, the distinction between "a change in quantity demanded" and "a change in demand." Not to do so is considered a major error by economists. Remember that a change in quantity demanded is caused by a change in the product's own price, while a change in demand is caused by changes in demand determinants.

2. Remember that a change in quantity demanded involves a movement along an existing demand curve, while a change in demand involves a shift of the entire demand curve.

3. Use of the ceteris paribus assumption is essential. The impact of a change in any variable on demand can only be assessed if all other variables are unchanged.

4. The demand determinants are best learnt, so that you can determine quickly whether or not a change in a variable will shift the demand curve.

♦ The Role of Supply
1. Again, terminology is important. Make the distinction between "a change in quantity supplied" and "a change in supply." Recall that a change in quantity supplied is caused by a change in the product's own price, while a change in supply is caused by changes in supply determinants.
2. A change in quantity supplied involves a movement along an existing supply curve, while a change in supply involves a shift of the entire supply curve.
3. As before, the ceteris paribus assumption is used to isolate the impact of the variable that changes, as all other variables are assumed constant.
4. Again, it is best to learn the supply determinants. You will then be sure to use only a supply determinant to shift the supply curve.

♦ How Competitive Markets Work
1. The market model is an exercise in analytical thought. When the role of demand is being considered, all aspects of supply are assumed ceteris paribus. Similarly, when the role of supply is being considered, all aspects of demand are assumed ceteris paribus. This keen separation of the two components of the market prevents us from making often heard mistakes, such as "Demand increased, therefore supply increased."
2. Having analyzed the two separate market components, demand and supply, we then combine both components. This enables us to arrive at the equilibrium price that clears the market, i.e., where quantity supplied equals quantity demanded.
3. To attain a new equilibrium position, a change in demand is accompanied by a change in quantity supplied. The demand curve shifts, and there is a movement along the supply curve towards a new equilibrium. Similarly, a change in supply is accompanied by a change in quantity demanded. The supply curve shifts, and there is a movement along the demand curve towards a new equilibrium. See the section on Thinking About Economics" on page 41.
4. The competitive market model is a simplification, so we must not expect it to always conform to reality. We should remember that it is based on the assumptions of the market economy outlined in the text's introductory chapter. These assumptions are private ownership of resources, freedom to exercise self-interest, dependence on markets and prices, and laissez faire.
5. A most important assumption of the market model discussed in Chapter 2 is that of competition. In business, competition may imply outwitting a business opponent to increase market share. In economics, competition means a large number of buyers. It is all these buyers and sellers who move the market from positions of disharmony to one of harmony where, at equilibrium price, quantity demanded equals quantity supplied.

Key Concepts

demand	supply
quantity demanded	quantity supplied
law of demand	market supply
demand schedule	law of supply
demand curve	supply schedule
change in quantity demanded	supply curve
market demand	change in quantity supplied
demand determinants	supply determinants
increase in demand	increase in supply
decrease in demand	decrease in supply
normal products	market equilibrium
inferior products	surplus
substitute products	shortage
complementary products	

Fill in the Blanks and True False Questions

1. **T F** The demand curve and demand schedule are different ways of representing the same information.

2. The inverse relationship that exists between a product's price and the amount that consumers choose to purchase is known as the _____ _____ _____.

3. When all consumers' quantity demanded for a given product are summed at all possible prices, the result is _____ demand.

4. If purchases of computer games decline when their price is constant, there has been a decrease in the _____ of computer games.

5. When consumer incomes fall, the demand for normal products _____, while demand for inferior products _____.

   Place the following terms in the correct order in the blanks above.

   increases   decreases

6. Skis and ski boots are _____ products.

7. **T F** The demand for photographic film falls when the price of cameras drops.

8. **T F** The demand for cheddar cheese increases when the price of mozzarella cheese drops.

9. Supply is shown in a table using a _____ _____, and in a graph using a _____ _____.

10. In a supply relationship, price is the _____ variable and quantity supplied is the _____ variable.

Place the following terms in the correct order in the blanks above.

independent   dependent

11. **T F** The supply of cod decreases when the price of fishing boats rises.

12. The point where price and quantity remain constant in a competitive market is known as market _____.

13. **T F** At market equilibrium, neither surpluses nor shortages can exist.

14. Price falls whenever price is above its equilibrium level, causing quantity demanded to _____ and quantity supplied to _____.

Place the following terms in the correct order in the blanks above.

increase   decrease

15. **T F** A shortage of oranges will cause the price of oranges to increase.

Multiple Choice Questions

1. An increase in quantity demanded is represented by:
   A. a rightward shift of the demand curve
   B. a downward movement along the existing demand curve
   C. a leftward shift of the demand curve
   D. the increase in supply which is caused by the increase in quantity demanded
   E. an upward movement along the existing demand curve

2. Which of the following determinants explains why the demand for ice-cream varies between summer and winter?
   A. consumer preferences
   B. consumer incomes
   C. prices of other products
   D. consumer expectations about prices
   E. increased supply to consumers

3. Fresh salmon is a normal product if:
   A. the demand for this product increases when incomes decrease
   B. the quantity demanded of this product increases when incomes increase
   C. the demand for this product increases when the price of asparagus, a complement, decreases
   D. the demand for this product increases when incomes increase
   E. the demand for this product increases when the price of lobster, a substitute, increases

4. In the market for pasta, which of the following will cause the demand curve to shift to the right?
   A. a decrease in the price of potatoes, a substitute
   B. an increase the price of tomatoes, a complement
   C. a decrease in the number of buyers
   D. an increase in the price of pasta
   E. research finding that pasta promotes good health and longevity

5. The amount of wheat grown by Canadian farmers rises when wheat prices increase. This illustrates:
   A. an increase in supply
   B. the law of supply
   C. a decrease in supply
   D. a change in expectations
   E. a change in technology

6. Along a given supply curve for strawberries, the following are held constant with the exception of:
   A. the number of strawberry farms
   B. the price of land for growing strawberries
   C. expectations that the price of strawberries will rise
   D. the price of strawberries
   E. the number of buyers of strawberries

Figure 1   Use this graph to answer questions 7 and 8.

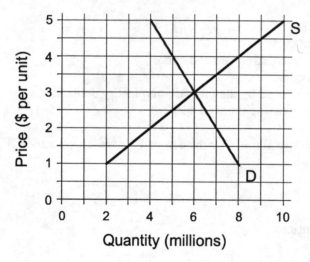

7. In Figure 1 above, what is the equilibrium quantity in this market?
   A. 2 million
   B. 3 million
   C. 4 million
   D. 6 million
   E. 8 million

8. In Figure 1 above, what is the equilibrium price in this market?
   A. $1.00
   B. $2.00
   C. $3.00
   D. $4.00
   E. $5.00

9. A surplus exists when:
   A. quantity demanded is greater than quantity supplied
   B. the demand curve is above the supply curve at a given quantity level
   C. price is below equilibrium price
   D. the demand curve is below the supply curve at a given quantity level
   E. quantity demanded is less than quantity supplied

10. A rise in the price of chicken causes which of the following effects in the market for beef?
    A. equilibrium price and quantity both fall
    B. equilibrium price and quantity both rise
    C. equilibrium price rises and equilibrium quantity falls
    D. equilibrium price falls and equilibrium quantity rises
    E. equilibrium price remains the same and equilibrium quantity increases

11. A fall in consumer incomes causes which of the following effects in the market for beef?
    A. equilibrium price and quantity both fall
    B. equilibrium price and quantity both rise
    C. equilibrium price rises and equilibrium quantity falls
    D. equilibrium price falls and equilibrium quantity rises
    E. equilibrium price remains the same and equilibrium quantity falls

12. Preferences for vegetarian diets cause one of the following effects in the market for beef:
    A. equilibrium price and quantity both fall
    B. equilibrium price and quantity both rise
    C. equilibrium price rises and equilibrium quantity falls
    D. equilibrium price falls and equilibrium quantity rises
    E. equilibrium price remains the same and equilibrium quantity falls

13. A fall in the price of cattle feed causes which of the following effects in the market for beef?
    A. equilibrium price and quantity both fall
    B. equilibrium price and quantity both rise
    C. equilibrium price rises and equilibrium quantity falls
    D. equilibrium price falls and equilibrium quantity rises
    E. equilibrium price remains the same and equilibrium quantity increases

14. The price of CD players will increase if:
    A. the supply of CD players increases
    B. the price of CDs, a complement, decreases
    C. there is a surplus of CD players
    D. the demand for CD players decreases
    E. the technology of CD players is improved

15. Foot and mouth disease, and the resulting reduction of the sheep population, causes the following effects in the market for wool:
    A. equilibrium price and quantity both fall
    B. equilibrium price and quantity both rise
    C. equilibrium price rises and equilibrium quantity falls
    D. equilibrium price falls and equilibrium quantity rises
    E. equilibrium price remains the same and equilibrium quantity falls

Short Answer Questions

Figure 2   Use this table to answer question 1.

Price per bagel	Quantity Demanded (bagels per week)			Quantity Demanded in market (bagels per week)
	Renata	Sheila	Li	
$0.30	1	0	0	_____
0.25	2	1	0	_____
0.20	3	2	0	_____
0.15	4	3	1	_____
0.10	5	4	2	_____
0.05	6	5	3	_____

1. Renata, Mila and Li are the only three consumers in the market for bagels. They have demand schedules as specified in Figure 2 above.
   a. On one pair of axes, draw the individual demand curves (D_r, D_s, and D_l) for Renata, Sheila, and Li.
   b. Complete the column for the quantity demanded in the market for bagels, and on a separate pair of axes, draw the market demand schedule (D_m) for bagels.
   c. What is the relationship between the price of bagels and the quantity demanded of bagels? What law specifies this relationship?
   d. How does the market demand curve for bagels compare with the three individual demand curves for bagels? Explain.

Figure 3   Use this table to answer question 2.

Price per kg.	Quantity Demanded (millions of kg. per year) (D_m)	Quantity Supplied (millions of kg. per year) (S_m)	Surplus (+) or Shortage (-)
$2.50	10	55	_____
2.25	15	45	_____
2.00	20	35	_____
1.75	25	25	_____
1.50	30	15	_____
1.25	35	5	_____

2. Figure 3 above shows the market demand and supply schedules for blueberries.
   a. What is the relationship between the price of blueberries and the quantity supplied of blueberries? What law specifies this relationship?
   b. Complete the column for surpluses and shortages.
   c. What is the equilibrium price of blueberries? the equilibrium quantity?
   d. At a price of $2.25, what occurs in this market?
   e. At a price of $1.25, what occurs in this market?

3. Explain the effect of the following events on demand and supply in the market for bananas.
   a. A banana blight destroys half of the banana trees in the tropics.
   b. A medical report suggests that bananas are an excellent remedy for digestive ailments.
   c. A new, fast-growing variety of bananas has been genetically engineered.
   d. The price of chocolate increases and growers transfer resources from bananas to the production of cocoa for chocolate.

4. Indicate the impact on the change in equilibrium price and quantity when each of the following events occur.
   a. Supply increases and demand is unchanged.
   b. Supply decreases and demand is unchanged.
   c. Demand increases and supply is unchanged.
   d. Demand decreases and supply is unchanged.

Solutions to Questions for Chapter 2

Fill in the Blank and True False Questions

1. **T** The schedule can be used to plot the curve, and the coordinate of the points on the curve can be used to create the schedule.
2. **law of demand**
3. **market**
4. **demand** Don't confuse this with a decrease in quantity demanded, which is caused by a rise in a product's own price.
5. **decreases, increases** Since the demand for normal products varies directly with consumer incomes, a drop in income leads to a fall in their demand. In contrast, a drop in consumer incomes causes a rise in the demand for inferior products, because their demand varies inversely with incomes.
6. **complementary** Because these items are consumed together, they are complementary products. (By the way, notice the spelling of this term. These goods are not complimentary, since this would mean they were free!)
7. **F** Cameras and film are complementary products, so there is a negative relationship between the change in the price of cameras and the change in demand for film.
8. **F** Because these two types of cheese are substitute products, a drop in the price of mozzarella means that consumers will buy more mozzarella and less cheddar.
9. **supply schedule, supply curve** Schedules are always shown in tables and curves in graphs.
10. **independent, dependent** Because price determines quantity supplied, price is the independent variable and quantity supplied is the dependent variable.
11. **T** A rise in a resource price means producers who use the resource will produce less than before.
12. **equilibrium**
13. **T** Surpluses and shortages occur only when a competitive market has yet to reach equilibrium.
14. **increase, decrease** The trends highlighted in the question ensure that quantities demanded and supplied converge on the equilibrium quantity.

15. **T** A shortage of oranges means that buyers will bid up the price of this product.

Multiple Choice Questions

1. **B** A downward movement along the negatively sloped demand curve is an increase in quantity demanded.
2. **A** For goods such as ice-cream, consumer preferences vary between summer and winter.
3. **D** Products for which demand changes directly with changes in income are known as normal products.
4. **E** If it is reported that pasta promotes good health, consumer preferences for pasta will be reflected in a rightward shift of the demand curve for this product.
5. **B** The law of supply specifies a direct relationship between a change in a product's own price and a change in quantity supplied.
6. **D** The price of strawberries is the only variable that causes a movement along a given supply curve for strawberries.
7. **D** This is where quantity demanded equals quantity supplied.
8. **C** Equilibrium price is the price at which quantity demanded equals quantity supplied.
9. **E** The surplus is the excess of quantity supplied over quantity demanded.
10. **B** This is because the rise in the price of chicken, a substitute for beef, leads to an increase (rightward shift) is the demand for beef, causing both equilibrium price and quantity to increase.
11. **A** A fall in consumer incomes leads to a decrease (leftward shift) in demand for a normal product such as beef, causing both equilibrium price and quantity to decrease.
12. **A** In the beef market, the demand curve shifts to the left as demand decreases.
13. **D** A drop in the price of a resource used in beef production (cattle feed) leads to an increase (rightward shift) in the supply of beef, reducing equilibrium price and raising equilibrium quantity.
14. **B** If the price of CDs decreases, then the demand for CD players will increase. With a given supply curve, the resulting shortage will cause the price of CD players to increase.
15. **C** A leftward shift of the supply curve results in an increase in equilibrium price and a decrease in equilibrium quantity.

Short Answer Questions

1. a.

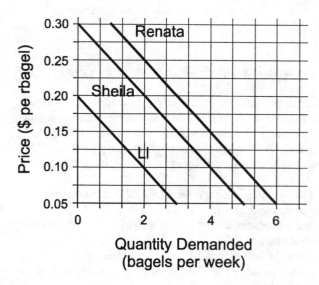

b. Summing across, the market demand schedule is 1, 3, 5, 8, 11, 14.

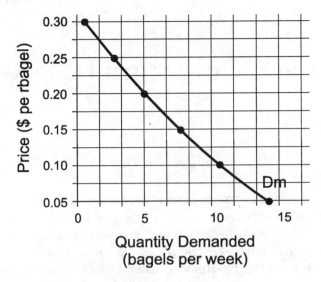

c. As the price of bagels falls, the quantity demanded increases. The relationship is inverse, as specified by the law of demand.

d. Except at the price range between $0.30 and $0.25, when there is only one buyer in the market, the market demand curve is flatter than the individual demand curves, since it is the horizontal summation of these curves.

2. a. As the price of blueberries rises, the quantity supplied increases. The relationship is direct, as specified by the law of supply.

b. Summing across, the surpluses and shortages are (in millions) +45, +30, +15, 0, -15, -30.

c. The equilibrium price is $1.75, and the equilibrium quantity is 25 million kg.

d. At a price of $2.25, there is a surplus of blueberries, with quantity supplied (45 million kg.) exceeding quantity demanded (15 million kg.) by 30 million kg. Sellers, trying to get rid of excess stock, reduce the price of blueberries, which causes buyers to increase the quantity demanded while sellers decrease their quantity supplied. The surplus shrinks until equilibrium is attained.

d. At a price of $1.25, there is a shortage of blueberries, with quantity demanded (35 million kg.) exceeding quantity supplied (5 million kg.) by 30 kg. Buyers, trying to get more blueberries, will offer a higher price, which causes sellers to increase the quantity supplied while buyers reduce their quantity demanded. The shortage shrinks until equilibrium is attained.

3. a. A shift of the supply curve for bananas to the left.

b. A shift of the demand curve for bananas to the right.

c. A shift of the supply curve for bananas to the right.

d. A shift of the supply curve for bananas to the left.

4. a. equilibrium price decreases and equilibrium quantity increases

b. equilibrium price increases and equilibrium quantity decreases

c. equilibrium price and quantity both increase

d. equilibrium price and quantity both decrease

Chapter 3

Competitive Dynamics and Government

Learning Objectives

In this chapter you will:
- learn about the price elasticity of demand, its relation to other demand elasticities, and the impact of the price elasticity of demand on sellers' revenues
- learn about the price elasticity of supply and the links between production periods and supply
- consider how governments use price controls to override the "invisible hand" of competition
- examine spillover costs and benefits, and the ways that governments address these issues

Chapter Highlights

- Price Elasticity of Demand
    1. Price elasticity of demand measures the responsiveness of consumers to changes in price. Demand is elastic when a change in price causes a proportionately larger change in quantity demanded, so that the value of the price elasticity of demand is greater than one ($e_d > 1$). Demand is inelastic when a change in price causes a proportionately smaller change in quantity demanded, so that the value of the price elasticity of demand is less than one ($e_d < 1$).
    2. When a change in price causes an equivalent proportionate change in quantity demanded then demand is unit-elastic, and the value of the price elasticity of demand is one ($e_d = 1$).
    3. Demand is perfectly elastic if there is an infinite response in quantity demanded to a change in price ($e_d = \infty$). Demand is perfectly inelastic if there is no response in quantity demanded to a change in price ($e_d = 0$).
    4. When demand is inelastic, a price increase will increase total revenue; however, when demand is elastic a price reduction is required to increase total revenue. When demand is unit-elastic, total revenue remains the same whatever the change in price.
    5. The value of the price elasticity of demand is found by dividing the ratio of the change in quantity demanded over average quantity demanded by the ratio of the change in price over average price.
    6. Price elasticity of demand is determined by four factors: the proportion of income spent on the product, the availability of substitutes for the product, the ranking of the product as a necessity or a luxury, and the lapse of time after a change in price.
    7. Income elasticity measures the response in the amount demanded of a product to a change in consumer income. Cross-price elasticity measures the response in the amount demanded of one product to a change in the price of another product.

- Price Elasticity of Supply
    1. Price elasticity of supply measures the responsiveness of producers to a change in price, with supply being elastic when a change in price causes a proportionately larger change quantity supplied, and supply being inelastic when a change in price causes a proportionately smaller change in quantity supplied.

2. Time is the most important determinant of the price elasticity of supply, based on three different production periods: the immediate run, the short run, and the long run.

3. In the immediate run, resources cannot be changed, so quantity supplied is fixed. The supply curve is therefore perfectly inelastic, and is drawn vertically. The value of price elasticity of supply is zero ($e_s = 0$).

4. In the short run, only some resources can be changed. These are called variable resources. They permit some response to a change in price. However, there is at least one fixed resource which limits the short-run response. The value of price elasticity of supply is greater than zero, but less than infinity ($0 < e_s < \infty$).

5. In the long run all resources are variable. This permits a great response to the change in price. However, the degree of elasticity of the supply curve will be affected by the cost of resources.

6. There are two main types of long-run supply curves: if costs are constant, the price of the product will also be constant, and the supply curve will be perfectly elastic ($e_s = \infty$); if costs are increasing, the price of the product will rise, and the supply curve will slope upwards ($e_s < \infty$).

7. The value for the price elasticity of supply is calculated in the same way as the value of the price elasticity of demand, except that quantity supplied is now used.

♦ Price Controls
1. Government sometimes intervenes in markets by setting price controls. Price controls may be price floors or price ceilings.
2. A price floor is always greater than equilibrium price.
3. A price ceiling is always less than equilibrium price.
4. Price floors create surpluses, while price ceilings cause shortages.
5. The sizes of surpluses and shortages are affected by price elasticities of demand and supply.
6. Social costs often arise from the surpluses and shortages created by price controls. The government must evaluate the benefits and costs of price controls whenever they are used.

♦ Spillover Effects
1. Spillover effects occur when a third party, other than the buyer or the seller, is affected by a market transaction.
2. A spillover effect may be positive. In this case the third party receives a benefit. Governments can support markets that create spillover benefits by subsidizing these products.
3. A spillover effect may be negative. In this case the third party experiences a cost. Governments can discourage markets that create spillover costs by taxing these products.
4. When positive spillover benefits greatly outweigh private benefits then the government itself can decide to produce these public goods. Public goods are those for which users cannot be excluded from the benefits of a product by the charging of a price. Public goods are best provided by government. Sometimes goods used in common are abused or destroyed from overuse. Then the government can privatize these goods to ensure that they are maintained.

Helpful Hints

♦ Price Elasticity of Demand
  1. Price elasticity of demand is useful for setting prices. On a linear demand curve, the prices that maximize total revenue are found in the range of unit elasticity. Refer to Figure 3.6 in the text. At prices where price elasticity of demand is greater than one, ($e_d > 1$), total revenue is increased if price is reduced. At prices where price elasticity of demand is less than one, ($e_d < 1$), total revenue is increased if price is increased. At the prices associated with unit elasticity, ($e_d = 1$), total revenue is maximized.
  2. Terminology is important when price elasticity of demand is being discussed. First, we do not make the mistake of referring to a product as elastic or inelastic. For example, we do not say that "eggs are inelastic;" rather, we say that "the demand for eggs is inelastic." Second, with price elasticity "a *change* in quantity demanded" is caused by "a *change* in price." We do not confuse this with the law of demand which states only that at a higher (lower) price a smaller (larger) quantity is demanded. Elasticity is used to measure relative changes at specific ranges on a given demand curve.
  3. Price elasticity is more that just the slope of a demand curve. Look carefully at the formula:

$$e_d = \ (\Delta Q_d \div \text{average } Q_d)/(\Delta P \div \text{average } P)$$

It can be written as:

$$= \ (\Delta Q_d / \text{average } Q_d) \quad x \quad (\text{average } P/\Delta P)$$

$$= \ (\Delta Q_d / \Delta P) \quad x \quad (\text{average } P/\text{average } Q_d)$$

The ratio $(\Delta Q_d/\Delta P)$ is the inverse of the slope, while the ratio (average P/average Q_d) locates a specific range on the demand curve. If the ratio of averages is in a range where prices are high and quantities are low then the value of e_d will be greater than where prices are low and quantities are high. See Figure 3.6 in the text. In other words, we must know both the changes and the location of the changes on the demand curve.
  4. Remember that the concept of elasticity is applicable to price decreases as well as price increases, i.e., a change can be either a decrease or an increase.
  5. When price elasticity of demand is calculated, the negative sign is always ignored. We consider the absolute value – i.e., $\left| e_d \right|$.

♦ Income and Cross-Price Elasticities
  1. Unlike price elasticity of demand, when income and cross-price elasticities are calculated the sign is important. Positive signs indicate a normal product (for income elasticity) and a substitute product (for cross-price elasticity); negative signs indicate an inferior product (for income elasticity) and a complementary product (for cross-price elasticity).

Sign	Income elasticity e_i	Cross-price elasticity e_{xy}
positive	Normal products	Substitute products
negative	Inferior products	Complementary products

2. Income elasticity involves a shift of the entire demand curve. We have already seen this in the discussion of normal and inferior products on page 32 in Chapter 2.
3. Income elasticity is important for sellers. Think of the increased revenues for stores that sell inferior products at a time when incomes decline during periods of economic recession.
4. Cross-price elasticity involves a shift of the entire demand curve. Look again at the discussion of substitute and complementary products on pages 32 and 33 in Chapter 2.

♦   Price Elasticity of Supply
1. Note that in the immediate run the product is in some sense perishable, e.g., fresh strawberries in July, fashion items in the spring, or models of automobiles for the current year. In the immediate run, producers will offer perishable goods at sale prices.
2. The value for e_s is positive except for two cases: first, the immediate run when e_s is zero, and second the long-run supply curve, if a perfectly competitive market were a decreasing cost industry. This curve would be negatively sloped and therefore would not obey the law of supply.

♦   Price Controls
1. The terms 'floor' and 'ceiling' are used quite contrary to the way they are used in the building trades. With price controls, floors are above and ceilings are below. Remember that a floor prevents a price from falling further, which it normally would as it moves downwards towards equilibrium price. In addition, a ceiling prevents a price from rising further, which it normally would as it moves upwards towards equilibrium price.
2. Price floors and price ceilings prevent the automatic resolution of surpluses and shortages, as previously discussed in Chapter 2 of the text.

♦   Spillover Effects
1. While the market model with a large number of buyers and sellers operating under the principle of laissez faire is designed to work perfectly, the economic system of the real world does not. In the real world, spillover effects occur. It is the role of government to seek optimal solutions for these spillovers.
2. Spillovers can create new market opportunities. For example, oil spills have permitted the creation of companies selling clean-up services.
3. A public good is indivisible and non-exclusive. An example is a national park. Each visitor can enjoy all its beauty without detracting from or preventing the enjoyment of any other visitor. A private good, once purchased, is excluded from the use of others.

Key Concepts

price elasticity of demand
elastic demand
inelastic demand
perfectly elastic demand
perfectly inelastic demand
total revenue
unit-elastic demand
income elasticity
cross-price elasticity
price elasticity of supply
elastic supply
inelastic supply
immediate run

perfectly inelastic supply
short run
long run
constant-cost industry
perfectly elastic supply
increasing-cost industry
decreasing-cost industry
price floor
price ceiling
spillover effects
spillover costs
spillover benefits
public good

Fill in the Blank and True False Questions

1. The extent to which a price change affects quantity demanded is known as the price _____ of demand.

2. From the perspective of businesses in a market, the quantity demanded of a product multiplied by the product's price is _____ _____.

Figure 1 Use this graph to answer questions 3 and 4.

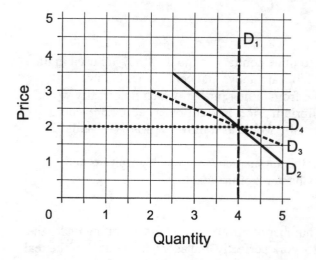

3. In Figure 1, the demand curve D_1 is _____, and the demand curve D_4 is _____.

Place the following terms in the correct order in the blanks above.

perfectly elastic   perfectly inelastic

4. For demand curve D_2 on the graph in Figure 1, a price rise from $2 to $3 causes total revenue to _____, which means that D_2 is _____. In contrast, for demand curve D_3, a price rise from $2 to $3 causes total revenue to _____, which means that D_3 is _____.

Place the following terms in the correct order in the blanks above.

inelastic   elastic   decrease   increase

5. When the price of electricity changes, the quantity supplied of the item changes by a smaller percentage. This is an example of _____supply.

6. In the time period known as the _____ _____, quantity supplied by businesses does not change.

7. A(n) _____-_____ industry is one which is not a significant user of any resource, while a(n)_____-_____ industry is a significant user of at least one resource.

8. Order the following where 1 = most inelastic, 4 = most elastic.

long-run supply in a constant-cost industry   immediate-run supply

long-run supply in an increasing-cost industry   short-run supply

1. _____
2. _____
3. _____
4. _____

9. A controlled price set by government below the equilibrium price is known as a price _____, and one above the equilibrium price is known as a price _____.

10. Because demand and supply for wheat are inelastic in the short run, a worldwide drought will tend to cause a greater fluctuation in wheat's equilibrium _____ than in its equilibrium _____.

11. **T F** When demand is elastic, total revenue and price vary in opposite directions.

12. **T F** Supply is elastic when small price changes lead to large variations in the amounts supplied by producers.

13. **T F** Key money is sometimes paid for rental units due to the surplus of apartments caused by rent controls.

14. Lighthouses and national defense are examples of _____ goods.

Multiple Choice Questions

1. The price of a town's busfare is increased by 30 percent. As a result daily ridership on the town's buses decreases by 20 percent. The price elasticity of demand for bus rides is:
   A. perfectly elastic
   B. elastic
   C. unit elastic
   D. inelastic
   E. perfectly inelastic

2. An increase of 10 percent in tuition fees results in a 2 percent decrease in applications for college admission. The price elasticity of demand for college education is:
   A. perfectly elastic
   B. elastic
   C. unit elastic
   D. inelastic
   E. perfectly inelastic

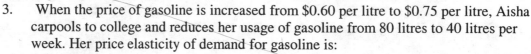

3. When the price of gasoline is increased from $0.60 per litre to $0.75 per litre, Aisha carpools to college and reduces her usage of gasoline from 80 litres to 40 litres per week. Her price elasticity of demand for gasoline is:
   A. (-)0.3
   B. (-)1.1
   C. (-)2
   D. (-)3
   E. (-)9

4. Hans' purchase of chocolate bars from the college vending machine declines from 15 to 12 bars a week when the price increases from $1.50 to $2.00. His price elasticity of demand for chocolate bars is:
   A. (-)0.78
   B. (-)0.85
   C. (-)1.25
   D. (-)1.33
   E. (-)6.00

5. If in a perfectly competitive market with 3000 producers of soybeans, a single soybean farmer raises his selling price above the price prevailing in the market his total revenue will be:
   A. the same as before
   B. one three-thousandths of the total revenue of all producers
   C. maximized
   D. greater than before
   E. zero

6. If a seller who faces a linear downsloping demand curve increases the price of their product in order to maximize total revenue, the price will be increased to the region where price elasticity of demand is:
   A. infinite
   B. greater than one
   C. equal to one
   D. less than one
   E. equal to zero

7. If a product makes up a small portion of consumers' incomes, is considered to be a necessity, and has few close substitutes, its demand tends to be:
   A. perfectly elastic
   B. elastic
   C. unit elastic
   D. inelastic
   E. perfectly inelastic

8. If canned salmon is an inferior product then:
   A. consumers will buy this product if the price of fresh salmon decreases
   B. an increase in income will cause an increase in its demand
   C. a decrease in income will cause a decrease in its demand
   D. a decrease in income will cause an increase in its demand
   E. consumers will buy more of this product if its price increases

9. If CDs are substitutes for cassette tapes then:
   A. an increase in the price of CDs will cause a decrease in the demand for cassette tapes
   B. a decrease in the price of CDs will cause an increase in the demand for cassette tapes
   C. a surplus of cassette tapes will cause a decrease in the price of CDs
   D. a decrease in the purchase of cassette tapes will cause an increase in the demand for CDs
   E. a decrease in the price of CDs will cause a decrease in the demand for cassette tapes

10. The price elasticity of supply refers to:
    A. the extent to which quantity supplied is affected by changes in price
    B. the extent to which price is affected by changes in quantity supplied
    C. the extent to which quantity supplied is affected by changes in a supply determinant such as a resource price
    D. the extent to which price is affected by changes in a supply determinant such as a resource price
    E. the extent to which suppliers are affected by expected prices of resources

11 In the short run, as the prices of winter coats increase, which of the following actions is a coat manufacturer unable to undertake in order to increase the quantity supplied of coats?
    A. hire more workers on the production line
    B. offer existing labour overtime work
    C. expand the factory and install new machines
    D. advertise the line of coats
    E. offer incentives to employees to work harder

12 In the long run supply curves in competitive markets become:
   A. more elastic, since producers have more time to adjust price
   B. less elastic, because producers have more time to adjust the quantity they supply
   C. more elastic, since producers have more time to adjust the quantity they supply
   D. less elastic, because producers have more time to adjust price
   E. more or less elastic, since producers have more time to adjust to consumer demand

13. When price floors are imposed in agriculture the winners are the:
   A. farmers
   B. taxpayers
   C. consumers
   D. society
   E. government

14 Rent controls benefit:
   A. society as a whole
   B. landlords
   C. middle-class tenants
   D. poorer tenants
   E. government

15 Spillover effects are:
   A. always in the form of costs
   B. illustrated by the case of positive surges of hydroelectric power
   C. negative or positive internal effects of producing or consuming a product
   D. negative or positive effects of government activity
   E. negative or positive external effects of producing or consuming a product

Short Answer Questions

1. Calculate the appropriate elasticity coefficient in each of the following cases. For income or cross-price elasticities, identify whether the product(s) are luxuries, necessities, inferior products, substitutes, or complementary. For price elasticities of demand or supply, identify whether demand or supply is elastic or inelastic.

   a. Because of a drop in average consumer incomes from $75 000 to $35 000, weekly purchases of bread fall from 20 000 to 18 000 loaves.
   b. A decrease in the average price of digital cameras from $750 to $500 reduces the purchases of polaroid cameras from 30 000 to 20 000 per month.
   c. A rise in the average price of paperback romance novels from $10 to $15 causes weekly purchases of these novels to decline from 4000 to 3000.
   d. A fall in the average price of beef from $4 to $3 a kilogram reduces the amount supplied each month by beef producers from 300 000 to 150 000 kilograms.

Figure 2   Use this graph to answer question 2.

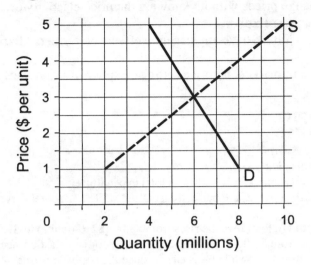

2. a.   Outline the results in the market shown in Figure 2 if a price floor of $4 is imposed by the government.
    b.   What will occur if, instead of a price floor, a price ceiling of $4 is imposed by the government?
    c.   Outline the results in this market if a price ceiling of $2 is imposed by the government.
    d.   What will occur if, instead of a price ceiling, a price floor of $2 is imposed by the government.

Figure 3   Use this graph to answer question 3.

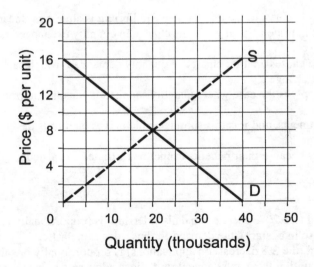

3. a.   Given the information for a perfectly competitive market in Figure 3, identify the equilibrium price and quantity in this market.
    b.   On the graph above, draw the supply curve that includes spillover costs if these costs are $8 per unit of output.
    c.   Using your graph identify the preferred quantity if in this market with spillover costs of $8 per unit of output.
    d.   Identify one way that government could intervene to ensure that the preferred quantity you identified in part c is achieved.

4. Why does the price elasticity of demand vary along a given demand curve?
5. Sellers should not attempt to change prices without knowing the price elasticity of demand that they face. Do you agree? Explain
6. Do technological advances in agriculture have any negative effects on farmers? Explain your answer.
7. Should the government intervene in markets by price setting? Explain your answer.

Solutions to Questions for Chapter 3

Fill in the Blank and True False Questions
1. **elasticity** This is also known as demand elasticity.
2. **total revenue** From the point of view of consumers, it is known as total expenditure.
3. **perfectly inelastic, perfectly elastic** Vertical curves are perfectly inelastic, while horizontal curves are perfectly elastic.
4. **increase, inelastic, decrease, elastic** With D_2, total revenue rises from $8.00 ($2 x 4 units) to $9.00 ($3 x 3 units). With D_3, total revenue falls from $8.00 to $6.00 ($3 x 2 units). D_2 is inelastic since price and total revenue move in the same direction, while D_3 is elastic since the opposite is true.
5. **inelastic** This illustrates inelastic supply, which is the case where quantity supplied is insensitive to price changes.
6. **immediate run** The period is so short that suppliers have no chance to adjust the amount they offer for sale.
7. **constant-cost, increasing-cost** An industry that is a major user of a resource exhibits increasing costs, since, when quantity supplied expands in the long run, higher demand for the resource pushes up its price.
8. The correct order is **immediate-run supply** (which is perfectly inelastic), **short-run supply, long-run supply in an increasing-cost industry**, and **long-run supply in a constant-cost industry** (which is perfectly elastic).
9. **ceiling, floor** To be effective, a price ceiling must be below and a price floor must be above equilibrium price.
10. **price, quantity** A drought shifts the supply curve to the left. A new equilibrium is attained. Because the demand curve is inelastic the change in price is great while the change in quantity exchanged is small.
11. **T** With elastic demand, a change in price causes a larger change in quantity demanded, which causes total revenue to vary counter to the price change.
12. **T** This statement is true, since elastic supply is the case where quantity supplied is sensitive to price changes.
13. **F** Rent controls cause a shortage of apartments, and it is this shortage which gives landlords the power to charge key money.
14. **public** They are included in this category because their benefits cannot be restricted to particular consumers.

Multiple Choice Questions
1. **D** Since the change in quantity demanded (the 20% decrease in daily ridership) is proportionally less than the change in price (the 30% increase in busfare), the demand for bus rides is inelastic.
2. **D** Since the change in quantity demanded (the 2% decrease in applications) is proportionally less than the change in price (the 10% increase in tuition fees), the demand for college admissions - is inelastic.
3. **D** e_d = (ΔQ_d ÷ average Q_d)/(Δ price ÷ average price)

= $[(40 - 80) ÷ ((40 + 80)/2)]/[(0.75 - 0.60) ÷ ((0.75 + 0.60)/2)]$

= (-)3

This is an elastic response to the increase in the price of gasoline. Carpooling is a substitute for driving one's own car.

4. **A** $[(12 - 15) \div ((12 + 15)/2)]/[(2.00 - 1.50) \div ((2.00 + 1.50)/2)] = 0.78$
5. **E** In a perfectly competitive market with a large number of buyers and sellers, each seller sells at the price determined in the market. At a price greater than the prevailing market price, nothing will be sold and the producer's total revenue will be zero. Buyers have 2999 other suppliers from whom to purchase at a lower price. Of course, at a price less than equilibrium price the seller will sell all he has available for sale, but total revenue will be smaller than that of other sellers in the market.
6. **C** Along a linear, down-sloping demand curve the value of price elasticity of demand varies. Total revenue is greatest where e_d is equal to a value of one.
7. **D** A product that meets all of these conditions will tend to have an inelastic demand curve.
8. **D** Consumers will increase the demand for inferior products when incomes decrease.
9. **E** When two products are substitutes there is a direct relationship between the change in price one product and the change in the demand for the other.
10. **A** This is the definition of price elasticity of supply.
11. **C** In the short run there is at least one fixed input. This will be factory and machines which cannot be adjusted during the current production run.
12. **C** In the long run all inputs are variable so that producers can make adjustments which will increase the quantity supplied.
13. **A** The farmers win because their total revenue increases. Taxpayers lose because they finance the cost of purchasing the surplus. Consumers lose because they pay a price greater than equilibrium price. Society loses because of the misallocation of resources.
14. **C** Middle-class tenants benefit because they have the opportunity to acquire desirable units. Society loses because resources are misallocated. Landlords are no longer free to set their own prices. Poorer tenants are pushed into the unregulated housing market. Government must absorb the administrative costs of rent controls and provide housing for poorer tenants.
15. **E** This is the definition of spillover effects.

Short Answer Questions

1. a. $e_i = $ ($\Delta Q_d \div$ average Q_d)/(Δ income $\div$ average income)

   $= [(18\ 000 - 20\ 000) \div ((18\ 000 + 20\ 000)/2)]/[(35\ 000 - 75\ 000) \div ((35\ 000 + 75\ 000)/2)]$

   $= 0.1$

   Since e_i is positive and less than one, bread is a necessity.
   b. $e_{xy} = $ ($\Delta Q_d \div$ average Q_d)/($\Delta P_y \div$ average P_y)

   $= [(20\ 000 - 30\ 000) \div ((20\ 000 + 30\ 000)/2)]/[(500 - 750) \div ((500 + 750)/2)]$

   $= 1$

   Since e_{xy} is positive, the two products are substitutes.
   c. $e_d = $ ($\Delta Q_d \div$ average Q_d)/(Δ price $\div$ average price)

   $= [(3000 - 4000) \div ((3000 + 4000)/2)]/[(15 - 10) \div ((15 + 10)/2)]$

   $= (-)0.7$

   Since $|e_d|$ is less than one, demand is inelastic.
   d. $e_s = $ ($\Delta Q_s \div$ average Q_s)/(Δ price $\div$ average price)

   $= [(150\ 000 - 300\ 000) \div ((150\ 000 + 300\ 000)/2)]/[(3 - 4) \div ((3 + 4)/2)]$

   $= 2.3$

   Since e_s is greater than one, supply is elastic.

2. a. A surplus of 3 million units is created in this market.
    b. In this case, the price ceiling is above the equilibrium price and therefore has no effect.
    c. A shortage of 3 million units is created in this market.
    d. In this case, the price floor is below the equilibrium price and therefore has no effect

3   a. $8, 20 000 units.
    b. Remember that the impact of spillover costs in a perfectly competitive market can be shown graphically by an upward shift in the supply curve by the dollar amount of the spillover cost per unit of output. Therefore, the new supply curve (S_1) is shown by a parallel upward shift from S, with a new vertical intercept of $8, and an intersection with D at $12 and 10 000 units.
    c. 10 000 units, where S_1 and D intersect.
    d. The government can impose an excise tax of $8 per unit.

4. The price elasticity of demand is the ratio of the relative change in quantity demanded and the relative change in price. On a given demand curve, when prices are high, quantity demanded is low. Relative price changes at high prices are small, while relative quantity changes at low quantities are large. So the value of e_d will be greater than 1. Conversely, when prices are low quantity demanded is high. Relative price changes at low prices are large, while relative quantity changes at high quantities are small. So the value of e_d will be less than 1.

5. Yes. If the seller's goal is to maximize total revenue, then price increases will increase total revenue whenever demand is inelastic, but will reduce total revenue whenever demand is elastic. In the case of unit elasticity, total revenue remains constant despite a change in price. Along linear downsloping demand curves, the value of elasticity varies. In every case, total revenue will increase as price is set closer to unit elasticity, where maximum total revenue is attained.

6. Yes. When technological advances take place in agriculture, costs of production are affected and the supply curve shifts to the right. Because demand for most agricultural goods is highly price inelastic, a rightward shift of the supply curve causes a large decrease in equilibrium price and, consequently, in total revenue to farmers.

7. When Adam Smith's 'invisible hand' is left to operate, there is an automatic movement towards equilibrium in perfectly competitive markets. However, in some markets (such as the market for rental accommodation) it is possible to argue that equilibrium price is excessive for some consumers. In other markets (such as agricultural markets) it is possible to argue that producers face too much price volatility to make participation in the market worthwhile. Governments may choose to intervene by using price ceilings and price floors to arrive at prices that are considered fair to buyers and sellers. Nevertheless, government intervention can create problems, since price ceilings create shortages and price floors create surpluses. The size of the shortages and surpluses will be affected by the elasticities of demand and supply. The persistent shortages caused by price ceilings lead to underground markets in which prices and other conditions are not under government control. The persistent surpluses caused by price floors create the dilemma of disposing of the surpluses or restricting quantity supplied.

Chapter 4

Costs of Production

Learning Objectives

In this chapter, you will:

- consider the major organizational forms of business – sole proprietorships, partnerships, and corporations
- learn about economic costs (explicit and implicit) of production and economic profit
- analyze short-run (total, average, and marginal) products and the law of diminishing marginal returns
- derive short-run (total, average, and marginal) costs
- examine long-run results of production (increasing returns to scale, constant returns to scale, and decreasing returns to scale) and long-run costs

Chapter Highlights

- Business Organization
  1. A business combines economic resources to produce goods or services for economic gain. Businesses are usually organized as sole proprietorships, partnerships or corporations.
  2. A sole proprietorship is owned by a single person. A partnership is owned by two or more people. Owners of sole proprietorships and partnerships are subject to unlimited liability, i.e., creditors may make claims against their personal assets.
  3. A corporation, having independent legal status, permits corporate shareholders limited liability. This confines risk to the amount invested in shares. Most Canadian manufacturing businesses are corporations.

- Production, Costs, and Profit
  1. The production process transforms inputs – natural, capital and human resources – into outputs of value, i.e., goods and services.
  2. Production takes place in three sectors: primary, secondary and service (or tertiary). The primary sector includes mining, forestry, fishing and agriculture. The secondary sector includes manufacturing and construction. The service sector includes trades, finance and banking, and information industries.
  3. Production processes may be capital-intensive or labour-intensive. Productive efficiency requires the use of the least costly mix of inputs.
  4. Economic costs may be explicit or implicit. Explicit costs are accounting costs. Implicit costs are the costs of resources provided by owners. Normal profit is an implicit cost. It is the minimum return that the owners must receive to ensure they remain in business. Opportunity costs – arising from sacrificed opportunity – are reflected in economic costs, and are therefore the basis of both explicit and implicit costs.
  5. Economic profit is the difference between total revenue and economic cost. Economic profit may be positive, zero, or negative. Negative economic profit is an economic loss.

◆ Production in the Short Run

1. The short run is the period during which the quantity of at least one input is fixed. Fixed inputs are machines and buildings in manufacturing, and land in agriculture. Variable inputs, which can be adjusted in the short run, are labour and materials. When the short run is discussed, fixed inputs are usually assumed to be capital, and variable inputs are assumed to be labour.

2. Total product (q) is the output produced with the use of fixed and variable inputs. As additional units of labour are combined with capital, total product will increase. The extra product produced with an additional unit of labour is called marginal product (MP), which is found by dividing the change in total product by the change in labour, ($\Delta q/\Delta L$), where Δ means "change in." As units of labour are added to capital, marginal product first increases, then decreases. The decreases in marginal product are due to the law of diminishing returns.

3. There is a predictable relationship between marginal product and total product. The marginal product curve attains its maximum where diminishing returns begin to apply to total product. The marginal product decreases and becomes zero where the total product attains its maximum. At higher employment levels, marginal product becomes increasingly negative, while total product decreases.

4. Average product (AP) is total product divided by the quantity of labour employed (q/L). Average product first increases and then decreases as additional units of labour are employed. There is a unique relationship between marginal and average values. For example, average product always rises when marginal product is greater than average product. Conversely, average product always falls when marginal product is less than average product. Finally, average product is always constant (ie. at its maximum value) when marginal product equals average product.

5. Production can be divided into three stages. The first is where total product is increasing at an increasing rate, so marginal product and average product are increasing. The second is where total product increases at a decreasing rate, so marginal product declines. The third is where total product is declining, so marginal product is negative.

◆ Costs in the Short Run

1. Short-run costs correspond to short-run inputs. Fixed cost (FC) is incurred with fixed inputs such as capital. Variable cost (VC) is incurred with variable inputs such as labour. Total cost (TC) is the sum of fixed and variable costs.

2. Fixed cost is constant – it does not change with output. In contrast, variable cost increases with output. The extra cost of an additional unit of output is called marginal cost (MC), and is found by dividing the change in total cost by the change in output ($\Delta TC/\Delta q$). This is the same as dividing the change in variable cost by the change in output ($\Delta VC/\Delta q$). As additional units of output are produced, marginal cost first decreases, then increases. The increases in marginal cost are due to the law of diminishing returns, since once the marginal product of each new worker begins to fall then the marginal cost of each new unit of output begins to rise.

3. Average variable cost (AVC) is variable cost divided by the units of output (VC/q). Average variable product first decreases and then increases as output expands. There is a predictable relationship between marginal cost and average variable cost. Average variable cost always falls when it is greater than marginal cost. Conversely, average variable cost always rises when it is less than marginal cost. Finally, average variable cost is always constant (i.e., reaches its minimum) when its equals marginal cost.

4. Average cost (AC) is the sum of average variable cost and average fixed cost (AC = AVC + AFC). Average cost is also found by dividing total cost by output (AC = TC/q). The relationship between marginal cost and average variable cost is repeated between marginal cost and average cost. Average cost always falls when it is greater than marginal cost. Conversely, average cost always rises when it is less than marginal cost. Finally, average cost is always constant (i.e., reaches its minimum) when its equals marginal cost.

5. The average variable cost and marginal cost curves are mirror images of the average product and marginal product curves, keeping in mind that labour is on the horizontal axis of the product diagram, and output is on the horizontal axis of the cost diagram. When the average product and marginal product curves are rising, the average variable cost and marginal cost curves are falling; when the average product and marginal product curves are falling, the average variable cost and marginal cost curves are rising. The maximum and minimum points of the AVC and AP curves correspond, as do the maximum and minimum points of the MC and MP curves.

◆ Production and Costs in the Long Run
1. In the long run, all inputs are variable. The amount of capital changes with plant size. The long-run average cost curve is the combination of single points from successive short-run average cost curves. The resulting saucer-shaped curve reflects increasing, constant and decreasing returns to scale.
2. Increasing returns to scale (or economics of scale) arise when changes in all inputs permit proportionately greater changes in output. This is the result of the division of labour, as well as specialization in the use of capital and management. Constant returns to scale arise when a change in all inputs permits an equivalent proportional change in output. Decreasing returns to scale (or diseconomies of scale) arise when changes in all inputs provide a proportionately smaller change in output. This results from management difficulties and limited resources.
3. In the long run, plants in various industries, to varying extents, reflect increasing returns to scale in initial stages of expansion, followed by constant returns to scale and then decreasing returns to scale in later stages of expansion.

Helpful Hints

◆ Business Organization
1. Businesses, whether sole proprietorships, partnerships, or corporations, are the means whereby production is organized in the market system. Their operation is supported by the legal framework of the market system.
2. Sole proprietorships and partnerships are necessary for permitting expressions of the entrepreneurial spirit. The protection of limited liability provided to shareholders by corporations has facilitated the growth of this type of business. Through corporations, investment funds maybe pooled and managerial skills attracted.
3. A major disadvantage of corporations is double taxation. Earnings are taxed first as corporate profits, and again as income from dividends.

◆ Production, Costs and Profit
1. The concepts and definitions set out in this chapter are important for later analyses. They should receive careful attention. They are essential to an understanding of the discussion of perfect competition, monopoly and imperfect competition in Chapters 5 and 6.

2. The recognition of implicit costs by economists enables an adequate assessment of the extent of opportunity cost. Implicit costs, although overlooked by accountants, who concern themselves largely with explicit costs, are important in applications in later chapters, such as the distinction between normal profit and economic profit, the potential for business to survive losses in the short run, and the assessment of long-run economic efficiency.

3. Remember that normal profit is a cost. It is economic profit, not normal profit, that will be useful in determining the long-run viability of businesses.

♦ Production in the Short Run

1. The law of diminishing marginal returns is a subset of the law of variable proportions. The law of variable proportions recognizes the fact that the proportions of inputs vary as a variable input is added to a fixed input in the short run. Initially, the addition of the variable input will result in increasing returns. Eventually, the addition of too many units of the variable input inhibits production and results in diminishing returns.

2. The relationships between the marginal cost curve and the average variable cost and average cost curves are best seen on a graph. When the marginal cost curve is below either of the average curves, the averages are falling or being pulled down. When the marginal cost curve is above either of the average curves, the averages are rising, or being pulled up. Consequently, the marginal cost curve intersects both average curves at their minimum points. To do this the marginal cost curve begins to turn up before the average variable cost curve, and, in turn, the average variable cost curve turns up before the average cost curve. Practice drawing the shapes of the curves, noting their relationships to each other.

3. If the average fixed cost curve is removed from the graph showing the family of short-run cost curves (Figure 4.8 on p. 102), it can be derived as the distance between the average cost and average variable cost curves.

♦ Production and Costs in the Long Run

1. The long-run average cost curve is similar to that of the short-run average cost curve in that both are saucer-shaped. However, the reason for the saucer-shape of the long-run average cost curve is increasing, constant and decreasing returns to scale; the reason for the saucer-shape of the short-run average cost curve is increasing returns then diminishing returns.

2. Notice that minimum points of the short-run average cost curves in Figure 4.9 (p. 105) coincide with the long-run average cost curve only when returns to scale are constant. When returns to scale are increasing and the long-run curve is declining, the relevant points of coincidence on each of the short-run curves occur before these curves reach their minimum points. When returns to scale are decreasing and the long-run curve is rising, the points of coincidence on each of the short-run curves occur after these curves reach their minimum points.

Key Concepts

business	variable inputs
sole-proprietorship	total product
partnership	average product
corporation	marginal product
production	law of diminishing marginal returns
inputs	fixed costs
output	variable costs
labour-intensive process	total cost
capital-intensive process	marginal cost
productive efficiency	average fixed cost
explicit costs	average variable cost
implicit costs	average cost
normal profit	increasing returns to scale
economic costs	constant returns to scale
economic profit	decreasing returns to scale
fixed inputs	long-run average cost

Fill in the Blank and True False Questions

Figure 1 Use this table to answer questions 1 to 3.

	Workers	**Computers**
Process A	1	3
Process B	4	2

1. Figure 1 shows two possible combinations of workers and computers that can be used to produce a given daily output. Process A is more _____- intensive, while process B is more _____-intensive.

2. For each of the two possible combinations of workers and computers shown in Figure 1, if daily costs are $100 for each worker and $50 for each computer, then _____ is preferable to _____, since the total daily cost of the given output using process A is _____ and using process B is _____.

   Place the following answers in the correct order in the blanks above.

   Process A   Process B $500 $250

3. For each of the two possible combinations of workers and computers shown in Figure 1, if daily costs are $30 for each worker and $100 for each computer, then _____ is preferable to _____, since the total daily cost of the given output using process A is _____ and using process B is _____.

   Place the following answers in the correct order in the blanks above.

   Process A   Process B $320 $330

4. **T F** A company's normal profit is one of its explicit costs.

5. **T F** For any business, economic profit is always greater than accounting profit.

6. When a marginal value exceeds its associated average value, then the _____ value is necessarily _____, and, when a total value increases at a decreasing rate, then the associated _____ value is necessarily _____.

    Place the following terms in the correct order in the blanks above.

    rising   falling   marginal   average

7. **T F** The cost of materials is a fixed cost for most businesses.

8. When a business hires its first worker, its total cost rises by $_____ and its ouput rises by two units. Therefore, the marginal cost of each of these units of output is $_____.

    Place the following answer in the correct order in the blanks above.

    3   6

9. A photocopy shop can make 10 000 copies an hour with fixed costs of $200 and an average variable cost of $0.01 a copy. Based on this information, enter the value for each of the shop's short run costs.

    variable cost   _____
    total cost   _____
    average cost   _____
    average fixed cost   _____

10. **T F** Each hour, Dunkin' Donuts can make 100 donuts at a total cost of $90, or it can make 101 donuts at a total cost of $91. The marginal cost of the 101st donut is therefore $0.90.

11. If a company raises all of its inputs by 5 percent, which causes its output to rise by 10 percent, the company's production exhibits _____ returns to scale. In contrast, if the company reduces all of its inputs by 10 percent and its output falls by 5 percent, the company's production exhibits _____ returns to scale.

12. If a company raises all of its inputs by 10 percent and its output also rises by 10 percent, this is a case of _____ returns to scale.

13. **T F** If production exhibits constant returns to scale, then long-run average cost remains the same.

14. When production exhibits increasing returns to scale, long-run average cost _____ as output expands, while in the case of decreasing returns to scale, long-run average cost _____ as output expands.

    Place the following answer in the correct order in the blanks above.

    falls   rises

15. **T F** Businesses tend to be large when they use production techniques characterized by increasing returns to scale.

16. Shareholders receive income in the form of _____, while bondholders receive income in the form of _____.

17. According to John Kenneth Galbraith, managers of corporations are interested in maximizing the company's _____, while shareholders of a corporation are interested in maximizing the company's _____.

Place the following answer in the correct order in the blanks above.

sales revenue   profit

Multiple Choice Questions

1. Which of the following statements is false?
   A. There are about one million businesses in Canada.
   B. The majority of businesses are sole proprietorships, partnerships or corporations.
   C. More than three-quarters of Canadian business have annual sales revenues of over $5 million.
   D. Just 5000 businesses in Canada account for almost half the total revenue received by Canadian businesses as a whole.
   E. In 1995 about 98 percent of Canadian manufacturing businesses were corporations, which accounted for 98 percent of the total sales revenues of manufacturers.

2. Which of the following is an implicit cost?
   A. medical benefits paid to workers
   B. rent that could have been earned by leasing a business's premises to another firm
   C. costs of materials
   D. insurance premiums paid by a business
   E. interest on a bank loan

3. Normal profit is:
   A. total revenue minus total cost
   B. total cost minus total revenue
   C. total revenue minus economic profit
   D. the maximum return that owners must receive
   E. the minimum return that owners must receive

4. A business's economic profit is found by subtracting the following from the business's total revenue:
   A. all explicit costs
   B. all implicit costs
   C. some implicit costs
   D. all economic costs
   E. all accounting costs

Figure 2 Use this table to answer questions 5 to 8.

Interest on bank loan	$10 000
Rent on store premises	$20 000
Normal profit	$5 000
Wages for employees	$60 000
Cost of inventories, hydro, and other miscellaneous expenses	$15 000
Owner's potential wage at another job	$40 000

5. Figure 2 shows the annual costs for Fit-Right Shoestore. Based on these costs, total implicit costs for Fit-Right Shoestore are:
   A. $150 000
   B. $120 000
   C. $45 000
   D. $60 000
   E. $105 000

6. Based on the costs outlined in Figure 2, total explicit costs for Fit-Right Shoestore are:
   A. $150 000
   B. $120 000
   C. $45 000
   D. $60 000
   E. $105 000

7. Based on the costs outlined in Figure 2, total economic costs for Fit-Right Shoestore are:
   A. $150 000
   B. $120 000
   C. $45 000
   D. $60 000
   E. $105 000

8. Based on Figure 2, if annual sales revenue for Fit-Right Shoes is $155 000, then the store is making an economic profit of:
   A. $50 000
   B. $5 000
   C. $45 000
   D. -$50 000
   E. -$5 000

Figure 3 Use this table to answer questions 9 to 11.

Workers	Total product (windows per hour)	MC
0	0	20
1	20	100
2	120	30
3	150	10
4	160	-10
5	150	

44

9. Given the short-run production choices for Spit-and-Polish Window Cleaners in Figure 3, marginal product rises when the following workers are hired.
   A. the 1st worker
   → B. the 1st and 2nd workers
   C. the 1st, 2nd, and 3rd workers
   D. the 1st, 2nd, 3rd, and 4th workers
   E. all 5 workers

10. Given the production choices for Spit-and-Polish Window Cleaners shown in Figure 3, marginal product falls but is still positive when the following workers are hired:
   A. the 2nd worker
   B. the 2nd and 3rd workers
   → C. the 3rd and 4th workers
   D. the 3rd, 4th, and 5th workers
   E. the 3rd worker

11. Given the production choices for Spit-and-Polish Window Cleaners shown in Figure 3, marginal product falls and becomes negative when the following workers are hired:
   A. the 2nd, 3rd, 4th, and 5th workers
   B. the 3rd, 4th, and 5th workers
   C. the 4th worker
   D. the 4th and 5th workers
   → E. the 5th worker

12. In the short run, when total product is increasing at a decreasing rate:
   A. marginal product is negative
   B. total cost is increasing at an increasing rate
   C. marginal product is increasing
   D. total cost is increasing at a decreasing rate
   E. marginal cost is decreasing

Figure 4 Use this graph to answer questions 13 and 14.

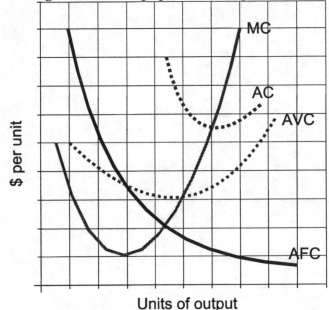

13. Based on Figure 4, the law of diminishing marginal returns starts to apply:
    A. at the minimum point on the average variable cost curve
    B. at the minimum point on the average cost curve
    C. at the minimum point on the marginal cost curve
    D. from the point where the average fixed cost curve begins to decline
    E. from the point where the marginal cost curve intersects the average variable cost curve

14. For the business whose short-run cost curves are shown in Figure 4, as output expands:
    A. average cost always stays constant
    B. average fixed cost always falls
    C. average variable cost always rises
    D. marginal cost always rises
    E. marginal cost always falls

15. Increasing returns to scale can be due to:
    A. the division of labour
    B. specialized capital
    C. specialized management
    D. all of the above
    E. none of the above

Short Answer Questions

1. Dress-Up Dry Cleaners is a premium cleaning service whose fixed inputs are buildings and machines. Its variable input is labour, and its output is cleaned garments.
    a. The table below sets out the relationship between the labour employed and daily total product for Dress-Up. Complete the table.

Labour	Total Product	Marginal Product	Average Product
0	0		
1	6	_____	_____
2	14	_____	_____
3	24	_____	_____
4	36	_____	_____
5	50	_____	_____
6	61	_____	_____
7	70	_____	_____
8	75	_____	_____
9	78	_____	_____

b. The fixed cost for Dress-Up is $100 a day, while the daily wage for each worker is $30. Based on this information, complete the following table:

Labour	Total Product	Fixed Cost	Variable Cost	Total Cost	Marginal Cost	Average Fixed Cost	Average Variable Cost	Average Cost
0	____	____	____	____				
1	____	____	____	____	____	____	____	____
2	____	____	____	____	____	____	____	____
3	____	____	____	____	____	____	____	____
4	____	____	____	____	____	____	____	____
5	____	____	____	____	____	____	____	____
6	____	____	____	____	____	____	____	____
7	____	____	____	____	____	____	____	____
8	____	____	____	____	____	____	____	____
9	____	____	____	____	____	____	____	____

c. Explain the relationships between marginal product and marginal cost, and between average product and average variable cost. How does average fixed cost behave as output increases?
d. What value does marginal cost have when it crosses the minimum point of average variable cost? average cost?
e. Draw two graphs, one below the other, making sure to place the number of units of labour on both of the horizontal axes. On the top graph, draw the total product curve. On the bottom graph, draw the marginal product and average product curves
f. On another graph, with the number of units of output on the horizontal axis, plot the marginal cost, average variable cost and average cost curves.

2. Dress Up Dry Cleaners is on the short-run average cost curve specified in question 1 above, and is employing 4 units of labour and producing 36 cleaned garments per day. The company may replace its current capital with either equipment A or B, with average costs shown below. Will it buy either A or B, or keep its current capital? Why?

Total Product	Equipment A Average Cost	Equipment B Average Cost
6	$16.00	$15.00
14	10.00	8.00
24	8.00	7.00
36	7.00	6.00
50	6.00	6.50
61	6.75	7.50
70	8.50	9.00
75	10.00	11.00
78	13.25	15.00

3. Outline the advantages and disadvantages of:
   a. proprietorships and partnerships
   b. corporations

4. Will a business with a positive accounting profit always have a positive economic profit? Explain.

Solutions to Questions for Chapter 4

Fill in the Blank and True False Questions

1. **capital, labour** Process A is more capital-intensive because it uses 3 computers per worker, while Process B uses only half a computer per worker.
2. **A, B, $250, $500** Daily costs for process A are $250 [(1 worker x $100) + (3 computers x $50)], and for process B are $500 [(4 workers x $100) + (2 computers x $50)]. Process A is preferable because it is less costly than process B.
3. **B, A, $330, $320** Daily costs for process A are $330 [(1 worker x $30) + (3 computers x $100)], and for process B are $320 [(4 workers x $30) + (2 computers x $100)]. Process B is preferable because it is less costly than process A.
4. **F** Normal profit is an implicit cost, since it must be estimated by a company's owner(s).
5. **F** Accounting profit is always greater, because economic profit requires subtracting an additional category of costs from accounting profit.
6. **average, rising, marginal, falling** An average value rises when a higher marginal value is added to the associated total, while a total value increases less rapidly when marginal product is falling.
7. **F** Because the cost of materials varies with output, it is a variable cost.
8. **6, 3** A $6 rise in total cost, when divided by the additional two units, gives a marginal cost of $3.
9. **$100, $300, $0.03, $0.02** Variable costs are average variable cost (1 cent) multiplied by total product (10 000 copies), total cost is variable cost ($100) plus fixed cost ($200), average cost is total cost ($300) divided by total product, and average fixed cost is fixed cost ($200) divided by total product.
10. **F** Marginal cost is $1 (the $1 change in total cost divided by the one extra unit of total product).
11. **increasing, decreasing** With increasing returns to scale output rises more rapidly than inputs, while the opposite is true in the case of decreasing returns to scale.
12. **constant** With constant returns to scale, output and inputs rise by the same proportion.
13. **T** Long-run average cost does remain the same with constant returns to scale, since costs per unit do not vary as output changes.
14. **falls, rises** In the case of increasing returns to scale, the more rapid rise in output allows long-run average costs to fall as production increases. On the other hand, the more rapid rise of inputs in the case of decreasing returns to scale means than long-run average costs rise as production increases.
15. **T** With increasing returns to scale, large firms have a cost advantage over small firms.
16. **dividends, interest**
17. **sales revenue, profit** According to Galbraith, managers focus on sales revenue (because it determines their salaries and power in the corporation), and shareholders focus on profit (since it determines their dividends and the extent to which their share prices will rise).

Multiple Choice Questions

1. **C** More than three quarters of Canadian businesses have annual sales revenues of less than $5 million.
2. **B** This type of rent is an implicit cost because it must be estimated by the business's owners. Medical benefits, costs of materials, and insurance premiums are explicit costs because they are actual payments made by the business.
3. **E** Normal profit is the minimum amount that owners must receive to remain in the business.
4. **D** Economic profit represents a pure profit after all economic costs – both explicit and implicit – have been taken into account.
5. **C** Total implicit costs for this business are the owner's potential wage at another job ($40 000) and normal profit ($5 000).

6. **E** Total explicit costs are the interest on the bank loan ($10 000), rent on store premises ($20 000), wages for employees ($60 000), and miscellaneous costs ($15 000).

7. **A** Economic costs include all the costs listed in the table.

8. **B** Economic profit is total revenue minus economic costs ($155 000 - $150 000).

9. **B** Marginal product increases from 20 to 100 windows when the first and second workers are hired.

10. **C** Marginal product decreases from 100 windows to 30 windows when the 3rd worker is hired and decreases to 10 workers when the 4th worker is hired.

11. **E** Marginal product falls from 10 windows to -10 windows when the 5th worker is hired.

12. **B** This is due to the onset of diminishing returns.

13. **C** Marginal product starts to fall when marginal cost starts to rise – in other words at the marginal cost curve's minimum point.

14. **B** Average fixed cost always declines as output gets larger.

15. **D** The division of labour, specialized capital and specialized management are all possible reasons for increasing returns to scale.

Short Answer Questions

1a. The two main advantages of proprietorships and partnerships are the independence and flexibility for owners, and the fact that there are few legal restrictions in establishing a company. There are two main disadvantages: unlimited liability, and the inability to accumulate financial capital.

b. The main advantage of a corporation is limited liability, which encourages participation by shareholders. One disadvantage is the expense of establishing a corporation is the expense of establishing the company. Another possible disadvantage is that owners (shareholders) are not involved with management.

2. No. Explicit costs are payments for which the firm has received invoices – they are accounting costs. Implicit costs apply to resources provided by the entrepreneur. Economic costs include implicit as well as explicit costs. If total revenue exceeds explicit cost there will be an accounting profit. If total revenue does not cover explicit and implicit costs, economic profit will be negative.

3a.

Labour	Total Product	Marginal Product	Average Product
0	0		
		6	
1	6		6
		8	
2	14		7
		10	
3	24		8
		12	
4	36		9
		14	
5	50		10
		11	
6	61		10.2
		9	
7	70		10
		5	
8	75		9.4
		3	
9	78		8.7

b.

Total Product	Fixed Cost	Variable Cost	Total Cost	Marginal Cost	Average Fixed Cost	Average Variable Cost	Average Cost
0	$100	$0	$100				
				$5.00			
6	100	30	130		$16.67	$5.00	$21.67
				3.75			
14	100	60	160		7.14	4.29	11.43
				3.00			
24	100	90	190		4.17	3.75	7.92
				2.50			
36	100	120	220		2.78	3.33	6.11
				2.14			
50	100	150	250		2.00	3.00	5.00
				2.73			
61	100	180 .	280		1.64	2.95	4.59
				3.33			
70	100	210	310		1.43	3.00	4.43
				6.00			
75	100	240	340		1.33	3.20	4.53
				10.00			
78	100	270	370		1.28	3.46	4.74

c. When marginal product is increasing, marginal cost is decreasing, and when marginal product is decreasing, marginal cost is increasing. Therefore, marginal product attains its maximum when marginal cost is at its minimum. When average product is increasing, average variable cost is decreasing, and when average product is decreasing, average variable cost is increasing. Therefore, average product attains its maximum when average variable cost attains its minimum. Average fixed cost decreases throughout the entire range of output. It becomes smaller and smaller as output increases, but never attains zero.

d. At the minimum of average variable cost, marginal cost attains the same value. In this example, minimum average variable cost is $2.95 with 6 workers. This means that marginal cost intersects average variable cost at $2.90. At the minimum of average cost, marginal cost attains the same value. In this example, minimum average cost is $4.43 with 7 workers. This means that marginal cost intersects average variable cost at $4.43.

e.

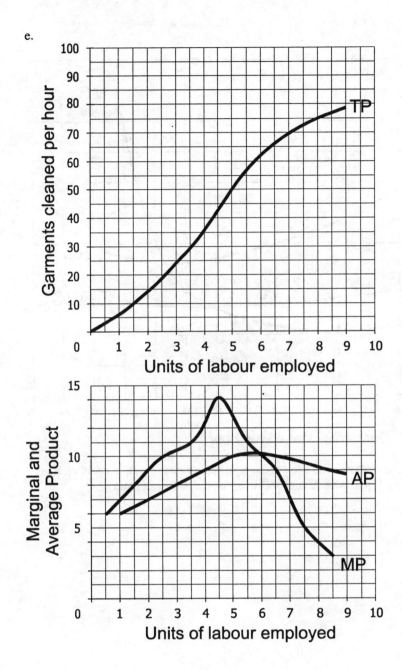

f.

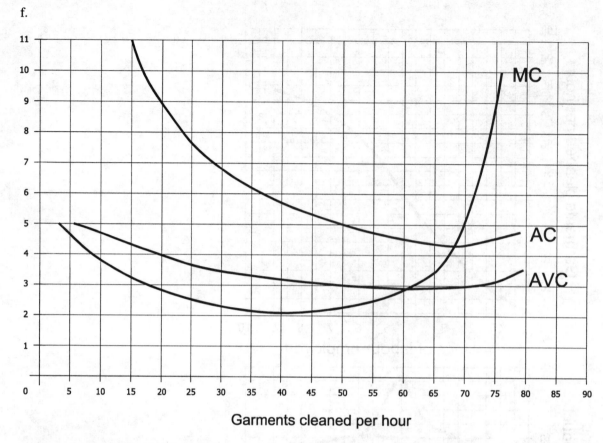

Garments cleaned per hour

4. The business will buy Equipment B, since this gives a lower average cost at a daily output of 36 cleaned garments ($6.00, as opposed to $7.00 for Equipment A, and $6.11 for the current equipment).

Chapter 5

Perfect Competition

Learning Objectives

In this chapter you will:
- consider the four market structures and main differences between them
- learn about the profit-maximizing rule and how perfect competitors use it in the short run
- examine how perfectly competitive markets adjust in the long run and the benefits they provide to consumers

Chapter Highlights

- Market Structures
  1. Product markets are classified into four structures: perfect competition, monopolistic competition, oligopoly, and monopoly. Market structure is determined by the number of businesses, the degree of product standardization, and the ease of entry and exit.
  2. Perfectly competitive markets have three main characteristics: a very large number of buyers and sellers, a standardized product, and easy entry and exit. Monopolistically competitive markets have a fairly large number of producers, some differences in product, and easy entry and exit. Oligopolies have just a few businesses, with products that may or may not vary, and restricted entry. Monopolies are single businesses providing a unique product with few close substitutes.
  3. Oligopolies and monopolies depend on entry barriers, which include increasing returns to scale, market experience, restricted ownership of resources, legal obstacles, market abuses, and advertising. Natural monopolies that experience increasing returns to scale can exclude potential entrants through the large financial requirements for entry. Predatory pricing is an illegal tactic for excluding entrants.
  4. Market power is least for perfect competitors, who are price-takers, and greatest for monopolists, who are price-makers. Market power for monopolists and oligopolists can extend to price discrimination among different buyers.

- Perfect Competition in the Short Run
  1. In perfect competition, equilibrium price is determined by the interaction of a large number of buyers and sellers. A perfect competitor can sell as much as possible at the market-determined price, so the business's demand curve is perfectly elastic or horizontal.
  2. Total revenue is price multiplied by quantity of output ($TR = P \times q$). Average revenue, which is total revenue divided by quantity of output ($AR = TR/q$), is equal to price ($AR = P$). Marginal revenue is the change in total revenue caused by a change in output ($MR = \Delta TR/\Delta q$). Because average revenue is constant for a perfect competitor, marginal revenue always equals average revenue, which is the same as price ($MR = AR = P$).
  3. For businesses in any market, profit is maximized when marginal revenue equals marginal cost ($MR = MC$). This is known as the profit-maximizing output rule.

4. A perfect competitor reaches its breakeven point when, at the profit-maximizing output, price equals minimum average cost (P = minimum AC). At this price, the business covers its normal profit, and economic profit is zero. At any price higher than the breakeven point, economic profit is positive. At any lower price, economic profit is negative, so that normal profit is no longer covered.

5. The shutdown point for a perfect competitor is where price equals minimum average variable cost (P = minimum AVC). At any lower price, the business cannot cover its variable costs, and so will shut down. The business can continue to operate in the short run at any price greater than minimum average variable cost but less than minimum average cost. At these prices, the business will minimize its losses, since variable costs and some fixed costs will be covered.

6. The portion of a perfect competitor's marginal cost curve that lies above the minimum average variable cost is the business's supply curve. The market supply curve for a perfectly-competitive industry is the sum of all the individual supply curves of the businesses in the industry.

♦ Perfect Competition in the Long Run
1. In a perfectly competitive industry, economic profits attract new businesses, while losses cause businesses to leave. When new businesses enter, economic profits for existing business are eroded. On the other hand, when businesses leave, losses are eliminated. Therefore, in the long run businesses in a perfectly competitive industry break even.

2. It follows that long run equilibrium for perfect competitors occurs when only normal profit is being made, and economic profit is zero. Businesses are covering all their costs, and charging the lowest possible price to consumers.

♦ Benefits of Perfect Competition
1. In long run equilibrium, price equals minimum average cost, which meets the condition of minimum-cost pricing. Also, price equals marginal cost, which meets the condition of marginal-cost pricing.

2. With minimum-cost pricing, businesses choose the least costly combination of inputs, and pass all these cost savings on to consumers. With marginal-cost pricing, the opportunity cost of an additional unit of output is equal to the extra benefit derived from that unit of output, which ensures the appropriate use of resources to provide the quantities of products desired by society.

Helpful Hints

♦ Market Structures
1. In actual economies, perfect competition and monopoly are relatively rare. Most markets are imperfectly competitive, which means they are either monopolistically competitive or oligopolistic. Oligopolies with standardized or diversified products are particularly common in Canada.

♦ Perfect Competition in the Short Run
1. Remember that the analysis of perfect competition is an extension of the market model set out in Chapter 2. View the model as an ideal. As a measuring rod it is an exceedingly useful guide, but it is often only an approximate representation of real-world markets.

2. The profit-maximizing output rule is an example of a type of marginal analysis that can be applied in a wide variety of contexts. Consider the extent to which your actions,

conscious or sub-conscious, are directed by marginal decisions. You will attend the next class because you expect the extra benefit derived from the class to exceed the extra opportunity cost of attending. If the extra cost is greater than the extra benefit you will find something better to do. This rule applies not only to the next class you attend, but to the next meal you eat, the next jacket you purchase, and the next movie you attend. The list is endless.

3. The word 'profit' in 'profit-maximizing' should not create confusion about the outcome. The profit-maximizing rule, MR = MC, does not always lead to a profit. The rule is also known as the loss-minimizing output rule. But even if losses are being made, it is the best possible output for maximizing profit or minimizing loss.

4. To ensure that price remains above minimum average variable cost, companies can restructure to remain viable. Replacing labour with machines may provide opportunities for reducing day-to-day operating costs. Laying-off and restructuring are also ways to reduce costs and avoid shutting down.

◆ Perfect Competition in the Long Run
1. Remember that businesses that just cover normal profit are meeting implicit costs, and can continue in business. At the same time, consumers benefit from paying the lowest possible price for the product.
2. If demand or supply curves shift so that economic profits or losses are created, then businesses will enter or leave the industry until long run equilibrium is restored where price equals minimum average cost. New entrants account for an increase in the total output of the industry. When businesses leave, total output of the industry decreases.

◆ Benefits of Perfect Competition
1. The appeal of perfectly competitive markets is that consumers get the products they want, producers get an adequate return, and price is fair. This represents the operation of Adam Smith's "invisible hand."

Key Concepts

perfect competition
monopolistic competition
oligopoly
monopoly
entry barriers
natural monopoly
predatory pricing
market power
business's demand curve

average revenue
marginal revenue
profit-maximizing output rule
breakeven point
shutdown point
business's supply curve
minimum-cost pricing
marginal-cost pricing

Fill in the Blank and True False Questions

1. Perfect competitors in a single market sell _____ products while monopolistic competitors in a single market sell _____ products.

   Place the following answer in the correct order in the blanks above.

   standardized   differentiated

2. **T F** A monopolist sells a product with close substitutes.

3. A business that temporarily drops its price below average cost to drive out smaller competitors is engaging in _____ pricing.

4. Order the following terms based on the extent to which a business in each market structure possesses market power (1 = highest, 4 = lowest).

    oligopoly   monopoly   perfect competition   monopolistic competition

    1._____
    2._____
    3._____
    4._____

5. **T F** Price discrimination can be practised by any business that possesses market power.

6. **T F** A business's demand curve is perfectly elastic for any perfect competitor.

    Figure 1 Use this table to answer questions 7 and 9.

    Demand Schedule for a Fisherman

Price	Quantity (salmon per day)
$5	0
5	150
5	400
5	580
5	720
5	800

7. Given the salmon fisherman's demand schedule in Figure 1, when quantity demanded is 150, total revenue is $_____.

8. Given the salmon fisherman's demand schedule in Figure 1, when quantity expands from 150 to 400 total revenue rises by $_____ and the number of salmon sold rises by _____. Therefore the marginal value of each of these additional salmon is $_____.

9. **T F** Given the salmon fisherman's demand schedule in Figure 1, his average revenue when selling any quantity of salmon is $5.

10. A perfect competitor's supply curve is the part of the marginal cost curve above the _____ point.

11. **T F** The market supply curve in a perfectly competitive industry is found by adding the prices charged by each firm in the industry at every possible quantity of output.

12. In the long run, perfectly competitive markets in which firms are making _____ will contract, and those is which firms are making _____ will expand until _____ are being made.

    Place the following answers in the correct order in the blanks above.

    zero economic profits   economic losses   economic profits

13. **T F** In long run equilibrium, a perfectly competitive business will earn only a normal profit.

14. _____-cost pricing means that a product is made with the least costly combination of inputs and all of these cost savings are passed on to the consumer. _____-cost pricing means that a price fully reflects a product's opportunity cost.

15. According to Karl Marx, product prices in capitalist economies can be determined using the _____ theory of value.

16. The theories of Karl Marx suggest that the rate of exploitation in capitalist economies will gradually _____ over time due to a _____ in wages.

    Place the following answers in the correct order in the blanks above.

    decrease   increase

Multiple Choice Questions

1. The perfectly competitive market structure is defined as having:
   A. one seller of a product with no close substitutes
   B. many sellers of slightly different product
   C. few sellers of a standard product
   D. many sellers of a standard product
   E. few sellers of similar products

2. Which of the following is not a potential entry barrier in a market that is a monopoly or an oligopoly?
   A. some firms can take advantage of significant decreasing returns to scale
   B. established businesses enjoy a cost advantage because of market experience
   C. there are legal obstacles that stop newcomers from entering the market
   D. one or a few businesses control supplies of a resource
   E. established businesses have large advertising budgets that are difficult for newcomers to match

3. As output increases, the total revenue of the perfectly competitive firm will increase by:
   A. increasing amounts
   B. decreasing amounts
   C. decreasing then increasing amounts
   D. increasing then decreasing amounts
   E. constant amounts

*TR - TC
= Profit*

Figure 2 Use this table to answer questions 4 to 8.

MR

Short-Run Costs for a Fisherman

MR = MC

Total Product (salmon per day)	Marginal Cost	Average Cost	Average Variable Cost
0		--	--
	$4.00		
150		$5.33	$4.00
	2.40		
400		3.50	3.05
	3.33		
580		3.45	3.10
	4.29		
720		3.61	3.50
	7.50		
800		4.00	3.75

4. Given the salmon fisherman's costs in Figure 2, if the price of salmon is set at $5, his profit-maximizing quantity is:
   A. 150 salmon
   B. 400 salmon
   C. 580 salmon
   D. 720 salmon
   E. 800 salmon

5. Given the salmon fisherman's costs in Figure 2, if the price of salmon is set at $5, his economic profit at his profit-maximizing quantity is:
   A. $0
   B. $1000
   C. $2000
   D. $3000
   E. $4000

6. Given the salmon fisherman's costs in Figure 2, if the market price of salmon moves to $3.45, his profit-maximizing quantity becomes:
   A. 150 salmon
   B. 400 salmon
   C. 580 salmon
   D. 720 salmon
   E. 800 salmon

7. Given the salmon fisherman's costs in Figure 2, and with the market price of salmon set at $3.45, his economic profit at his profit-maximizing quantity is:
   A. $0
   B. $1000
   C. $2000
   D. $3000
   E. $4000

8. Given the salmon fisherman's costs in Figure 2, if the market price of salmon moves to $3.00, the fisherman's profit-maximizing quantity becomes:
   A. 0 salmon
   B. 150 salmon
   C. 400 salmon
   D. 580 salmon
   E. 720 salmon

9. Given the salmon fisherman's costs in Figure 2, at a price of $3.45 he reaches his:
   A. sole loss-minimizing point.
   B. sole profit-maximizing point.
   C. shutdown point
   D. breakeven point
   E. none of the above

Figure 3 Use this graph to answer questions 10 to 13.

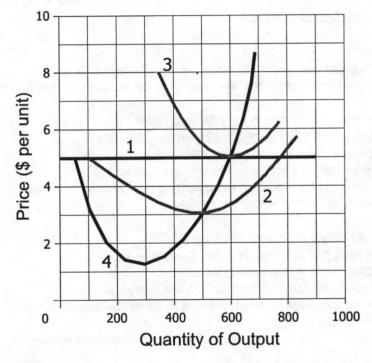

10. Based on the information for a salmon fisherman in Figure 3, which of the following statements is true?
    A. Curve 1 is marginal cost, curve 2 is average cost, curve 3 is average variable cost, and curve 4 is marginal revenue.
    B. Curve 1 is marginal revenue, curve 2 is average variable cost, curve 3 is marginal cost, and curve 4 is average cost.
    C. Curve 1 is average cost, curve 2 is marginal revenue, curve 3 is marginal cost, and curve 4 is average variable cost.
    D. Curve 1 is average variable cost, curve 2 is average cost, curve 3 is marginal cost, and curve 4 is marginal revenue.
    E. Curve 1 is marginal revenue, curve 2 is average variable cost, curve 3 is average cost, and curve 4 is marginal cost.

11. Based on the information for a salmon fisherman in Figure 3, his profit-maximizing quantity at a price of $5 is found at:
    A. the minimum point on the marginal cost curve
    B. the minimum point on the average variable cost curve
    C. the point where the average cost curve intersects the marginal revenue curve
    D. the point where the marginal cost curve intersects the marginal revenue curve
    E. the point where the average variable cost curve intersects the marginal revenue curve

12. Based on the revenue and cost curves for a salmon fisherman in Figure 3, his breakeven point is found at:
    A. the minimum point on the marginal cost curve
    B. the minimum point on the average variable cost curve
    C. the minimum point on the average cost curve
    D. the point at which the marginal cost curve intersects the marginal revenue curve
    E. the point at which the average variable cost curve intersects the marginal revenue curve

13. Based on the information for a salmon fisherman in Figure 3, his shutdown point is found at:
    A. the minimum point on the marginal cost curve
    B. the minimum point on the average variable cost curve
    C. the minimum point on the average cost curve
    D. the point at which the marginal cost curve intersects the marginal revenue curve
    E. the point at which the average variable cost curve intersects the marginal revenue curve

14. Which of the following does not describe minimum-cost pricing?
    A. the lowest possible cost of a perfectly competitive business
    B. the long-run equilibrium for a perfectly competitive business
    C. the long-run breakeven position for a perfectly competitive business
    D. the short-run breakeven position for a perfectly competitive business
    E. the price which covers all costs including normal profit

15. Which of the following does not describe marginal-cost pricing?
    A. the long-run equilibrium for a perfectly competitive business
    B. the practice of setting price where it equals marginal cost
    C. the practice of setting a price that fully reflects the product's opportunity cost
    D. distributing society's scarce resources among industries in a way that maximizes the overall satisfaction of consumers
    E. the practice of setting a price so that it maximizes the producer's opportunity cost

Short Answer Questions

1. Categorize the four market structures according to characteristics set out in the table below.

Characteristics	Number of Firms	Standard Product	Market Power for Firms	Ease of Entry and Exit
Perfect Competition	v. many	always	none	v. easy
Monopolistic Competition	many	never	none	easy
Oligopoly	few	sometimes	some	diff
Monopoly	one	not applicable	great	v. diff

2. Fish farming of a particular species has developed as a perfectly competitive industry with 10 000 businesses. The costs of a representative business are set out in the table below.

Output (kgs.)	Average Variable	Average Cost	Marginal Cost
0	-	-	
			$4.00
5	4.00	$24.00	
			2.00
15	2.70	9.30	
			1.54
28	2.14	5.57	
			1.67
40	2.00	4.50	
			4.00
45	2.20	4.40	
			10.00
47	2.60	4.70	

a. At what price would this business reach its breakeven point? its shutdown point?
b. What is this business's profit at a price of $7? a price of $3?
c. Explain how to find this business's supply curve and the entire industry's supply curve, using the prices of $7 and $3 as illustrations.
d. Graph the average variable cost, average cost, and marginal cost curves on a graph.

3. Using the data in question 3, explain what would happen in this industry in the long run if:
a. market price is $7
b. market price is $3

Solutions to Questions for Chapter 3

Fill in the Blank and True False Questions

1. **standardized, differentiated** Products in perfectly competitive markets must be standardized so that the outputs of various suppliers are indistinguishable, while those in monopolistically competitive markets are always differentiated, so that each supplier has some control over its own price.

2. **F** The product a monopolist sells must have no close substitutes, so that the business has significant control over its own price.

3. **predatory** This is known as predatory pricing, since the firm seeks to destroy its prey.

4. **monopoly, oligopoly, monopolistic competition, perfect competition**

5. **F** Not only must businesses possess market power, they must also be able to divide up their market into separate segments and stop resale by consumers.

6. **T** This is because the business is too small to have any impact on the market price, so it faces the prevailing price regardless of how much it produces.

7. **750** This is found by multiplying the $5 price by the quantity of 150.

8. **1250, 250, 5**

9. **T** Notice that price is $5 at every possible quantity level.

10. **shutdown** This point occurs where the marginal cost curve crosses the average variable cost curve. At prices below this point, the business will supply a zero quantity.

11. **F** It is the quantities supplied by each business that must be added together at every possible price.

12. **economic losses, economic profits, zero economic profits**
13. **T** At this point, a perfectly competitor will be making zero economic profit, which means it earns only a normal profit (which is considered part of economic costs).
14. **Minimum, Marginal**
15. **labour**
16. **increase, decrease** Marx predicted that exploitation will rise due to a fall in wages. Whether this has in fact occurred is another matter.

Multiple Choice Questions

1. **D** Perfectly competitive markets have many buyers and a standard product.
2. **A** It is increasing returns to scale that can serve as potential entry barrier.
3. **E** Total revenue increases by the same amount as price, which is constant.
4. **D** At this output, marginal cost goes from $4.29 to $7.50. Therefore, in this range is the point where marginal cost equals the $5 marginal revenue.
5. **B** This fisherman makes an economic profit of $1000, since, at his profit-maximizing daily output of 720 salmon, his total revenue is $3600 and his total cost is $2600.
6. **C** At this output, marginal cost goes from $3.33 to $4.29. Therefore, in this range is the point where marginal cost equals the $3.45 marginal revenue.
7. **A** This is because the fisherman's total revenue and total cost both equal $2000 at a daily output of 580 salmon.
8. **A** At a price of $3.00, the fisherman is no longer covering even his variable costs, so it is better to produce nothing.
9. **D** This name refers to the fact that the fisherman is making zero economic profit.
10. **E** The marginal revenue line is always horizontal for a perfect competitor.
11. **D** This is how the profit-maximizing rule is applied to the graph.
12. **C** At this point, price and average cost are equal at the profit-maximizing output, giving a zero economic profit.
13. **B** At this point, price and average variable cost are equal at the loss-minimizing output, which means that total revenue just covers variable costs.
14. **D** Minimum-cost pricing is attained in the long run for perfect competitors, not in the short run.
15. **E** Marginal-cost pricing maximizes consumer satisfaction, not producers' opportunity costs.

Short Answer Questions

1.

Characteristics	Number of Firms	Standard Product	Market Power of Firms	Ease of Entry and Exit
Perfect Competition	very many	always	none	very easy
Monopolistic Competition	many	never	some	fairly easy
Oligopoly	few	sometimes	some	difficult
Monopoly	one	not applicable	great	very difficult

2a. This business's breakeven point is at a price of $4.40, where average cost reaches its minimum. The business's shutdown point is at a price of $1.54, where average variable cost reaches its minimum.
b. At a price of $7, the business will produce 45 kgs. of fish, since marginal cost is below $7 between 40 and 45 kgs. and above $3 between 45 and 47 kgs. Given that total revenue is $315 (= $7 x 45), and total cost is $198 (= $4.40 x 45), the business's economic profit is $117 (= $315 - $198). Meanwhile, at a price of $3, the business produce 40 kgs. of fish, since marginal cost is below $3 between 28 and 40 kilograms and above $3 between 40 and 45 kgs. Given that total revenue is $120 (= $3 x 40), and total cost is $180 (= $4.50 x 40), the business's economic loss is (-)$60 (= $120 - $180).
c. The business's supply curve is the MC curve above the shutdown point, while the industry's supply curve is found by multiplying each of the quantity levels on the business's supply curve by 10 000 (the number of businesses in the industry). So, at a price of $7, the quantity supplied by the business would be

approximately 45 kgs. (based on the related quantity on the MC curve at this monetary value), and at a price of $3, the quantity supplied by the business would be approximately 40 kgs. (again based on the MC curve). The associated values for the industry are therefore 450 000 kgs. for the $7 price and 400 000 kgs. for the $3 price.

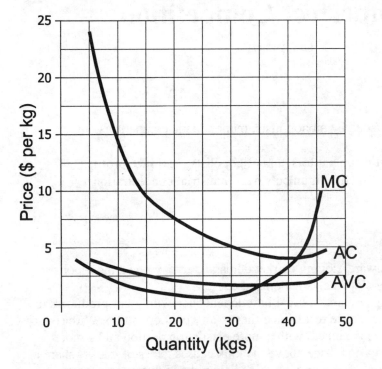

3a. At a $7 price, economic profits are being made in the industry. As new business are attracted, the market supply curve shifts to the right and equilibrium price falls until all economic profits are eroded. Long run equilibrium is attained at a price of $4.40 with an output of 45 kgs. per business. At this price and output, price equals marginal cost which is equal to minimum average cost. The minimum-cost rule and the marginal-cost rule are therefore satisfied.

b. At a $3 price, economic losses are being made in the industry. As businesses leave the industry, the market supply curve shift to the left, and equilibrium price rise until economic losses disappear at a price of $4.40 and an output of 45 kgs. per business. Again, the minimum-cost rule and the marginal-cost rule are satisfied.

Chapter 6

Monopoly and Imperfect Competition

Learning Objectives

In this chapter you will:
♦ consider the demand conditions faced by monopolists, monopolistic competitors, and oligopolists
♦ see how monopolists, monopolistic competitors, and oligopolists maximize profits
♦ learn about nonprice competition and the arguments over industrial concentration

Chapter Highlights

♦ Demand Differences
1. A monopolist faces the downward-sloping market demand curve, while a monopolistic competitor faces a negatively-sloped elastic demand curve.
2. An oligopolist's demand curve reflects mutual interdependence with other producers in the industry. Mutual interdependence results in either rivalry or cooperation. With rivalry, the oligopolist's demand curve is kinked, with a more elastic top portion and a more inelastic bottom portion. Increasing price above the kink causes a loss of market share as rivals maintain their lower price. Reducing the price below the kink causes a loss of market share as rivals match the price reduction. With cooperation – achieved through price leadership, collusion, or a cartel – oligopolists act as a single monopolist, facing a downward-sloping demand curve.

♦ Monopoly
1. The monopolist's downward-sloping demand curve permits equality between price and average revenue. However, marginal revenue is less than price, since when price is reduced to sell one more unit of output, the price on all other units sold must be reduced as well.
2. The profit-maximizing rule – marginal revenue equals marginal cost – is used to find the monopolist's output. The price corresponding to this output is found on the demand curve. This price, along with the average cost at this output, together determine economic profit.
3. In monopoly the conditions of minimum-cost pricing and marginal-cost pricing are not met. Price is not necessarily equal to minimum average cost, and price is greater than marginal cost.
4. In a monopoly, the location of the marginal revenue curve beneath the demand curve results in a lower output and higher price than would apply in a corresponding perfectly competitive market. At this price and output, the monopolist is making an economic profit.
5. Government regulation of natural monopolies limits excessive profits by imposing an average-cost price. The problem of estimating the average-cost price is partly overcome by estimating a fair rate of return based on a set accounting-profit rate.

- ♦ Imperfect Competition
  1. Imperfect competition includes the market structures of monopolistic competition and oligopoly. For a monopolistic competitor, the demand curve is downward sloping, with average revenue equal to price. As with a monopolist, a monopolistic competitor's marginal revenue is below average revenue, since reducing price to sell one more unit means reducing price on all other units as well.
  2. In the short run, the monopolistic competitor uses the profit-maximizing output rule to find the output where marginal revenue equals marginal cost. The price corresponding to this output is found on the demand curve, with economic profit determined by comparing price and average cost.
  3. In the long run, positive economic profits attract new businesses into a monopolistically competitive market. As these businesses enter the industry, the demand curves for existing businesses become more elastic and shift to the left. The profit-maximizing output will be less for each business, and, ultimately, price will equal average cost. Likewise, economic losses force out some monopolistic competitors in the long run. As businesses leave the market, the demand curves for remaining businesses become less elastic and shift to the right. The profit-maximizing output for each business will increase, and again price will ultimately equal average cost. Nevertheless, in monopolistic competition neither minimum-cost pricing nor marginal-cost pricing is attained in the long run.
  4. Oligopolists who are rivals, like all other businesses, use the profit-maximizing output rule. Their marginal revenue curve, which lies below the demand curve, has two segments that are misaligned because of the kink in the demand curve. Equality between marginal revenue and marginal cost occurs at the output defined by the kink. Oligopolists who are rivals do not attain the minimum-cost or the marginal-cost pricing conditions. At the profit-maximizing output, price is greater than marginal cost and there are no competitive pressures that force price towards average cost in the long run.
  5. Cooperating oligopolists charge a higher price than rival oligopolists, so minimum-cost and marginal-cost pricing are not attained.
  6. To enhance competition, anti-combines legislation has been implemented in Canada since 1889. In 1986 the laws were amended to facilitate international competitiveness and the benefits of increasing returns to scale. The Competition Tribunal oversees civil offenses under the Act, such as abuse of dominant position. Conspiracy, bid-rigging and predatory pricing are criminal offences which are tried in the courts.

- ♦ Traits of Imperfect Competition
  1. Imperfectly competitive businesses use non-price competition to attract consumers. The goals of non-price competition are to increase demand and to decrease the price elasticity of demand. The two strategies employed to do this are product differentiation and advertising. Product differentiation creates product differences that are either cosmetic or substantial. Advertising provides information and promotes consumer preference for a product. Advertising may be anti-competitive, enhancing the market power of established businesses, or pro-competitive, by giving new businesses a chance to make their presence known.
  2. Businesses gain from non-price competition when the extra revenue from a particular strategy exceeds extra cost. Consumers may either gain or lose, since they gain from convenience and choice, but pay higher prices.
  3. Concentration ratios, based on the percentage of total sales revenue earned by the four largest businesses in an industry, can be used to measure the structure of imperfectly competitive markets. A four-firm ratio of 50 percent is the benchmark for classifying an

      industry as an oligopoly (if the ratio is greater than 50 percent) or as being monopolistically competitive (if the ratio is less than 50 percent).

4. Industrial concentration permits cost savings from increasing returns to scale and sometimes the benefits of innovation. However, market power may be reflected in higher prices, and it is quite possible for competitive markets to be as innovative as concentrated ones.

Helpful Hints

♦ Monopoly
1. The horizontal intercept of the monopolist's marginal revenue curve always lies halfway between the horizontal intercept of the demand curve and the origin. At the horizontal intercept of the marginal revenue curve, marginal revenue equals zero, and total revenue is maximized.
2. The easiest way to find the profit-maximizing output and price for a monopolist is with the aid of a graph. Output is determined at the intersection of the MR and MC curves. To find the monopolist's price, a line is drawn perpendicular from the quantity axis, through the intersection of marginal revenue and marginal cost, to the demand curve. Meanwhile, this same vertical line will intersect average cost at the appropriate value, as read off the vertical axis. If the average cost curve lies below the demand curve, the monopolist is making an economic profit. If the average cost curve lies above the demand curve, the monopolist is making a loss.

♦ Imperfect Competition
1. Monopolistic competition lies between the market structures of perfect competition and monopoly. The analysis for monopolistic competition is similar to the analysis for monopoly, except that the demand curve is flatter.
2. Remember that the market structure of cooperating oligopolists coincides with that of a pure monopolist.
3. A supply curve can be defined only for perfectly competitive markets. Recall the definition of supply. In perfect competition, there are a multitude of possible prices, each with an associated quantity supplied. However, for monopoly, monopolistic competition, and oligopoly there is only one quantity, determined by the profit-maximizing output, with its corresponding price.

Key Concepts

mutual interdependence
market share
kinked demand curve
price leadership
collusion
cartel
average-cost pricing
accounting-profit rate
fair rate of return

anti-combines legislation
horizontal merger
vertical merger
conglomerate merger
non-price competition
product differentiation
concentration ratio
industrial concentration

Fill in the Blank and True False Questions

1. _____ _____ refers to the fact that the actions of an oligopolist affect all of its competitors.

2. While _____ can occur in an oligopoly without direct interaction among businesses in the market, _____ is a type of _____ that requires a formal agreement.

   Place the following answer in the correct order in the blanks above.
   collusion   price leadership   a cartel

3. **T F** Product differentiation and advertising both allow monopolistic competitors and oligopolists to permanently raise their profits.

4. **T F** If there are five businesses in a market, each with 20 percent of the market's total sales revenue, the market's four-firm concentration ratio is 80 percent.

5. A concentration ratio _____ the extent of competition in localized markets and _____ the extent of competition in markets with imports.

   Place the following answer in the correct order in the blanks above.

   overestimates   underestimates

6. _____ _____ refers to the domination of a market by one or a few large businesses.

7. **T F** The main defense of industrial concentration is that healthy profits are earned by owners of businesses in concentrated markets.

8. **T F** Any business's profit is maximized when total revenue equals total cost.

9. When monopolistic competitors make economic profits, businesses enter the market in the long run, shifting demand curves for existing firms to the _____. On the other hand, when economic losses are being made, businesses leave the market in the long run, shifting demand curves for remaining firms to the _____.

   Place the following answer in the correct order in the blanks above.

   right   left

10. **T F** A monopolistic competitor necessarily makes a positive economic profit in the long run.

11. The _____ demand curve explains why some oligopolists are reluctant to change price.

Figure 1 Use this graph to answer questions 12 to 15.

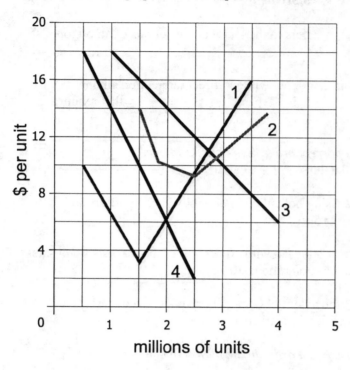

12. Based on the information for Hook-Up Cable shown in Figure 1, fill in the number of the appropriate curve for each of the revenue and cost concepts.

    marginal cost   _____
    demand   _____
    average cost   _____
    marginal revenue   _____

13. **T F** Given the demand curve for Hook-Up Cable shown in Figure 1, this business most likely operates in a market that is monopolistically competitive.

14. Given the demand curve for Hook-Up Cable in Figure 1, when price declines from $14 to $10 total revenue rises by $_____ and the number of subscribers rises by _____. Therefore the marginal revenue of each of these additional subscribers is $_____.

15. Given the revenue and cost information for Hook-Up Cable in Figure 1, the profit-maximizing price and quantity for this business are _____ and _____ subscribers.

16. **T F** Given the revenue and cost information for the Hook-Up Cable in Figure 1, the business is making a positive economic profit at its profit-maximizing price and quantity.

17. If a market that is initially perfectly competitive is transformed into a monopoly, equilibrium quantity _____ and equilibrium price _____.

    Place the following answer in the correct order in the blanks above.

    rises   falls

18. A public agency that regulates a monopoly usually tries to make the firm charge a price that just covers its _____ cost.

19. According to Joseph Schumpeter, the central player in the progress of capitalism is the _____, while the crucial player in the eventual decline of capitalism is the _____.

Multiple Choice Questions

Figure 2 Use this figure to answer questions 1 to 7.

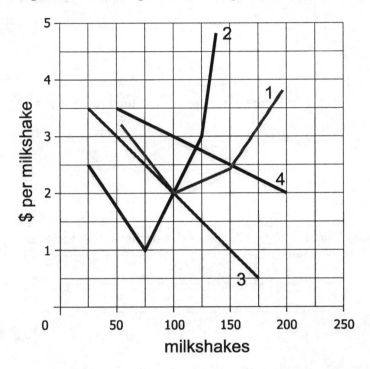

1. Based on the information for the Dairy Palace in Figure 2, which of the following statements is true?
    A. Curve 1 is marginal cost, curve 2 is average cost, curve 3 is demand, and curve 4 is marginal revenue.
    B. Curve 1 is average cost, curve 2 is marginal cost, curve 3 is marginal revenue, and curve 4 is demand.
    C. Curve 1 is average cost, curve 2 is marginal cost, curve 3 is demand, and curve 4 is marginal revenue.
    D. Curve 1 is marginal cost, curve 2 is average cost, curve 3 is marginal revenue, and curve 4 is demand.
    E. Curve 1 is demand, curve 2 is marginal revenue, curve 3 is marginal cost, and curve 4 is average cost.

2. Given the demand curve for the Dairy Palace shown in Figure 2, this business most likely operates in a market that is:
    A. perfectly competitive
    B. monopolistically competitive
    C. a collusive oligopoly
    D. a monopoly
    E. a rival oligopoly

3. Given the demand curve for the Dairy Palace in Figure 2, the appropriate total revenue at a price of $3.50 is:
    A. $612.50
    B. $437.50
    C. $300.00
    D. $175.00
    E. $87.50

4. Given the demand curve for the Dairy Palace in Figure 2, the appropriate total revenue at a price of $3.00 is:
    A. $375.00
    B. $312.50
    C. $300.00
    D. $187.50
    E. $62.50

5. Given the demand curve for the Dairy Palace in Figure 2, when price declines from $3.50 to $3, the marginal revenue of each of the new milkshakes sold is:
    A. $3.50
    B. $3.00
    C. $2.50
    D. $2.00
    E. $1.50

6. Given the revenue and cost information for the Dairy Palace in Figure 2, the profit-maximizing price and quantity for this business are:
    A. $4 and 0 milkshakes
    B. $3.50 and 50 milkshakes
    C. $3 and 100 milkshakes
    D. $2.50 and 150 milkshakes
    E. $2 and 200 milkshakes

7. Given the revenue and cost information for the Dairy Palace in Figure 2, the business is making:
    A. a positive economic profit at its profit-maximizing price and quantity.
    B. a negative economic profit at its profit-maximizing price and quantity.
    C. a zero profit at its profit-maximizing quantity.
    D. such a large loss that it closes down its operations.
    E. none of the above

8. Businesses that use non-price competition are attempting to:
    A. shift their demand curve to the left and make it more elastic
    B. shift their demand curve to the left and make it less elastic
    C. shift their demand curve to the right and make it more elastic
    D. shift their demand curve to the right and make it less elastic
    E. move along the existing inelastic demand curve

9. The appropriate range of the concentration ratio for oligopoly is:
    A. one hundred percent
    B. between fifty and ninety-nine percent
    C. between one and fifty percent
    D. zero percent
    E. between one and ninety-nine percent

10. The appropriate range of the concentration ratio for monopolistic competition is:
    A. one hundred percent
    B. between fifty and ninety nine percent
    C. between one and fifty percent
    D. zero percent
    E. between one and ninety nine percent

Figure 3 Use this graph to answer questions 11 to 15.

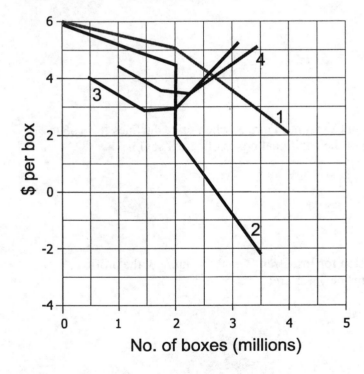

11. Based on the information for the Just-Bran Cereal in Figure 3, which of the following statements is true?
    A. Curve 1 is marginal cost, curve 2 is average cost, curve 3 is demand, and curve 4 is marginal revenue.
    B. Curve 1 is average cost, curve 2 is marginal cost, curve 3 is marginal revenue, and curve 4 is demand.
    C. Curve 1 is average cost, curve 2 is marginal cost, curve 3 is demand, and curve 4 is marginal revenue.
    D. Curve 1 is marginal cost, curve 2 is average cost, curve 3 is marginal revenue, and curve 4 is demand.
    E. Curve 1 is demand, curve 2 is marginal revenue, curve 3 is marginal cost, and curve 4 is average cost.

12. Given the demand curve for Just-Bran Cereal in Figure 3, the appropriate total revenue at a price of $5 is:
    A. $10.5 million
    B. $10 million
    C. $8 million
    D. $5.5 million
    E. $5 million

13. Given the demand curve for Just-Bran Cereal in Figure 3, the appropriate total revenue at a price of $3.50 is:
    A. $10.5 million
    B. $10 million
    C. $8 million
    D. $5.5 million
    E. $5 million

14. Given the demand curve for Just-Bran Cereal in Figure 3, when price declines from $5 to $3.50, the marginal revenue of each of the additional boxes of cereal sold is:
    A. $5.50
    B. $4.50
    C. $3.00
    D. $2.00
    E. $0.50

15. Given the revenue and cost information for Just-Bran Cereal in Figure 3, the profit-maximizing price and quantity for this business are:
    A. $6 and 0 boxes of cereal
    B. $5.50 and 1 million boxes of cereal
    C. $5 and 2 million boxes of cereal
    D. $3.50 and 3 million boxes of cereal
    E. $2 and 4 million boxes of cereal

Short Answer Questions

1. Gopher Golf Club, the only golf club in the small rural community of Hole-in-one, faces the following price, quantity, average cost, and marginal cost schedules.

Price	Quantity (players per day)	Total Revenue	Marginal Revenue	Average Cost	Marginal Cost
$225	0	0		-	
	>10	>2000	200		$60
200	10	2000		$160.00	
	>10	>1500	150		40
175	20	3500		100.00	
	>10	1000	100		20
150	30	4500		73.33	
	>10	>500	50		30
125	40	5000		62.50	
	>10	>	—		40
100	50	5000		58.00	
	>10	-500	-50		60
75	60	4500		58.33	
	>10	-1000	-100		70
50	70	3500		60.00	

    a. Complete the table above.
    b. What is the club's profit-maximizing output and price?
    c. What is the club's total cost, total revenue, and economic profit or loss?
    d. Draw a graph to verify your answers to b and c.
    e. Are the conditions of minimum-cost and marginal-cost pricing met by this business?

2.   Third Rival Ltd. is a competing oligopolist in a market of three businesses.

Price	Quantity	Total Revenue	Marginal Revenue	Marginal Cost	Average Cost
$13	8	104			$17.50
	>4	>40	10	$2	
12	12	144			12.33
	>4	>32	8	3	
11	16	176			10.00
	>4	>24	6	4	
10	20	200			8.80
	>2	>2	-1	5	
9	22	198			8.45
	>2	>6	-3	6	
8	24	192			8.25
	>2	>-10	-5	7	
7	26	182			8.15
	>2	>-14	-7	8	
6	28	168			8.14

a. Complete the above table.
b. What is Third Rival's profit-maximizing output and price?
c. What is the business's total cost, total revenue, and economic profit or loss?
d. Draw a graph to verify your answers to parts b and c.

e. Why is Third Rival unlikely to change its output and price from this point?

3. NewData is a computer software business operating in a monopolistically competitive market.

Price (per disc)	Quantity	Total Revenue	Marginal Revenue	Marginal Cost	Average Cost
$65	1500	____			$70
			____	$50	
60	3000	____			60
			____	21	
55	4500	____			47
			____	11	
50	6000	____			38
			____	18	
45	7500	____			34
			____	28	
40	9000	____			33
			____	40	
35	10 500	____			34

a. Complete the above table.
b. What is NewData's profit-maximizing output and price?
c. Calculate the business's total revenue, economic cost, and economic profit.
d. Explain the changes that will take place for NewData in the long run.

Solutions to Questions for Chapter 6

Fill in the Blank and True False Questions
1. **mutual interdependence**
2. **price leadership, a cartel, collusion**
3. **F** Any increase in profits provided by product differentiation or advertising may be temporary - almost certainly so in the case of monopolistic competition where positive economic profits attract new rivals in the long run.
4. **T** Since all firms have an identical 20 percent market share, the top four firms (which can be any four in the market) have a concentration ratio (or combined market share) of 80 percent.
5. **overestimates, underestimates** Because concentration ratios are national in scope, they overestimate the extent of competition in localized markets. However, since they exclude foreign competitors, they underestimate the extent of competition markets with imports.
6. **industrial concentration**
7. **F** The main defenses are that big firms can provide lower prices and more innovative products because of their ability to take advantage of increasing returns to scale and to engage in research and development.
8. **F** The profit-maximizing point occurs where total revenue exceeds total cost by the largest possible amount.
9. **left, right** With new rivals, demand curves for those already in the market decreases. With the exit of firms, the demand curves for those that remain increases.
10. **F** In the long run, the monopolistic competitor can expect to make zero economic profit.
11. **kinked**
12. **marginal cost = 1, demand = 3, average cost = 2, marginal revenue = 4**
13. **F** Because of its relatively inelastic demand curve, this business likely operates as a monopolist.
14. **2 million, 1 million, 2**

15. **$14, 2 million** This is the output and associated price where marginal revenue and marginal cost intersect.

16. **T** At the business's profit-maximizing quantity of 2 million subscribers, total revenue exceeds total cost giving a positive economic profit.

17. **falls, rises** Quantity falls because the monopolist cuts back on output in order to make marginal revenue equal marginal cost. As quantity drops, the associated price on the demand curve rises.

18. **average** This is done in an attempt to ensure that the monopoly breaks even.

19. **entrepreneur, bureaucrat** Schumpeter stressed the progressive innovation of entrepreneurs and the destructive rule-making of bureaucrats. According to Schumpeter, the innovations of entrepreneurs allow capitalism to progress, while the rules and regulations imposed by bureaucrats finally destroy capitalism.

Multiple Choice Questions

1. **B** Remember that demand is always above marginal revenue and average cost intersects marginal cost at the minimum point on the average cost curve.

2. **B** Monopolistic competitors face an elastic demand curve such as the one shown in the graph.

3. **D** This is found by multiplying the $3.50 price by the associated quantity of 50 milkshakes.

4. **C** This is found by multiplying the $3 price by the associated quantity of 100 milkshakes.

5. **C** This is because total revenue rises by $125 while quantity rises by 50, giving a marginal revenue for each additional milkshake of $2.50.

6. **C** At an output of 100 milkshakes, the marginal revenue and marginal cost curves intersect and the maximum price that can be charged is $3.

7. **A** A positive economic profit is being made since the demand curve is higher than the average cost curve.

8. **D** The businesses are trying to shift their demand to the right and make it less elastic.

9. **B** This range of concentration ratios means that only a few businesses control the market.

10. **C** This range of concentration ratios means that there are a relatively large number of businesses in the market.

11. **E** Remember that demand is always above marginal revenue and average cost intersects marginal cost at the minimum point on the average cost curve.

12. **B** This is found by multiplying the $5 price by the associated quantity of 2 million boxes.

13. **A** This is found by multiplying the $3.50 price by the associated quantity of 3 million boxes.

14. **E** This is because total revenue rises by $.5 million while quantity rises by 1 million, giving a marginal revenue for each additional cereal box of $0.50.

15. **C** At an output of 2 million boxes of cereal, the marginal revenue and marginal cost curves intersect and the maximum price that can be charged is $5.

Short Answer Questions

1a.

Price	Quantity (players per day)	Total Revenue	Marginal Revenue	Average Cost	Marginal Cost
225	0	0		-	
			200		60
200	10	2000		160.00	
			150		40
175	20	3500		100.00	
			100		20
150	30	4500		73.33	
			50		30
125	40	5000		62.50	
			0		40
100	50	5000		58.00	
			-50		60
75	60	4500		58.33	
			-100		70
50	70	3500		60.00	

b. At Gopher Golf's profit-maximizing quantity of 40 players and the associated price of $125, marginal revenue equals marginal cost, since between 30 and 40 players the $50 marginal revenue exceeds the $30 marginal cost, while the opposite is the case between 40 and 50 players.

c. Since the club's total revenue is $5000 and total cost is $2500 (= $62.50 x 40), its economic profit is $2500.

d.

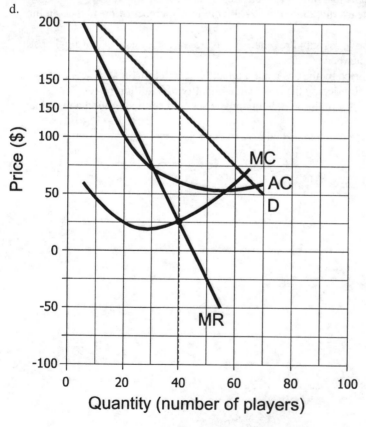

e. Neither the minimum-cost pricing nor the marginal-cost pricing conditions is met, since price is greater than both minimum average cost and marginal cost.

2a.

Price	Quantity	Total Revenue	Marginal Revenue	Marginal Cost	Average Cost
13	8	$104			$17.50
			$10	$2	
12	12	144			12.33
			8	3	
11	16	176			10.00
			6	4	
10	20	200			8.80
			-1	5	
9	22	198			8.45
			-3	6	
8	24	192			8.25
			-5	7	
7	26	182			8.15
			-7	8	
6	28	168			8.14

b. At Third Rival's profit-maximizing output of 20 units and its associated price of $10.00, marginal revenue and marginal cost meet, since between 16 and 20 units the $6 marginal revenue exceeds the $4 marginal cost, while the opposite is the case between 20 and 22 units.

c. Since the business's total revenue is $200 and total cost is $176 (= $8.80 x 20), economic profit is $24.

d.

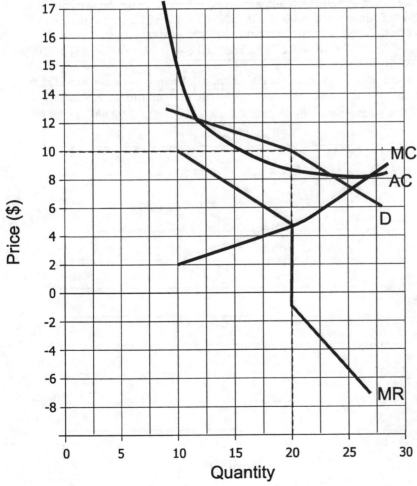

e. Given the broad vertical range on this business's MR curve, Third Rival is unlikely to change its price and quantity. Only if the MC curve shifts so that it no longer intersects within this vertical range of the MR curve will the business's price and quantity be adjusted.

3a.

Price (per disc)	Quantity	Total Revenue	Marginal Revenue	Marginal Cost	Average Cost
$65	1500	97 500			70
			55	50	
60	3000	180 000			60
			45	21	
55	4500	247 500			47
			35	11	
50	6000	300 000			38
			25	18	
45	7500	337 500			34
			15	28	
40	9000	360 000			33
			5	40	
35	10 500	367 500			34

b. At NewData's profit-maximizing output of 7500 units and associated price of $45.00, the marginal revenue and marginal cost curves meet, since between 6000 and 7500 discs, the $25 marginal revenue exceeds the $18 marginal cost, while the opposite is the case between 7500 and 9000 discs.

c. Since the business's total revenue is $337 500 (= $45 x 7500) and total cost is $255 000 (= $34 x 7500), economic profit is $82 500 (= $337 500 – 255 000).

d. Economic profit will attract new entrants. NewData's demand curve will become more elastic and shift to the left, reducing economic profits until they reach zero at long-run equilibrium. But since NewData always remains on the downward sloping portion of the average cost curve, neither the minimum-cost nor marginal-cost pricing conditions are met.

Chapter 7

Wages, Rent, Interest, and Profit

Learning Objectives

In this chapter you will:
- consider how businesses choose the profit-maximizing amount of a resource they use when they are price-takers in the product markets in which they sell their products
- look at the case where businesses are price-makers in their product markets and analyze the factors that change resource demand and affect the price elasticity of resource demand
- learn about the factors that affect wages, including productivity, education, experience, job conditions, regional disparities, market power, and discrimination
- look at the incomes from other resources – rent, interest, and profit

Chapter Highlights

- How Resource Markets Operate
    1. In resource markets, prices are influenced by the interaction of supply and demand. Households sell economic resources to businesses and receive incomes in return. Economic resources are land, capital, labour, and entrepreneurship. Incomes are rent, interest, wages, and profit.
    2. Demand for resources is determined indirectly by the demand for final products. Resources are demanded if they create extra profit from the sale of the final product. The assessment of the extra profit derived from the use of additional resources is based on marginal productivity theory. This theory highlights three concepts: the marginal product of the resource, the marginal revenue received from an additional unit of output of the product, and the marginal cost of the resource.
    3. Marginal revenue product combines marginal product and marginal revenue. It is the marginal product of the resource multiplied by the marginal revenue from each unit sold. (In a perfectly competitive market, marginal revenue is constant.) The marginal revenue product curve is the business's demand curve for the resource. It shows how many units of the resource are demanded at each possible resource price. The business's resource demand curve is negatively sloped.
    4. The marginal resource cost is the extra cost of each additional unit of a resource. The marginal resource cost curve is the business's resource supply curve. It shows how many units of the resource are supplied at each possible resource price. When a business is a price-taker in the resource market, the business's resource supply curve is horizontal.
    5. The profit-maximizing employment rule for resources is that marginal revenue product should equal marginal resource cost (MRP = MRC). Therefore the intersection of the business's resource demand curve with its resource supply curve determines the amount of the resource used. A business should employ resources up to the point where marginal revenue product equals marginal revenue cost.
    6. In a perfectly competitive resource market, the resource market demand curve shows combinations of the quantities of resource demanded and the resource prices. It is the sum of all the resource demand curves of businesses in the market. Likewise, the resource

market supply curve shows combinations of the quantities of resource supplied and the resource prices. It is the sum of the quantities supplied by resource suppliers at each resource price. The resource market supply curve is positively sloped since higher resource prices generally encourage suppliers to increase quantities supplied. The equilibrium price and the equilibrium quantity of the resource are determined by the intersection of the resource market demand curve with the resource market supply curve.

♦ Other Topics Relating to Resource Demand
1. When a business, such as a monopolist or an imperfect competitor, is a price-maker in its product market then the marginal revenue product curve, and therefore the resource demand curve, is less elastic than that of a perfect competitor. Marginal revenue product declines because of the decreasing price of the product as well as the decreasing marginal product of the resource.
2. When the price-maker in the product market is a price-taker in the resource market the marginal resource cost curve, which is the resource supply curve, is horizontal. The profit-maximizing employment level occurs at the point where the business's resource demand curve and its resource supply curve intersect. It is here that marginal revenue product equals marginal revenue cost, and the profit-maximizing employment rule is attained.
3. Resource demand is affected by changes in product demand, changes in other resource prices, and technological innovation. Changes in product demand affect product price, which, in turn, affects marginal revenue product, and consequently, the demand for the resource. When changes in the price of one resource are inversely related to changes in demand for another resource, the two resources are complementary. Conversely, when changes in the price of one resource are directly related to changes in the demand for another resource, the two resources are substitutes. Technological innovation will increase the marginal product of complementary resources.
4. Price elasticity of resource demand is less the greater the rate of decline in the marginal product of a resource, the more price inelastic the product demand, the smaller the resource's proportion of a business's total costs, and the fewer the substitute resources.

♦ Wages and Their Determinants
1. The seven main determinants of wage levels in the labour market are labour productivity, education, experience, job conditions, regional disparities, market power, and discrimination.
2. Labour productivity is the output per worker in a given period. It is affected by the ability to do the job, the use of complementary resources, and technology. An increase in labour productivity is reflected in a rise in the marginal revenue product of labour.
3. There is a positive correlation between education and pay. Education postpones entrance into the labour force, but the costs of further education are offset by the benefits of future income gains. Education enhances human capital – the income-earning potential of a person's skills and knowledge.
4. On-the-job experience increases a worker's productivity. Also, experience is reflected in workplace privileges or seniority rights. Seniority rights are correlated with pay and promotion opportunities.
5. Job conditions, regional disparities, and market power each have an effect on wages. Market power is achieved mainly through industrial and craft unions. An industrial union includes workers in an industry, whatever their occupations. A craft union includes workers in a particular occupation.
6. Job discrimination, reflecting criteria other than a worker's credential or performance, may also create wage disparities.

◆ Other Resource Incomes
1. Resource incomes, other than wages, are rent, interest, and profit. Rent is the payment for use of a resource that is fixed in amount, such as land. The supply curve for land, being fixed, is perfectly inelastic. Meanwhile, the demand curve for land is negatively sloped, reflecting an inverse relationship between rent and quantity demanded. In a perfectly competitive land market, equilibrium rent is determined at the intersection of the demand and supply curves. The demand curve will shift with a change in the price of the product the land is used to produce.
2. Interest is the payment made for borrowing money. It is based on a percentage rate of the principal, which is the amount borrowed. The rate of interest varies directly with the borrower's credit risk, and the length of the loan period; it varies inversely with the amount of collateral, and the size of the loan.
3. Profit is the incentive for entrepreneurial effort. Economic profit is total revenue minus all implicit and explicit costs. Normal profit, an implicit cost, is an essential return for business activity.

Helpful Hints

◆ How Resource Markets Operate
1. The operation of resource markets is usually introduced with a discussion of labour because labour can be measured in standardized units – either the number of workers or labour hours. Land is also easily measure in this way. Even though in theory marginal analysis is relevant to all resources, it is difficult to apply this analysis to other resources, because capital and entrepreneurial resources are not easily broken into discrete portions.
2. A decreasing marginal product, multiplied by a constant marginal revenue (in perfect competition) will result in a decreasing marginal revenue product; hence the negative slope of the marginal revenue product (or demand) curve for a business that is a price-taker in its product market. Meanwhile, a decreasing marginal product, multiplied by a falling marginal revenue (in monopoly or imperfect competition) will result in an ever faster decrease in marginal revenue product; hence the less elastic downsloping marginal revenue product (or demand) curve for a business that is a price-maker in its product market.
3. Note the difference between a price-taker and a price-maker. When a business is a price-taker in its product market the market is perfectly competitive. This means price is constant as output increases. In contrast, when a business is a price-maker in its product market, the market is either monopolistic or imperfectly competitive. This means price falls as output increases.
4. The profit-maximizing employment rule is similar to the profit-maximizing output rule discussed in Chapter 5 of the text. In each case, two marginal concepts are equated with one another – one revenue-related and the other cost-related. This confirms, yet again, the general applicability of marginal analysis.

◆ Other Topics Relating to Resource Demand
1. Note the variable being measured on the horizontal axis in Figures 7.1, 7.2, and 7.3. The profit-maximizing employment rule relates to the use of inputs, so the quantity of resource input is the relevant variable on the axis. This corresponds to the profit-

maximizing analysis for output, in Chapters 5 and 6, where the quantity of output is on the horizontal axis.

♦ Other Resource Incomes
1. Remember that land is not just real estate. It includes all natural resources whose quantities are fixed in both the short run and long run. Indeed, the analysis for rent is applicable to all "free gifts of nature" available in fixed quantities, including special talents.
2. While rent – sometimes called pure economic rent – is the term used to describe payments for use of resources that are fixed, the term used for resources that are fixed in the short run only is quasi-rent. The much-used term "rent-seekers" applies to those who compete for limited productive resources so they can receive a monetary gain –either in the form of pure rent or quasi-rent.

Key Concepts

marginal productivity theory
marginal revenue product
marginal resource cost
business's labour demand curve
business's labour supply curve
profit-maximizing employment rule
labour market demand curve
labour market supply curve
complementary resources
substitute resources
labour productivity

human capital
seniority rights
industrial union
craft union
job discrimination
rent
principal
interest
credit risk
collateral

Fill in the Blank and True False Questions

1. According to _____ _____ theory, a business should use a resource based on the extra profit provided by each new unit of the resource.

2. **T F** When a business is a price-taker in the labour market, the business's labour demand curve is horizontal and the business's labour supply curve is upward-sloping.

3. _____ _____ _____ refers to the extra total revenue associated with hiring a new unit of a resource.

4. _____ _____ _____ refers to the extra cost associated with hiring a new unit of a resource.

5. According to the _____ _____ _____ rule, a business should hire additional units of a resource until the marginal revenue and marginal cost associated with the last unit of the resource are equal.

Figure 1 Use this table to answer questions 6 and 7.

Employment Choices for a Beekeeper

Workers	Total Product (litres per hour)	Total Revenue
0	0	$0
1	8	12
2	14	21
3	18	27
4	20	30

6. **T F** Given the information for the beekeeper in Figure 1, this business sells its product in a perfectly competitive market.

7. Given the information for the beekeeper in Figure 1, when the second worker is hired the beekeeper's total revenue rises from $_____ to $_____, giving a marginal revenue product of $_____.

Figure 2 Use this table to answer questions 8 to 9.

Employment Choices for an Ice Cream Seller

Workers	Total Product (cones per hour)	Total Revenue
0	0	$0.00
1	50	100.00
2	90	157.50
3	120	180.00

8. **T F** Given the information for the ice cream seller in Figure 2, this business sells its product in a perfectly competitive market.

9. Given the information for the ice cream seller in Figure 2, when the third worker is hired total revenue rises from $_____ to $_____, giving a marginal revenue product of $_____.

10. Marginal revenue product falls more quickly when new workers are added by a business that is a _____ in its product market than by a business that is a _____ in its product market.

Place the following answer in the correct order in the blanks above.
         price-taker   price-maker

11. Sandra decides what college degree to pursue based on her estimates of the income she will receive with each degree minus the costs of acquiring each degree. For her, education is an investment in _____ _____.

12. **T F** Because a job such as fire fighting has potential dangers, incomes paid to firefighters are lower than they would otherwise be.

13. **T F** Market power is a factor in pushing up wages in unionized occupations and also pushing up salaries in many professions.

14. While _____ unions are more common in skilled occupations such as those in the entertainment industry, _____ unions are more common in semiskilled occupations such as those in the forestry industry.

15. **T F** In Canada, women earn about 55 percent of what men earn.

16. Any resource that is in fixed supply may earn an economic _____.

Figure 3 Use this graph to answer questions 17 and 18.

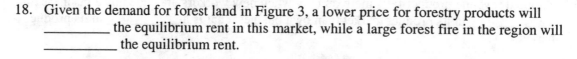

17. Given the demand for forest land in Figure 3, the equilibrium rent is $_____ if the supply of forest land is 2000 hectares.

18. Given the demand for forest land in Figure 3, a lower price for forestry products will _____ the equilibrium rent in this market, while a large forest fire in the region will _____ the equilibrium rent.

Place the following answers in the correct order in the blanks above.

increase   decrease

19. According to David Ricardo, population growth causes a _____ in the quality of land brought into agricultural production and a _____ in food prices.

    Place the following answers in the correct order in the blanks above.

    fall   rise

20. According to David Ricardo, _____ gain, _____ lose, and _____ are relatively unaffected by the changes that accompany population growth.

    Place the following answers in the correct order in the blanks above.
    employers   workers   landowners

21. Henry George suggested that all taxes should be replaced with a 100 percent tax on land _____.

Multiple Choice Questions

1. The theory that businesses use resources on the basis of how much extra profit these resources provide is called:
   A. resource profit theory
   B. marginal revenue theory
   C. resource productivity theory
   D. marginal profitability theory
   E. marginal productivity theory

2. When a business hires labour in a perfectly competitive resource market the business's supply curve of labour is:
   A. perfectly inelastic
   B. inelastic
   C. unit elastic
   D. elastic
   E. perfectly elastic

3. Which of the following statements is not true? Marginal revenue product
   A. is found by multiplying marginal product by marginal revenue.
   B. is the change in total revenue associated with each new unit of a resource.
   C. is equated with marginal resrouce cost to find the profit-maximizing employment level.
   D. is used to find how many workers are demanded at each possible wage.
   E. is used to find how many workers are supplied at each possible wage

4. In the case of two complementary resources (such as computers and computer operators), a rise in the price of one will:
   A. decrease the supply of the other resource.
   B. increase the supply of the other resource.
   C. decrease the demand of the other resource.
   D. increase the demand of the other resource.
   E. increase the price of the other resource.

5. In the case of two substitute resources (such as computers and typewriters), a fall in the price of one will:
   A. decrease the supply of the other resource
   B. increase the supply of the other resource
   C. decrease the demand of the other resource
   D. increase the demand of the other resource
   E. decrease the price of the other resource

6. Labour productivity is a measure of
   A. wage per worker
   B. output per worker
   C. labour income per worker
   D. education per worker
   E. ability per worker

7. The main reason for differences in the wages of individual workers in Canada is:
   A. different levels of labour productivity
   B. unequal job conditions
   C. regional disparities
   D. the market power possessed by some workers
   E. experience possessed by some workers

8. An industrial union includes all:
   A. workers in the same occupation
   B. workers in the same industry
   C. workers in the same building
   D. workers in the same corporation
   E. workers in the same country

9. A craft union includes all:
   A. workers in the same occupation
   B. workers in the same industry
   C. workers in the same building
   D. workers in the same corporation
   E. workers in the same country

10. Which of the following is not an important reason why women's average wages are lower than for men?
    A. women have traditionally been restricted to a narrow range of occupations
    B. women are less likely than men to retire early
    C. women are more likely than men to work part-time
    D. women are sometimes paid a lower wage than men for substantially the same work
    E. women often experience prejudice from employers

11. Which of the following individuals is most likely to earn an economic rent?
    A. a pensioner whose income comes from financial capital
    B. an entrepreneur who has started a successful software company
    C. a university professor of economics
    D. a world-famous architect
    E. the owner of a car-rental business

12. Rent is:
    A. the payment for leasing an apartment.
    B. the return to owners of capital.
    C. the return for the use of a resource that is fixed in supply.
    D. the return for the use of a renewable resource.
    E. the payment for innovation.

13. The supply curve for land is:
    A. perfectly elastic
    B. elastic
    C. unit elastic
    D. inelastic
    E. perfectly inelastic

14. The interest rate charged on a particular bank loan depends on all of the following except:
    A. the borrower's credit risk
    B. the loan period
    C. whether or not collateral is pledged against the loan.
    D. the lender's credit risk.
    E. the size of the loan.

15. Which of the following factors leads to a higher interest rate on a loan?
    A. a lower credit risk associated with the borrower
    B. a shorter period during which the loan is repaid
    C. a greater amount of collateral on the loan
    D. a smaller amount borrowed
    E. the high costs of branch banking

Short Answer Questions

1. A lobster fisherman sells his catch for $3 per kilogram in a perfectly competitive product market and hires labour in a perfectly competitive labour market at a daily wage of $50.

Labour	Total Product (kgs. per day)	Marginal Product (kgs. per day)	Product Price	Total Revenue ($ per day)	Marginal Revenue Product ($ per hour)	Marginal Resource Cost ($ per hour)
0	0		$3	——		
		——			——	$50
1	24		3	——		
		——			——	50
2	45		3	——		
		——			——	50
3	63		3	——		
		——			——	50
4	78		3	——		
		——			——	50
5	90		3	——		
		——			——	50
6	99		3	——		
		——			——	50
7	105		3	——		

a. Complete the table.
b. Determine this fisherman's profit-maximizing employment level for labour.
c. Graph the marginal revenue product and the marginal resource cost curves for this fisherman, and show the profit-maximizing employment level on your graph.

2. In question 1 above, the price per unit of output increases to $7.

Labour	Total Product (kgs. per day)	Marginal Product (kgs. per day)	Product Price	Total Revenue ($ per day)	Marginal Revenue Product ($ per hour)	Marginal Resource Cost ($ per hour)
0	0		$7	——		
		——			——	$50
1	24		7	——		
		——			——	50
2	45		7	——		
		——			——	50
3	63		7	——		
		——			——	50
4	78		7	——		
		——			——	50
5	90		7	——		
		——			——	50
6	99		7	——		
		——			——	50
7	105		7	——		

a. Fill the above table, given the new output price.
b. How many workers will now be employed by the fisherman?
c. What has happened to the marginal revenue product curve? Show this change on the graph you drew in question 1, along with the new profit-maximizing employment level.

3. Hi Gloss Pottery sells its product in an imperfectly competitive product market and hires labour in a perfectly competitive labour market at $550 per day.

Labour	Total Product (pots per day)	Marginal Product (pots per day)	Product Price	Total Revenue ($ per day)	Marginal Revenue Product ($ per hour)	Marginal Resource Cost ($ per hour)
0	0		$75	___		
		___			___	550
1	20		65	___		
		___			___	550
2	38		55	___		
		___			___	550
3	54		45	___		
		___			___	550
4	68		35	___		
		___			___	550
5	80		25	___		

a. Complete the table.
b. Determine High Gloss Pottery's profit-maximizing employment level of labour.
c. Graph the marginal revenue product and the marginal resource cost curves for this business, and show the profit-maximizing employment level on your graph.

Solutions to Questions for Chapter 7

Fill in the Blank and True False Questions
1. **marginal productivity**
2. **F** The business's labour demand curve is downward-sloping, since the business will demand less labour at higher wages. The fact that the business is a price-taker in the labour market means that its labour supply curve is horizontal at the prevailing market wage.
3. **marginal revenue product** It is called this since it can be found by multiplying the relevant values of marginal product and marginal revenue.
4. **marginal resource cost**
5. **profit-maximizing employment**
6. **T** Because the beekeeper's total revenue and total product change by the same proportion, the price of honey for the beekeeper is constant at $1.50, which means honey is being sold in a perfectly competitive market.
7. **12, 21, 9**
8. **F** This firm faces a declining price as its output expands, since total revenue and total product do not change by the same proportions. Therefore, this product market is imperfectly competitive.
9. **157.50, 180, 22.50**

10. **price-maker, price-taker** When a business is a price-maker in its product market, both its marginal product and price fall as output expands. In the case of a business that is a price-taker in its product market, only its marginal product falls with expanding output.

11. **human capital**

12. **F** Income paid to firefighters should be higher than otherwise to compensate for this job risk.

13. **T** Many professional organizations operate in a way similar to craft unions, gaining market power by restricting entry into their professions.

14. **craft, industrial** Craft unions are more common in occupations where it is possible to restrict entry on the basis of required skills, while industrial unions are more common in other occupations.

15. **F** In fact, Canadian women's earnings are about 73 percent the average earnings of Canadian men.

16. **rent** The payment for this type of resource is known as an economic rent.

17. **80** As in any perfectly competitive market, this equilibrium occurs at the intersection of the demand and supply curves.

18. **decrease, increase** Lower prices for forestry products cause a leftward shift in the demand for forestry land, decreasing equilibrium rent. A forest fire leads to a leftward shift in the supply of forestry land, increasing equilibrium rent.

19. **fall, rise** The higher food prices are determined by production costs on the increasingly poor land brought into cultivation.

20. **landowners, employers, workers** Landowners gain due to the rent rise accompanying higher food prices, employers lose since they must pay higher wages, and workers are relatively unaffected because their higher wages merely cover higher food prices.

21. **rent** He believed a 100 percent tax on land rent was the fairest and most efficient means of raising government revenues.

Multiple Choice Questions

1. **E** It is known as marginal productivity theory.

2. **E** There are many buyers and sellers in the labour market so the wage for each unit of labour is constant. It is determined by the intersection of the labour market demand and supply curves.

3. **E** It is the labour supply curve that shows how many workers are supplied at each possible wage.

4. **C** This is because a rise in the price of computers will decrease employment of both computers and computer operators.

5. **C** This is because a fall in the price of computers will cause some businesses to switch from typewriters to computers.

6. **B** Labour productivity is the ratio of output to labour in a given period.

7. **A** While all these factors affect wage disparities, labour productivity is the most important.

8. **B** Industrial unions include workers in an entire industry.

9. **A** Craft unions include workers in an entire skilled occupation.

10. **B** There is no great difference in retirement ages for men and women.

11. **D** The architect's income is primarily from highly scarce creative talents whose payment is in the form of economic rent.

12. **C** Rent is the payment for a fixed resource.

13. **E** Land is a resource with a fixed supply.

14. **D** The interest rate on a particular loan depends on the credit risk of the borrower, not the lender.

15. **D** This is because administrative costs are greater as a proportion of a small loan than a large loan.

Short Answer Questions

1a.

Labour	Total Product (kgs. per day)	Marginal Product (kgs. per day)	Product Price	Total Revenue ($ per day)	Marginal Revenue Product ($ per day)	Marginal Resource Cost ($ per day)
0	0		$3	0		
		24			72	50
1	24		3	72		
		21			63	50
2	45		3	135		
		18			54	50
3	63		3	189		
		15			45	50
4	78		3	234		
		12			36	50
5	90		3	270		
		9			27	50
6	99		3	297		
		6			18	50
7	105		3	315		

b. The profit-maximizing employment level of 3 workers is found by comparing marginal revenue product and marginal resource cost. Between 2 and 3 workers, the marginal revenue product of $54 exceeds the marginal resource cost of $50, whereas between 3 and 4 workers, the opposite is true.

c.

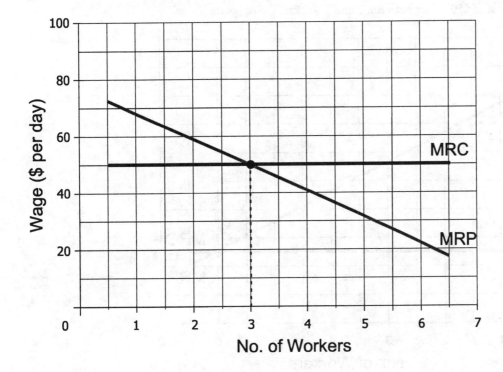

2a.

Labour	Total Product (kgs. per day)	Marginal Product (kgs. per day)	Product Price	Total Revenue ($ per day)	Marginal Revenue Product ($ per day)	Marginal Resource Cost ($ per day)
0	0		$7	0		
		24			168	50
1	24		7	168		
		21			147	50
2	45		7	315		
		18			126	50
3	63		7	441		
		15			105	50
4	78		7	546		
		12			84	50
5	90		7	630		
		9			63	50
6	99		7	693		
		6			42	50
7	105		7	735		

b. The marginal revenue product curve has shifted to the right. The new profit-maximizing employment level is 6 workers, since between 5 and 6 workers the marginal revenue product of $63 exceeds the marginal resource cost of $50, while between 6 and 7 workers the opposite is true.

c.

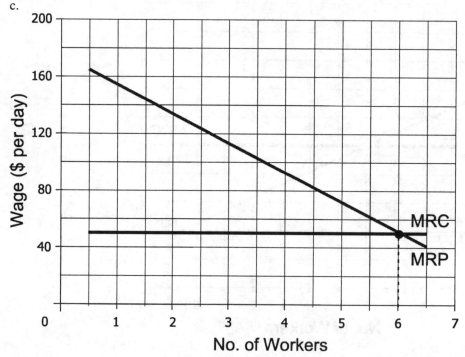

92

3a.

Labour	Total Product (pots per day)	Marginal Product (pots per day)	Product Price ($ per day)	Total Revenue Product ($ per day)	Marginal Revenue Cost ($ per day)	Marginal Resource
0	0		$75	$0		
		20			$1300	$550
1	20		65	1300		
		18			790	550
2	38		55	2090		
		16			340	550
3	54		45	2430		
		14			-50	550
4	68		35	2380		
		12			-380	550
5	80		25	2000		

b. The profit-maximizing employment level is 2 workers, since between 1 and 2 workers the marginal revenue product of $790 exceeds the marginal resource cost of $550 per day, while between 2 and 3 workers the opposite is true.

c.

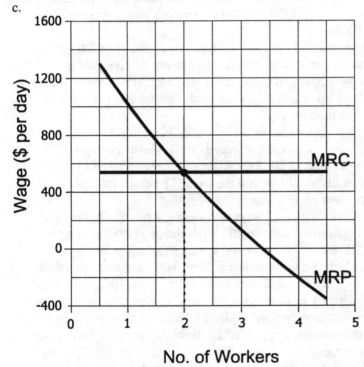

93

Chapter 8

The Distribution of Income

Learning Objectives

In this chapter you will:
♦ learn about the distribution of income among Canadian households, how this distribution is measured, and the factors underlying the distribution
♦ consider the causes of poverty and the way poverty is measured
♦ analyze the effectiveness of government intervention to change the distribution of income

Chapter Highlights
♦ The Distribution of Income
1. The distribution of income is measured through ranking households by income, classifying these households into five groups, and showing the share of income received by each group. In 1998, the fifth of Canadian households with the lowest income received 4.3 percent of pre-tax income, while the fifth of households with the highest income receive 45.5 percent of pre-tax income. In 1951, the corresponding shares were 4.4 percent and 42.8 percent respectively.
2. The shares of income can be presented as a cumulative distribution. In 1998, 20 percent of Canadian households received 4.3 percent of income, 40 percent of households received 14.2 percent of income, 60 percent of households received 30 percent of income, 80 percent of households received 55 percent of income, and, finally, 100 percent of households received 100 percent of income.
3. The Lorenz curve is used to graph this cumulative distribution. With households represented on the horizontal axis and income represented on the vertical axis, both expressed in percentages, the distribution of income in Canada is represented by an arc. The arc lies between the 45-degree diagonal line and the axes. The diagonal represents perfect equality and the axes represent perfect inequality.
4. Three main factors determine the distribution of income received from profit, rent and interest. The factors are risk-taking, ability, and wealth. High incomes are the outcome of successful risk-taking, special abilities, and the ownership of assets.
5. Poverty, as defined by Statistics Canada's low-income cut-off, is the expenditure of 64 percent or more of income on food, clothing and shelter. In 1998, 3.7 million Canadians lived below this poverty line, of which 1 million were children. Poverty is greater among unattached women, single-parent families, persons under 24 and over 64 years of age, the less educated, the unemployed, those employed part-time, those employed in low-wage jobs, and in poorer provinces in Canada.
6. Whether to use a relative or an absolute measure of poverty in Canada is controversial. The low-income cut-off, LICO, is a relative measure. The proposed market basket measure (MBM) is based on an absolute definition of items considered necessities. With LICO, 17.5 percent of Canada's population is considered poor. With MBM, only 12 percent of the population is considered poor.

♦ The Canadian Welfare Society
1. Canada is a welfare society whose mixed economy helps ensure the well-being of its citizens. Equity is maintained by government transfer payments and taxation. Transfer payments were originally based on the principle of universality, whereby benefits were provided to all. However, Canada is moving towards means-testing to direct transfers towards the most needy. In 1998, the poorest fifth of households received 21.4 percent of transfer payments, while the richest fifth received 13.6 percent.
2. Taxation, to be equitable, may be based on the principle of benefits received, or the principle of ability to pay. Ability to pay is related to income. A progressive tax increases as a proportion of income, as income increases. A regressive tax decreases as a proportion of income, as income increases. A proportional tax remains constant as a proportion of income, for all incomes.
3. In 1998, the poorest fifth of Canadian households paid 6.3 percent of their incomes as income tax, while the richest fifth paid 24.5 percent of their incomes as income tax.
4. Canada's taxes do not always redistribute income towards lower income groups. Personal income taxes are progressive, but excise and sales taxes are regressive. Property taxes are regressive to the extent that the poor pay a larger portion of their income for housing. To the extent that corporate income taxes reduce the income of shareholders they are progressive, but to the extent they result in higher prices to consumers they are regressive.

Helpful Hints

♦ The Distribution of Income
1. Note that the data on the distribution of income in Canada indicates some widening of the gap between rich and poor. Comparing the distribution of income in 1998 and 1951, the income share to the richest fifth rose from 42.8 to 45.5 percent, while the share to the lowest two fifths declined from 15.6 to 14.2 percent.
2. It is interesting to see the extent to which the disparity in the distribution of wealth is greater than that for income. For example, in 1984 the richest 20 percent of Canadians held over 68 percent of the wealth. One of the main reasons for the large disparity is that, for many poorer households, wealth is negative rather than positive. In other words, these households' debts exceed their assets.
3. The Gini coefficient is a succinct measure of the distribution of income, which is useful for comparisons between countries. It is found by dividing the area between the Lorenz curve and the 45-degree diagonal line by the entire area beneath the diagonal line.

♦ The Canadian Welfare Society
1. Who values a dollar more – a rich person, or a poor person? Most would answer that a poor person does, since the poor person needs the dollar for necessities. But would we have been wrong if we had answered a rich person? After all, a rich person remains rich because each dollar is valued. Moreover, the rich person will use each dollar to create more wealth. So the answer to this question reflects a value judgement. The Canadian concern with well-being of the poor reflects the system of values of our society. It is these values that maintain our welfare society.
2. Views on taxation and income equity vary with political persuasion. Right wing economists tend to call for reductions in taxes, transfer payments and the role of government. Left wing economists promote government involvement in using taxes and transfer payments to reduce economic inequities. Right wing economists promote

"laissez faire" and the free operation of the market in the belief that this will generate more income for all. Left wing economists promote government intervention to remedy market imperfections. They believe that the market system, operating without government intervention, leads to an overly unequal distribution of income.

Key Concepts

Lorenz curve	means testing
wealth	benefits received
poverty	ability to pay
poverty line	progressive tax
welfare society	regressive tax
universality	proportional tax

Fill in the Blank and True False Questions

Figure 1 Use this graph to answer questions 1 to 4.

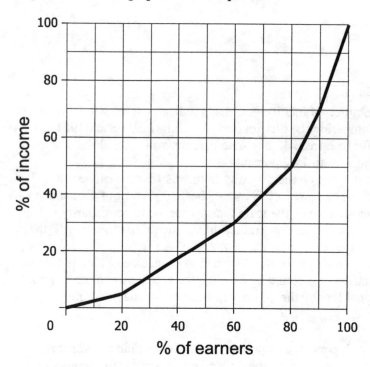

1. Figure 1 contains a _____ curve.

2. Figure 1 shows that the lowest three-fifths of income-earners together receive 30 percent and the lowest four-fifths of income-earners receive 50 percent of the economy's total income. Therefore, the second highest fifth of income-earners receives _____percent of total income.

3. Figure 1 shows that the lowest four-fifths of income-earners together receive 50 percent of the economy's total income. Therefore, the highest fifth of income-earners receives _____percent of total income.

4. The Lorenz curve in Figure 1 shows the distribution of income after transfer payments but before personal income taxes. In the case of Canada, this curve is _____ of the curve for income before personal taxes and transfer payments and _____ of the curve for income after personal taxes and transfer payments.

   Place the following answers in the correct order in the blanks above.

   southeast   northwest

5. **T F** In an economy with a perfectly equal distribution of income, the Lorenz curve is a 45-degree line.

6. **T F** Efficiency in the Canadian economy would be improved if all Canadians earned the same income.

7. **T F** Income equity is usually interpreted to mean that all incomes should be equal.

8. **T F** In Canada, a household is classified as poor if its members spend less than 64 percent of their income on food, clothing, and shelter.

9. **T F** Because of the added expenses of living in outlying regions of Canada, the yearly income associated with the poverty is higher in rural areas than in urban centres.

10. About _____ percent of families and _____ percent of unattached individuals were classified as poor in Canada in 1998.

    Place the following answers in the correct order in the blanks above.

    9.1   30.3

11. The incidence of poverty is _____ for unattached women than for unattached men, and _____ for unattached individuals over the age of 65 than for unattached individuals under the age of 25.

    Place the following answers in the correct order in the blanks above.

    higher   lower

12. In recent years, the principle of _____ has been replaced by the principle of _____ in the design of the federal government's transfer payments to households.

13. **T F** Transfer payments have a significant effect on the distribution of income.

14. A tax on gasoline used to finance road construction is an example of the _____ principle of taxation, while a personal income tax used to finance welfare programs is an example of the _____ principle of taxation.

15. Sales taxes are an example of a _____ tax while personal income taxes are an example of a _____ tax.

   Place the following answers in the correct order in the blanks above.

   progressive   regressive

16. According to Thomas Malthus, food production grows in a(n) _____ progression and population grows in a(n) _____ progression.

17. Thomas Malthus's population theory has not been relevant for industrialized countries such as Canada because birth rates in these countries have been _____ and the rate of technological change has been _____ than Malthus envisioned.

   Place the following answers in the correct order in the blanks above.

   lower   higher

Multiple Choice Questions

Figure 2 Use this graph to answer questions 1 to 4.

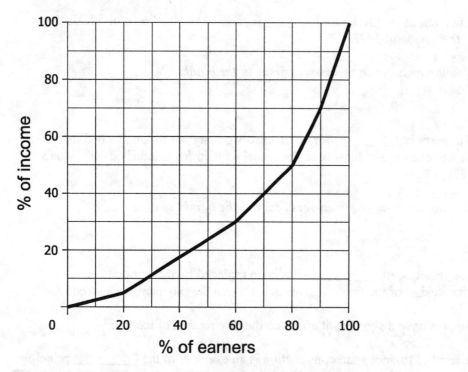

1. Given the information in Figure 2, the lowest fifth of income-earners receives approximately what percentage of this economy's total income?
   A. 5
   B. 10
   C. 15
   D. 20
   E. 25

2. Given the information in Figure 2, the lowest two-fifths of income-earners together receive approximately what percentage of this economy's total income?
    A. 5
    B. 10
    C. 15
    D. 20
    E. 25

3. Given the information in Figure 2, the second lowest fifth of income-earners receives what percentage of this economy's total income?
    A. 5
    B. 10
    C. 15
    D. 20
    E. 25

4. Given the information in Figure 2, and your answers to the previous questions, the middle fifth of income-earners receive what percentage of this economy's total income?
    A. 5
    B. 10
    C. 15
    D. 20
    E. 50

5. Which of the following factors is not a cause of income inequality in Canada?
    A. Canada's personal income tax system
    B. the market power enjoyed by some Canadian workers
    C. The unequal distribution of wealth among Canadians
    D. risk-taking by some Canadian income-earners
    E. disparities in labour productivity

6. Using the Lorenz curve, which of the following situations would indicate a redistribution of income which would attain the greatest equality?
    A. a reduction in the share going to the lowest quintile
    B. an increase in the share going to the highest quintile
    C. a reallocation of shares between the second and fourth quintiles
    D. a reallocation of shares between the first and fifth quintiles
    E. a reallocation of shares so that each quintile receives the same percentage of income as any other

7. Using the Lorenz curve diagram, the extent of inequality in the distribution of income is shown by:
    A. the slope of the Lorenz curve.
    B. the length of the Lorenz curve.
    C. the divergence of the Lorenz curve from the 45-degree diagonal line.
    D. the divergence of the Lorenz curve from the vertical axis.
    E. the divergence of the Lorenz curve from the horizontal axis.

8. Based on the incidence of poverty in Canada in 1998, the probability of avoiding poverty is greatest with which level of education:
    A. less than high school
    B. high school
    C. some post-secondary
    D. post-secondary diploma
    E. university degree

9. Based on the incidence of poverty in 1998, the probability of being below the poverty line is greatest for which of the following age groups?
    A. less than 18 years
    B. 18-24 years
    C. 25-54 years
    D. 55-64 years
    E. 65+ years

10. Based on the incidence of poverty in 1998, the probability of being below the poverty line is greatest for which of the following household types?
    A. single-parent families with a female head
    B. single-parent families with a male head
    C. married couples with children
    D. elderly unattached females
    E. nonelderly unattached females

11. Based in the incidence of poverty in 1998, the probability of being below the poverty line is greatest for which of the following groups?
    A. elderly unattached males
    B. nonelderly unattached males
    C. elderly unattached females
    D. nonelderly unattached females
    E. all unattached individuals

12. A regressive tax is:
    A. a tax that stays the same as a proportion of income as income increases
    B. a tax that doubles as income rises
    C. a tax that rises as a proportion of income as income increases
    D. a tax that triples as income rises
    E. a tax that falls as a proportion of income as income increases

13. A proportional tax is
    A. a tax that stays the same as a proportion of income as income increases
    B. a tax that doubles as income rises
    C. a tax that rises as a proportion of income as income increases
    D. a tax that triples as income rises
    E. a tax that falls as a proportion of income as income increases

14. A progressive tax is:
    A. a tax that stays the same as a proportion of income as income increases
    B. a tax that doubles as income rises
    C. a tax that rises as a proportion of income as income increases
    D. a tax that triples as income rises
    E. a tax that falls as a proportion of income as income increases

15. When applied to transfer payments, the term "universality" means:
    A. the principle whereby benefits are applied to all the poor citizens of a nation.
    B. the principle whereby benefits are applied to all the world's population.
    C. the principle whereby benefits are applied to all citizens of a nation regardless of income
    D. the principle whereby benefits are applied to all rich citizens of a nation.
    E. the principle whereby benefits are applied to all who apply for benefits, regardless of income.

Short Answer Questions

1. In an certain economy, wealth is distributed among five inhabiting households in the following manner:

Families	Wealth	Percentage of Wealth	Cumulative Share of Wealth
Lowest	$25 000	_____	_____
Second	50 000	_____	_____
Third	75 000	_____	_____
Fourth	150 000	_____	_____
Highest	200 000	_____	_____

   a. Fill in the above table.
   b. Draw, labeling correctly, the appropriate Lorenz curve.

2. Compare the distribution of pre-tax income for Canadian households for the years 1951 and 1998. What observations can you make?

Percentage of Total Pre-Tax Income Received by Each Fifth of Households

	1951	1998
Lowest 20 percent	4.4	4.3
Second 20 percent	11.2	9.9
Third 20 percent	18.3	16.0
Fourth 20 percent	23.3	24.3
Highest 20 percent	42.8	45.5

3. Given the hypothetical income tax rates below:

Taxable Income	Marginal Tax Rate
$0 to $30 000	10 percent
$30 001 to $60 000	20 percent
$60 001 or more	30 percent

a. How much would someone with a taxable income of $25 000 pay in personal income tax?

b. How much would someone with a taxable income of $45 000 pay in personal income tax?

c. How much would someone with a taxable income of $80 000 pay in personal income tax?

Solutions to Questions for Chapter 8

Fill in the Blank and True False Questions

1. **Lorenz** This is named after the economist who first developed the curve.

2. **20** This group of households receives 20 percent of total income, which is the difference between the 50 percent of income received by the group that includes them and the 30 percent of income received by the group that excludes them.

3. **50** The highest fifth of income-earners receives the remainder (100 percent - 50 percent) of total income after the shares of all the other groups of households have been taken into account.

4. **northwest, southeast** This is because both transfer payments and personal income taxes make income more equally distributed and therefore move the Lorenz curve closer to the 45-degree line.

5. **T** In this case, any given share of households receive exactly the same share of income, which means that the horizontal and vertical coordinates of the Lorenz curve are identical at every point.

6. **F** Without some income inequality, there would be little incentive to engage in costly or unpleasant productive activities.

7. **F** Income equity commonly means the reduction rather than the elimination of income inequality.

8. **F** Household members must spend more than 64 percent of their income on necessities to be considered poor.

9. **F** The poverty line is lower in rural areas because of the lower cost of living outside of cities.

10. **9.1, 30** Poverty is much less common among families than among unattached individuals.

11. **higher, lower** Poverty is more common among unattached women than among unattached men, and is less common for elderly than for young unattached individuals.

12. **universality, means-testing** Means-testing has been replacing universality in the design of federal transfer payments, largely because of the high cost and limited effectiveness of universal programs in dealing with poverty.

13. **T** These programs have a major impact on the distribution of Canadian incomes.

14. **benefits-received, ability-to-pay** The road tax illustrates the benefits-received principle, since road users are the ones who pay for new roads. Personal income taxes used to finance welfare are an example of the ability-to-pay principle, since those with high incomes, rather than primary welfare users, pay the most.

15. **regressive, progressive** Sales taxes are regressive, since poor people spend a larger portion of their incomes on consumption items. Personal income taxes are progressive largely because of the rising marginal rates faced by taxpayers as their incomes increase.

16. **algebraic, geometric** Food production grows in an algebraic progression (1, 2, 3,...) and population grows in a geometric progression (1, 2, 4,...).

17. **lower, higher** Lower birth rates and higher rates of technological change than Malthus predicted have meant that his theory has not been borne out in industrialized countries.

Multiple Choice Questions

1. **A** This is the vertical coordinate of the curve at 20 percent of earners on the horizontal axis.

2. **C** This is the vertical coordinate of the curve at 40 percent of earners on the horizontal axis.

3. **B** This is the difference between the 15 percent of total income received by the group that includes them and the 5 percent of total income received by the group that excludes them.

4. **C** This is the difference between the 30 percent of total income received by the group that includes them and the 15 percent of total income received by the group that excludes them.

5. **A** Canada's personal income tax system reduces the inequality of incomes.

6. **E** This is the only distribution for which the Lorenz curve would coincide with the diagonal.

7. **C** Perfect equality is indicated by the 45-degree diagonal line, so the divergence of the Lorenz curve from the 45-degree diagonal line indicates the extent of inequality.

8. **E** There is a high correlation between levels of education and poverty. Thirty percent of household heads with less than high school education are below the poverty line, compared to 11 percent with a university degree.

9. **B** The percentage of household heads below the poverty line is greatest for 18 to 24 year olds.

10. **A** Among single parent families with a female head, 42 percent are below the poverty line.

11. **D** The greatest incidence of poverty is among nonelderly unattached females, with a rate of 38.8 percent.

12. **E** A regressive tax will fall as a proportion of income as income increases.

13. **A** A proportional tax will stay the same as a proportion of income as income increases.

14. **C** A progressive tax will rise as a proportion of income as income increases.

15. **C** When applied to transfer payments, universality means giving the same benefits to all citizens of a country.

Short Answer Questions

1a.

Families	Wealth	Percentage of Wealth	Cumulative Share of Wealth
Lowest	$25 000	5	5
Second	50 000	10	15
Third	75 000	15	30
Fourth	150 000	30	60
Highest	200 000	40	100
Total	500 000		

For the lowest-income family, the percentage share of wealth is found by dividing the family's wealth ($25 000) by the economy's total wealth ($500 000). A similar calculation is made for each of the remaining four families. To calculate the cumulative shares of wealth, the percentage shares are summed. For example, the two families with the lowest income have a cumulative share of 15 percent (= 5 + 10), and so on.

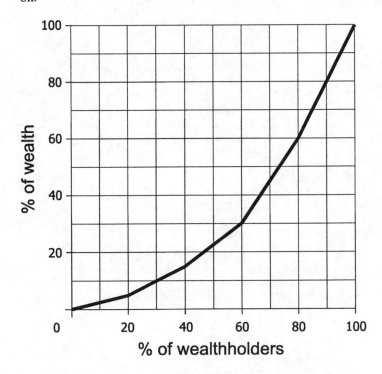

2. These figures show that there has been no considerable change in the shares of income. The income of the richest quintile has remained over 40 percent, while that of the poorest quintile is less than 5 percent. But the poor received a smaller share of income and the rich a larger share in 1998 than was the case in 1951. The share of the lowest quintile fell from 4.4 percent to 4.3 percent, while the share of the first and second quintiles also declined from 15.6 percent to 14.2 percent over the period. At the same time the share of the highest quintile rose from 42.8 percent to 45.5 percent while the share of the two highest quintiles also rose from 66.1 percent to 69.8 percent over the period. It is significant that the positive change of 3.7 for the two highest quintiles were larger than the negative change of -1.4 for the two lowest quintiles. This was made possible by the negative change of -2.3 for the third quintile over the period.

3a. This person pays a 10 percent marginal tax rate on all of their income, or $2500.
b. This person pays a 10 percent marginal tax rate on the first $30 000 of income ($3000) and a 20 percent tax rate on the remaining $15 000 ($3000). Therefore they pay a total of $6000 (= $3000 + $3000).
c. $15 000 This person pays a 10 percent marginal tax rate on the first $30 000 ($3000), 20 percent tax rate on the next $30 000 ($6000), and 30 percent on the remaining $20 000 ($6000) Therefore they pay a total of $15 000 (= $3000 + $6000 + $6000).

Microeconomics Review Test

This practice test includes multiple choice and short answer questions from Chapters 1 to 8.

Multiple Choice Questions

1. To represent the production possibilities curve for two goods:
    A. the quantity of one good is on the vertical axis and the price of the other good is on the horizontal axis.
    B. the quantity of one good is on the horizontal axis and the price of the other good is on the vertical axis.
    C. the price of one good is on one axis and the price of the other good is on the other axis.
    D. the quantity of one good is on one axis and the quantity of the other good is on the other axis.
    E. the quantity of each good is expressed as a percentage of the economy total output on each axis.

2. To represent the supply curve of good A, economists place:
    A. quantity demanded on the horizontal axis and price on the vertical axis.
    B. quantity demanded on the vertical axis and price on the horizontal axis.
    C. quantity supplied on the horizontal axis and price on the vertical axis.
    D. quantity supplied on the vertical axis and price on the horizontal axis.
    E. quantity supplied of good A on the horizontal axis and good B on the vertical axis.

3. In the rental housing market, rent controls are:
    A. the lower limit to the price of rental housing
    B. greater than equilibrium price
    C. less than equilibrium price
    D. a price floor
    E. the equilibrium price for rental housing

4. In the labour market, a minimum wage is
    A. less than the equilibrium price of labour
    B. greater than the equilibrium price of labour
    C. the equilibrium price of labour
    D. the price to which the price of labour will rise when the "invisible hand" operates
    E. a price ceiling

5. If long-run costs are increasing then the long-run supply curve of the perfectly competitive business will:
    A. slope downwards to the right
    B. slope upwards to the right
    C. be horizontal
    D. be vertical
    E. shift to accommodate increasing costs

6. Which of the following statements about long run average cost curve is true?
    A. When a business is facing increasing returns to scale, this curve is upward-sloping.
    B. When a business is facing decreasing returns to scale, this curve is downward-sloping.
    C. This curve is always symmetrical.
    D. This curve is based on the highest points from each possible short run average cost curve.
    E. This curve is used to find long run equilibrium for a perfectly competitive business.

7. Which of the following statements about the market supply curve is untrue?
    A. The market supply curve shows the relationship between price and quantity supplied.
    B. The market supply curve is the sum of all marginal cost curves above average cost.
    C. The market supply curve is the sum of all marginal cost curves above average variable cost.
    D. The market supply curve slopes upwards to the right.
    E. The market supply curve shows the quantities that suppliers will produce at each price in a perfectly competitive market.

8. The demand curve faced by a monopolistically competitive business is:
    A. perfectly elastic
    B. perfectly inelastic
    C. elastic
    D. inelastic
    E. unit elastic

9. A kinked demand curve represents the demand curve faced by a:
    A. monopolist
    B. perfectly competitive business
    C. rival oligopolist
    D. cooperative oligopolist
    E. monopolistically competitive business

10. In the long run, the only businesses that attain minimum-cost pricing are:
    A. monopolistic
    B. perfectly competitive
    C. rival oligopolists
    D. cooperative oligopolists
    E. monopolistically competitive

11. A business in perfectly competitive product and resource markets will find that:
    A. product price is constant and marginal resource cost varies.
    B. both product price and marginal resource cost vary.
    C. product price and marginal resource cost are irrelevant.
    D. both product price and marginal resource cost are constant.
    E. product price varies and marginal resource cost is constant.

12. When a business is a product price-maker, its marginal revenue product curve is:
    A. more elastic than that of a product price-taker.
    B. perfectly inelastic.
    C. less elastic than that of a product price-taker.
    D. perfectly elastic.
    E. unit elastic.

13. To maintain Canada as a welfare society the government:
    A. relies entirely on the market economy.
    B. implements a truly progressive tax system.
    C. has eliminated the incidence of poverty.
    D. has redefined the measurement of poverty.
    E. makes transfer payments to facilitate equity.

Short Answer Questions

1. In a perfectly competitive market for corn, market demand and market supply curves are represented by the schedules below.

Price	Quantity Demanded (millions of ears of corn)	Quantity Supplied (millions of ears of corn)
$1.75	3	9
1.50	4	8
1.25	5	7
1.00	6	6
0.75	7	5
0.50	8	4
0.25	9	3

a. Draw the market supply and market demand curves. What are the equilibrium price and quantity in this market?

b. Ideal weather conditions cause a bountiful harvest and the quantity supplied of corn increases by three million ears at every possible price. Draw the new market supply curve. What are the new equilibrium values for price and quantity?

c. The rapidly rising prices of petroleum increase the demand for a substitute automobile fuel manufactured from corn. Quantity demanded of corn increases by five million ears at every possible price. Draw the new market demand curve. What are the new equilibrium values for price and quantity?

d. At the equilibrium values found in part c, above, the revenue realized by corn producers is considered inadequate. The government imposes a price floor of $1.50. What is the result of this policy in this market?

2. The table below shows the revenue and cost conditions for a perfect competitor.

Price	Quantity Demanded	Total Revenue	Average Revenue	Marginal Revenue	Marginal Cost
$8	100	$＿＿	$＿＿		
				$＿＿	$5
8	200	＿＿	＿＿		
				＿＿	3
8	300	＿＿	＿＿		
				＿＿	5
8	400	＿＿	＿＿		
				＿＿	7
8	500	＿＿	＿＿		
				＿＿	9
8	600	＿＿	＿＿		
				＿＿	11
8	700	＿＿	＿＿		

a. Fill in the table.
b. What is the profit maximizing output of this firm?

3. Window Replacement Inc. is one of many firms selling new windows to homeowners. As a price-taker in both its product and resource markets, its product price is $30 per window, and the marginal resource cost is $165 per worker. Daily total product per worker is set out below.

Labour	Total Product	Marginal Product	Product Price	Total Revenue	Marginal Revenue Product	Marginal Resource Cost
0	0		$30	＿＿		
		＿＿			＿＿	$165
1	10		30	＿＿		
		＿＿			＿＿	165
2	19		30	＿＿		
		＿＿			＿＿	165
3	27		30	＿＿		
		＿＿			＿＿	165
4	34		30	＿＿		
		＿＿			＿＿	165
5	40		30	＿＿		
		＿＿			＿＿	165
6	45		30	＿＿		

a. Complete the table above.
b. How many workers will be employed?
c. How many windows per day will be installed?
d. Calculate the price elasticity of demand for labour using the values of $180 and $150 for marginal revenue product and the corresponding units of labour, 4.5 and 5.5 workers.

Solutions to Microeconomics Review Test

Multiple Choice Questions

1. **D** The quantity of one good goes on one axis and the quantity of the other good on the other axis.
2. **C** Quantity supplied goes on the horizontal axis and price on the vertical axis.
3. **C** Rent controls are price ceilings, which are below equilibrium price.
4. **B** A minimum wage is a price floor, which is above equilibrium price.
5. **B** The long-run supply curve for a business in an increasing-cost industry is upward sloping, reflecting the gradually rising price of an input as production rises.
6. **E** Long run equilibrium for a perfect competitor is found at the minimum point on this curve.
7. **B** The market supply curve is the sum of all marginal cost curves above average variable cost, not average cost.
8. **C** A monopolistically competitive business faces an elastic demand curve, since it sells a product with many close substitutes sold by other businesses in the industry.
9. **C** A rival oligopolist faces a kinked demand curve, which reflects the differing responses of its rivals when it raises or reduces its price.
10. **B** Only perfect competitors achieve minimum-cost pricing in long-run equilibrium.
11. **D** Both price and marginal resource cost are constant for a business that is a price-taker in both its product and resource markets.
12. **C** This is because, as output increases, not just marginal product but also price is falling for the product price-maker.
13. **E** The Canadian government uses transfer payments to enhance income equity.

Short Answer Questions

1a. The equilibrium price is $1.00, and the equilibrium quantity is 6 million ears.

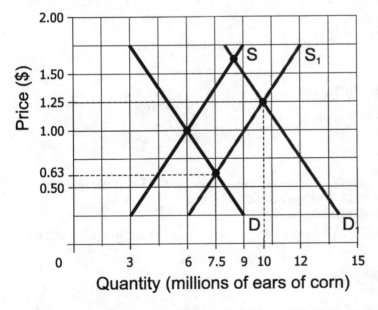

b. The new equilibrium price is $0.63, while the equilibrium quantity is now 7.5 million ears.
c. The equilibrium price is now $1.25, and the new equilibrium quantity is 10 million ears.
d. The result is a surplus of 2 million ears of corn per period

2a.

Price	Quantity Demanded	Total Revenue	Average Revenue	Marginal Revenue	Marginal Cost
$8	100	$800	$8		
				$8	$5
8	200	1600	8		
				8	3
8	300	2400	8		
				8	5
8	400	3200	8		
				8	7
8	500	4000	8		
				8	9
8	600	4800	8		
				8	11
8	700	5600	8		

b. The profit-maximizing output is 500 units, since marginal cost is less than the $8 marginal revenue between 400 and 500 units of output, and is greater than marginal revenue between 500 and 600 units.

3a.

Labour	Total Product	Marginal Product	Product Price	Total Revenue	Marginal Revenue Product	Marginal Resource Cost
0	0		30	0		
		10			300	165
1	10		30	300		
		9			270	165
2	19		30	570		
		8			240	165
3	27		30	810		
		7			210	165
4	34		30	1020		
		6			180	165
5	40		30	1200		
		5			150	165
6	45		30	1350		

b. This business will hire 5 workers, since marginal revenue product exceeds the $165 marginal resource cost between 4 and 5 workers and is less than $165 between 5 and 6 workers.

c. With 5 workers, the business will install 40 windows per day.

d. The price elasticity of demand for labour is (-)1.1 [= (5.5 −4.5) ÷ ((5.5 + 4.5)/2)] / [(150 − 180) ÷ ((150 + 180)/2)]

Chapter 9

Measures of Economic Activity

Learning Objectives

In this chapter you will:
♦ learn about Gross Domestic Product (GDP) and the two approaches to calculating it
♦ consider real GDP and per capita GDP and their possible uses and limitations when comparing living standards in different years or different countries
♦ analyze other economic measures developed from national income accounts

Chapter Highlights

♦ Gross Domestic Product
  1. Canada's national income accounts provide the data needed to calculate various measures of total income and total expenditures in the entire economy. These measures are used to judge how well the Canadian economy is doing, when compared with its own past performance as well as to the performance of other countries.
  2. Gross Domestic Product (GDP) is the total value at current prices of all final goods and services produced in an economy. The two approaches to measuring GDP are the income approach, which adds up all incomes in the economy, and the expenditure approach, which adds up all spending in the economy. Based on the GDP identity, these two approaches should give the same estimate of GDP
  3. Using the income approach, the main components of GDP are wages and salaries, corporate profits, interest income, and proprietors' incomes and rents. The three non-income components included in the income approach are indirect taxes, depreciation, and statistical discrepancy. These ensure that the income approach balances with the expenditure approach.
  4. Using the expenditure approach, GDP includes the value of all final goods and services, which are those products that will not be processed further and resold. But, as a practical matter, double counting of final products and intermediate products is avoided by using value added, which is the extra worth of the product at each stage of production.
  5. Financial exchanges and second-hand purchases are excluded from expenditure-based GDP. The four main elements that are included are personal consumption (C), gross investment (I), government purchases (G), and net exports (X-M). This is shown by the expenditure equation: $GDP = C + I + G + (X - M)$.
  6. Personal consumption includes expenditures on services, nondurable goods and durable goods. Gross investment includes all construction, purchases on equipment and machines by businesses and government agencies, as well as increases in inventories. Government purchases include current spending by governments on goods and services, but not transfer payments. Net exports are exports minus imports.

7. Net investment, which is the increase in an economy's capital stock each year, is found by subtracting depreciation from gross investment. Business investment is financed from saving by households as well as businesses' retained earnings.
8. Government purchases are financed by taxes (minus subsidies and transfer payments) as well as by government borrowing.
9. The rest of the world is linked to the Canadian economy not only by exports and imports, but also by foreign lending and foreign borrowing.

♦ GDP and Living Standards
1. Per capita GDP, or GDP per person, is often used to compare living standards in a country over time or living standards among different countries.
2. When comparing living standards over time, per capita GDP can be adjusted for inflation, resulting in per capita real GDP. When comparing living standards in different countries, per capita GDP is often expressed in a common currency, usually the US dollar.
3. GDP has limitations as an indicator of living standards. It understates economic activity because it excludes both nonmarket activities, such as the work of homemakers, and market transactions in the underground economy. It may also miss out on the value provided by higher-quality products. When comparing living standards in various countries, GDP is limited as a measure because it does not take into account the composition of output, income distribution, or leisure. Finally, it does not take into account the effects of economic activity on environmental quality.

♦ Other Economic Measures
1. Other measures of income and output include Gross National Product (GNP), which is total income acquired by Canadians both in Canada and elsewhere.
2. GNP is found by subtracting the net investment income going to the rest of the world from GDP. In Canada, GNP is less than GDP because of the high proportion of foreign ownership within the Canadian economy. But in some countries GNP exceeds GDP because these countries' residents have large amounts of foreign income-earning assets.
3. Net domestic income is the income earned by households supplying resources in Canada, and is found by subtracting indirect taxes, depreciation, and the statistical discrepancy from GDP.
4. Personal income is the income received by Canadian households, and is found by adding transfer payments and other payments to persons (such as interest payments by governments) from net domestic income, then subtracting earnings not paid out to persons (such as corporate profits) and net investment income to the rest of the world.
5. Disposable income is household income minus personal taxes and other personal transfers to government.

Helpful Hints

♦ Gross Domestic Product
1. In the simple circular flow model, only consumer goods and services are traded in product markets. But this does not apply once other flows have been added to this model, as shown in this chapter. Once financial markets, government, and the rest of the world are taken into account, product markets include not just purchases of final products by domestic consumers, but also by businesses, government, and foreigners. Therefore, the

element that distinguishes final products from intermediate products is not who
purchases them, but the nature of their use. Intermediate products are processed further
or resold, while final products are not.

2. In Canada, the income-based estimate of GDP in most years is higher than the
expenditure-based estimate. Therefore when the two estimates are balanced with the aid
of the statistical discrepancy, usually half of the discrepancy must be added to the
income-based estimate of GDP and subtracted from the expenditure-based estimate of
GDP. But the figures for the year 2000, which are highlighted in the text, show an
income-based estimate of Canadian GDP which is higher than the expenditure-based
estimate.

3. Some of the distinctions made in the calculation of GDP may appear arbitrary. For
example, in the interest income account that appears in the income-based estimate of
Canadian GDP, Statistics Canada includes only interest payments made by businesses,
and not those made by governments and consumers. This is because it is assumed that
only debts incurred by businesses are related to the creation of new capital, and therefore
the interest on this debt represents earned income for its recipients. Debts incurred by
governments are not viewed in this way, but instead are viewed as simple financial
transactions. But it is possible to argue that some government debt is related to the
creation of new capital – especially if capital is defined broadly to include the creation of
human capital through education. Statistics Canada's distinction – though open to debate
– is at least straightforward to measure.

♦   GDP and Living Standards
1. Evaluating whether GDP overstates or understates a particular change in economic
activity or living standards can be a tricky task. For example, during the past century in
Canada the importance of nonmarket activities, such as the unpaid work of homemakers,
has diminished as more women enter the labour force and tasks previously performed
outside of markets (such as child-care) become part of formal economic activity. If we
focus on this particular reason, changes in GDP have overstated the actual change in
living standards, because such activities that now take place in markets were still being
performed a century ago – it was simply not being captured by GDP in that period. In
contrast, most economists believe the underground economy (which is based on market
activity which goes unrecorded, often for tax-related reasons) has grown in size in
Canada over the past few decades. If we focus instead on this particular reason, changes
in GDP have understated the actual change in living standards because so much market-
based productive activity currently taking place is not being captured by GDP in the
current period. Similarly with the other limitations of GDP, some mean that GDP
overstates changes in living standards and others mean that GDP understates changes in
living standards.

♦   Other Economic Measures
1. Whether or not a country's GDP exceeds it GNP or its GNP exceeds its GDP depends on
whether the sign of the account known as net investment income to the rest of the world
is positive or negative. Remember that GNP is derived from GDP using this account,
based on the following formula:

GNP = GDP - net investment income to the rest of the world

In Canada, this net investment income account is positive, because the extent of foreign ownership in Canada means that the outward flow of investment income to the rest of the world exceeds the inward flow. Therefore Canada's GNP is less than its GDP. But in countries such as the United Kingdom, where the foreign assets of the country's residents exceed the domestic assets of that country owned by foreigners, GNP is greater than GDP. This is because the net investment income to the rest of the world is negative. When this negative number is subtracted from GDP, using the above formula, the result is a GNP figure larger than GDP.

Key Concepts

national income accounts
Gross Domestic Product
income approach
expenditure approach
GDP identity
retained earnings
final products
intermediate products
double-counting
value added
expenditure equation
personal consumption
nondurable goods
durable goods
gross investment
inventories
capital stock
depreciation
net investment

net investment
personal saving
government purchases
transfer payments
personal saving
government purchases
transfer payments
exports
imports
net exports
per capita GDP
real GDP
per capita real GDP
nonmarket activities
underground economy
Gross National Product
net domestic income
personal income
disposable income

Fill in the Blank and True False Questions

1. The _____ approach to calculating GDP measures activity in resource markets, while the _____ approach to calculating GDP measures activity in an economy=s product markets.

2. A country=s GDP equals $1 trillion using both the income approach and expenditure approach. This illustrates the concept known as the GDP _____.

3. **T F** To balance the estimates of GDP found using the income approach and expenditure approach, half the statistical discrepancy is added to the higher GDP estimate and half is subtracted from the lower GDP estimate.

4.   Order the following components of the expenditure approach based on their
     significance as a proportion of Canada's GDP (1 = highest, 4 = lowest)

     government purchases   statistical discrepancy   gross investment   net exports

     1.   _____
     2.   _____
     3.   _____
     4.   _____

5.   Gasoline purchased by a vacationing motorist is an example of a(n) _____
     product, while gasoline purchased by a commercial truckdriver is a(n) _____
     product.

          Place the following terms in the correct order in the blanks above.

                              intermediate   final

6.   **T F** To overcome the problem of double counting, the value added at each stage of
     production is excluded from GDP.

7.   If an economy=s capital stock is worth $10 billion at the beginning of the year and $12
     billion at the end of the year, _____ investment during the year has been $2
     billion.

8.   **T F** Gross investment does not include additions to inventories since these are
     products that will soon be sold.

9.   Investment is financed by _____ _____ that come from saving,
     as well as from businesses' own _____ _____.

          Place the following terms in the correct order in the blanks above.

                    retained earnings   investment funds

10. Government purchases create a monetary _____ product markets while taxes
     represent a monetary _____ households and businesses.

          Place the following terms in the correct order in the blanks above.

                         inflow into   outflow from

11. Purchases of Canadian exports by the rest of the world are _____ GDP, while
     Canadians' purchases of imports from the rest of the world are _____ GDP.

          Place the following terms in the correct order in the blanks above.

                         included in   excluded from

12. Canada's exports create a monetary _____ Canadian product markets while imports create a monetary _____ these markets.

   Place the following terms in the correct order in the blanks above.

   outflow from   inflow into

13. **T F** The most appropriate indicator of living standards when comparing various countries is each country=s per capita real GDP, each expressed in the country's own currency.

14. **T F** Because transactions in the underground economy are excluded from GDP, GDP can underestimate living standards.

15. **T F** Since the environmental damage caused by economic activity does not appear in GDP, GDP can overestimate living standards.

16. Gross _____ Product represent the total income acquired by a country's citizens, while Gross _____ Product represents the total value of products made in a country.

17. **T F** To find GNP, income earned by foreigners on their Canadian financial investments must be subtracted from GDP while income earned by Canadians on their foreign financial investments must be added to GDP.

Multiple-Choice Questions

1. The accounts that measure the level of activity in the entire Canadian economy are known as the:
   A. balance of payments accounts
   B. balance of trade accounts
   C. national income accounts
   D. national expenditure accounts
   E. balance of income accounts

2. The total dollar value of all final goods and services produced in an economy during a certain period is known as:
   A. net domestic income
   B. Gross Domestic Product
   C. Gross Domestic Income
   D. Gross National Product
   E. personal income

3. Which of the following is a component of GDP using the income approach?
   A. net exports
   B. personal consumption
   C. gross investment
   D. depreciation
   E. government purchases

4. In calculating GDP, landlords' rents are included with:
    A. indirect taxes
    B. depreciation
    C. proprietors= incomes
    D. corporate profits
    E. the statistical discrepancy

5. Which of the following is not included in gross investment?
    A. purchases of consumer durables
    B. purchases of equipment and machinery by government agencies
    C. purchases of equipment and machinery by businesses
    D. residential construction
    E. increases in inventories

6. Which of the following usually represents the largest component of Canada's income-based GDP?
    A. wages and salaries
    B. personal consumption
    C. corporate profits
    D. proprietors' incomes and rents
    E. depreciation

7. The most appropriate indicator of changes in living standards over time within a particular country is:
    A. per capita GDP
    B. real GDP
    C. per capita real GDP
    D. GDP
    E. net investment

8. The most appropriate indicator of living standards in two countries during a given year is:
    A. per capita GDP valued in US dollars
    B. real GDP valued in each country's currency
    C. GDP valued in US dollars
    D. GDP valued in each country's currency
    E. net investment valued in each country's currency

9. In which of the following cases will the change in per capita GDP overstate the rise in living standards in a country?
    A. the underground economy becomes more important.
    B. nonmarket activities become less significant as a proportion of the economy
    C. many of the country's products increase in quality
    D. citizens have more leisure time
    E. the country's government devotes a larger share of economic output to health care and education of its citizens

10. The total income acquired by Canadians both within Canada and elsewhere is known as:
    A. disposable income
    B. Gross Domestic Product
    C. Gross National Product
    D. personal income
    E. net domestic income

11. The income earned by households supplying resources in Canada is known as:
    A. disposable income
    B. Gross Domestic Product
    C. Gross National Product
    D. personal income
    E. net domestic income

12. The income received by Canadian households, before deducting personal taxes and other personal transfers to government, is known as:
    A. disposable income
    B. Gross Domestic Product
    C. Gross National Product
    D. personal income
    E. net domestic income

13. The income received by Canadian households, after deducting personal taxes and other personal transfers to government, is known as:
    A. disposable income
    B. Gross Domestic Product
    C. Gross National Product
    D. personal income
    E. net domestic income

14. In Canada, which of the following statements is true?
    A. GDP is less than GNP because net investment income to the rest of the world is positive.
    B. GDP is less than GNP because net investment income to the rest of the world is negative.
    C. GDP is greater than GNP because net investment income to the rest of the world is positive.
    D. GDP is greater than GNP because net investment income to the rest of the world is negative.
    E. GDP and GNP are equal because net investment income to the rest of the world is zero.

15. Which of the following is not one of the components of Mahbub ul Haq's Human Development Index?
    A. rate of adult literacy
    B. per capita GDP adjusted purchasing power parity
    C. the percentage of youth enrolled in school
    D. life expectancy
    E. the rate of infant mortality

Short Answer Questions

Figure 1   Use this table to answer question 1. All figures are in billions of dollars

Personal consumption	$140
Interest income	30
Indirect taxes	25
Exports	75
Proprietors' incomes and rents	50
Gross investment	40
Depreciation	10
Corporate profits	45
Imports	50
Government purchases	45
Wages and salaries	100
Government transfer payments	35
Statistical discrepancy	?

1. a.   Given the data in Figure 1, calculate estimates of GDP using both the income and the expenditure approaches.
   b.   Based on your answer to part a, what is the total value of the statistical discrepancy in this economy?
   c.   Use the statistical discrepancy you calculated in part b to provide the final value for GDP.

Figure 2   Use this table to answer question 2. All figures are in billions of dollars.

Personal consumption	$120
Other payments to persons	70
Corporate income taxes	30
Indirect taxes	30
Exports	55
Earnings not paid out to persons	80
Gross investment	50
Depreciation	20
Net investment income to the rest of the world	25
Government transfer payments	40
Personal taxes and other personal transfers to government	30
Imports	60
Government purchases	55
Statistical discrepancy	0

2. Given the data in Figure 2, calculate the following:
   a.   Gross Domestic Product (GDP)
   b.   Gross National Product (GNP)
   c.   Net Domestic Income (NDI)
   d.   Personal Income (PI)

e. Disposable Income (DI)

Figure 3 Use this table to answer question 3.

Value Added in Making a Loaf of Bread

Production Stage	Total Value Paid/Received	Value Added	Business That Adds Value
A. Wheat is milled into flour	$ 0.25	$__(1)__	flour miller
B. Flour is baked into loaf of bread	1.50	__(2)__	baker
C. Bread is sold by retailer to consumer	2.50	__(3)__	retailer

3. a. Fill in the table in Figure 3.
   b. With the aid of the table, explain how this loaf of bread appears in GDP, using the concept of value added.

Figure 4 Use this table to answer question 4.

Country	GDP (US$ billions)	Population (thousands)	Per Capita GDP (US$ billions)
Gemini	$ 358	14 409	____(1)____
Libra	240	134 395	____(2)____
Virgo	2349	384 329	____(3)____

4. a. Fill in the table in Figure 4.
   b. How would you rank these three countries in terms of living standards?
   c. What are the possible limitations in your ranking?

Solutions to Questions for Chapter 9

Fill in the Blank and True False Questions

1. **income, expenditure** Incomes flow through resource markets and expenditures through product markets.
2. **identity** This identity is true in theoretical terms, but in practice the income-based and expenditure-based estimates of GDP differ because of measurement difficulties.
3. **F** Half the statistical discrepancy is added to the lower GDP estimate and half is subtracted from the higher GDP estimate.
4. The correct order is **consumption, gross investment, net exports**, and the **statistical discrepancy**. In some years, such as the year 2000, gross investment exceeds government purchases (which is missing from this list). In other years, government purchases exceed gross investment. This is because of the volatility of gross investment.
5. **final, intermediate** The motorist's gasoline is a final product because it will not be resold, while the truckdriver's gasoline will be resold in the prices charged for the products being transported.
6. **F** The value added at each of stage of production is what is included, rather than excluded, from GDP.

7. **net** Net investment is the difference in capital stock in two successive years, after accounting for depreciation.

8. **F** Gross investment does include additions to inventories, since, like other forms of real capital, they are an income-producing asset (like other forms of real capital) used by businesses to facilitate the production and delivery of goods.

9. **investment funds, retained earnings**

10. **inflow into, outflow from** Because government purchases represent an expenditure in product markets, they create a monetary inflow, while taxes are a monetary outflow for both households and businesses.

11. **included in, excluded from** It is exports that are included in GDP, since they represent goods and services produced in Canada. In contrast, imports are excluded because they represent goods and services produced elsewhere (and are therefore part of GDP in other nations).

12. **inflow into, outflow from** Since exports represent expenditure by the rest of the world in Canadian product markets, they create a monetary inflow, while imports are a monetary outflow from Canada to product markets in other countries.

13. **F** The GDPs of the various countries must all be expressed in terms of one currency, such as the American dollar.

14. **T** In this case, GDP can underestimate living standards, because some transactions in the underground economy contribute to economic well-being.

15. **T** In this case, GDP can overestimate living standards, because the environmental damage excluded from GDP detracts from economic well-being.

16. **National, Domestic**

17. **T** The income earned on Canadian investments by foreigners must be deducted and the income earned on foreign investments by Canadians must be added to GDP in order to find GNP.

Multiple-Choice Questions

1. **C** This is the definition of the national income accounts.
2. **B** This is the definition of Gross Domestic Product.
3. **D** Only depreciation is component of GDP using the income approach. All the others are components of GDP using the expenditure approach.
4. **C** Landlords' rents are included with proprietors' incomes.
5. **A** Purchases of consumer durables are not included in gross investment.
6. **A** Wages and salaries are the largest component of GDP using the income approach.
7. **C** Per capita real GDP is the best indicator of changes in living standards over time in a given country.
8. **A** Per capita GDP valued in US dollars is the best indicator of living standards in two countries during a given year.
9. **B** If nonmarket activities become less important, then changes in GDP overstate the change in living standards.
10. **C** Gross National Product is the total income acquired by Canadians both within Canada and elsewhere.
11. **E** Net domestic income is the amount earned by households supplying resources in Canada.
12. **D** Personal income is the amount households receive before subtracting personal taxes and other personal transfers to government.
13. **A** Disposable income is the amount households receive after subtracting personal taxes and other personal transfers to government.
14. **C** Canada's net investment income to the rest of the world is positive, so that when this amount is deducted from GDP to find GNP then GDP exceeds GNP.
15. **E** The rate of infant morality is not included in the calculation of the HDI.

Short Answer Problems

1. a. GDP (income approach) = wages and salaries ($100 b.) + corporate profits ($45 b.) + interest income ($30 b.) + proprietors' incomes and rents ($50 b.) + indirect taxes ($25 b.) + depreciation ($10 b.) = $260 billion

GDP (expenditure approach) = personal consumption ($140 b.) + gross investment ($40 b.) + government purchases ($45 b.) + exports ($75 b.) – imports ($50 b.) = $250 billion

b. The total statistical discrepancy is the difference between the estimates using the two approaches, or $10 billion ($260 b. - $250 b.).

c. The final value of GDP is $255 billion, with half the statistical discrepancy ($5 b.) being added to the lower estimate ($250 b.), and half being subtracted from the higher estimate ($260 b.).

2. a. GDP (expenditure approach) = personal consumption ($120 b.) + gross investment ($50 b.) + government purchases ($55 b.) + exports ($55 b.) – imports ($60 b.) = $220 billion

b. GNP = GDP ($220 b.) – net investment income to the rest of the world ($25 b.) = $195 b.

c. NDI = GDP ($220 b.) – indirect taxes ($30 b.) – depreciation ($20 b.) – statistical discrepancy ($0) = $170 billion

d. PI = NDI ($170 b.) + government transfer payments ($40 b.) + other payments to persons ($70 b.) – earnings not paid out to persons ($80 b.) – net investment income to the rest of the world ($25 b.) = $175 billion

e. DI = PI ($175 b.) – personal taxes and other personal transfers to government ($30 b.) = $145 billion

3. a. (1) $0.25, (2) $1.25 [= $1.50 - $0.25], (3) $1.00 [= $2.50 - $1.50]

b. So that final and intermediate products are not double-counted, only the extra worth of the product at each stage of production is included in GDP. In the first stage of production, the value added by the flour miller is the total value of the flour sold to the baker ($0.25). In the second stage, the value added by the baker is $1.25, and in the third stage the value added by the retailer is $1.00. The total value added in all three production stages ($2.50 = $0.25 + $1.25 + $1.00) therefore equals the value of the final product.

4. a. (1) $24 846 (2) $179 (3) $6112

b. Gemini, Virgo, Libra

c. This GDP-based ranking does not take into account differences among the three countries in terms of the extent of nonmarket activities, the underground economy, product quality, composition of output, income distribution, leisure, and the environment.

Chapter 10

Inflation and Unemployment

Learning Objectives

In this chapter you will:
- ◆ learn about inflation, how it is measured, and its effect on nominal and real incomes
- ◆ examine the official unemployment rate, the different types of unemployment, and the definition of full employment

Chapter Highlights

- ◆ Inflation
    1. Inflation is most commonly measured by the consumer price index (CPI), which includes price changes in a representative basket of consumer products.
    2. The CPI uses quantities consumed by an average household in the base year. In the numerator of the CPI formula, base-year quantities are multiplied by current-period prices; in the denominator, they are multiplied by base-year prices. The result is multiplied by 100.
    3. To derive real income, nominal income is divided by the CPI expressed in hundredths.
    4. The CPI has limitations as a measure of inflation, since not everyone has the same consumption patterns. Also, some products improve in quality. Finally, changes in relative prices can affect spending patterns. Products whose prices rise most are bought less often. Products whose prices rise least (or decline) are bought more often. Overall, the CPI tends to overstate the rate of inflation.
    5. The GDP deflator measures price changes for all products, and uses quantities measured in the current year. In the numerator of the GDP deflator formula, current-year quantities are multiplied by current-period prices; in the denominator, they are multiplied by base-year prices. This result is multiplied by 100.
    6. Nominal GDP is divided by the relevant value of the GDP deflator, expressed in hundredths, to find real GDP. When the GDP deflator is greater than 100, nominal GDP is reduced or deflated to derive real GDP. In contrast, when the deflator is less than 100, nominal GDP is expanded or inflated to derive real GDP.
    7. Inflation affects real incomes. Some nominal incomes are fully indexed, so they automatically rise by the inflation rate, and are protected from any loss of purchasing power due to inflation. Other nominal incomes are partially indexed or fixed. Because these incomes do not rise by the inflation rate, there is a loss of purchasing power due to inflation.
    8. The nominal interest rate on loans, which stays fixed during the period of the loan, is the desired real interest rate for lenders plus an inflation premium to anticipate the rate of inflation. If inflation is greater than anticipated, then the actual real interest rate is less than the rate desired by lenders, which means that borrowers gain. In contrast, if actual inflation is less than anticipated, the actual real interest rate exceeds the rate desired by lenders, so that lenders gain.

♦ Unemployment

1. Unemployment is measured using a monthly labour survey conducted by Statistics Canada, which provides an estimate of the labour force population. This population is all Canadian residents 15 years of age or over and eligible to be in the labour force. There are several specific exclusions, including those living in the Northwest, Nunavut, and Yukon Territories, on First Nations reserves, in jails and psychiatric hospitals, and in the armed forces.

2. The labour force incorporates those in the labour force population who are employed or are actively seeking work. The participation rate is the percentage of the labour force population in the labour force. Participation rates for some demographic groups have fluctuated widely in recent decades, with the rate for women rising until the mid-1990s then leveling of, while the rate for young people rose until the late 1980s, then fell back to the same level as in the early 1970s.

3. The unemployment rate is the percentage of the labour force who are unemployed. This rate may understate unemployment because it excludes underemployment, or the underutilization of some workers. The official rate may also understate unemployment due to its exclusion of discouraged workers who have given up seeking work. Finally, this rate may overstate unemployment because some respondents to Statistics Canada's survey say they are unemployed when in fact they are working – often in the underground economy.

4. There are four main types of unemployment. Frictional unemployment occurs when someone is temporarily jobless, or is a new entrant in the labour force. Structural unemployment occurs when there is a mismatch between people and jobs. Cyclical unemployment happens when there is a downturn in the economy. Seasonal unemployment applies in seasonally based industries such as tourism and some resource sectors.

5. Full employment is the highest reasonable level of employment, and is measured using the concept of the natural unemployment rate. This rate includes both frictional and structural unemployment. Since the 1970s, this rate has generally risen, due to accelerating structural change in the economy, more liberal unemployment insurance, higher minimum wages in some provinces, and (at least up until the late 1980s) rising participation rates for young people. Canada's natural unemployment rate is estimated to be between 6 and 7 percent.

6. The economic costs of unemployment can be measured by comparing the actual level of real output in the economy with the potential output level, which would apply if unemployment were at its natural rate. According to Okun's law, for every percentage point that the unemployment rate exceeds the natural rate, actual output is 2.5 percent below its potential level.

Helpful Hints

♦ Inflation

1. There is an important difference between how quantities are defined when calculating the consumer price index (CPI) and when calculating the GDP deflator. The quantities used in both the numerator and denominator of the CPI formula are base-year quantities, while the quantities used in both the numerator and denominator of the GDP deflator formula are current-year quantities

2. It is possible to find nominal income using real income, and to find nominal GDP using real GDP. All that is required is the value of the appropriate price index. This can be shown by rearranging the two formulas.

In the case of individual income:

Real income = nominal income/CPI (in hundredths)

which can be rewritten as:

Nominal income = real income x CPI (in hundredths)

In the case of GDP:

Real GDP = nominal GDP/GDP deflator (in hundredths)

which can be written as:

Nominal GDP = real GDP x GDP deflator (in hundredths)

3. To calculate inflation rates, always use the percentage formula:

inflation rate = [((final index value – initial index value)/initial index value) x 100]

The number 100 is placed in the denominator only if this happens to be the initial value of the index.

4. If inflation is higher than expected, borrowers gain at the expense of lenders because the fixed nominal interest rate includes an inflation premium lower than the actual inflation rate. This means the expected real interest is higher than the actual real interest rate. In contrast, a lower inflation rate than expected causes lenders to gain at the expense of borrowers, since the expected real interest rate turns out to be lower than the actual real interest rate.

♦ Unemployment
1. Both the participation rate and the unemployment rate are affected by changes in the number of discouraged workers.

Recall the two formulas:

Participation rate = labour force/labour force population

Unemployment rate = unemployed in labour force/labour force

For example, if more unemployed workers become discouraged and stop looking for work, values in both formulas change. The participation rate falls due to the drop in the labour force, in the numerator of the first formula. In the second formula, the drop in the labour force affects both the numerator and the denominator. However, since the drop is a larger portion of the numerator, and a smaller portion of the denominator, the unemployment rate will fall. This is why knowledge of the unemployment rate, although by itself useful, is not sufficient. There is hidden unemployment which the decrease in the participation rate will reveal.

2. Remember that unemployment and output are always inversely related. So when the actual unemployment rate is *above* its natural level, real output is *below* its potential level, and vice versa.

3. When calculating an output gap using Okun's Law it is necessary to keep in mind that any percentage must be put in hundredths. For example, if real output could have been 2.5 percent higher than its actual level, then the actual level must be multiplied by .025 (ie. 2.5 expressed in hundredths) rather than by 2.5.

4. The natural unemployment rate is not completely fixed. For example, the Canadian government endeavours to minimize the natural rate of unemployment by using job-matching agencies to reduce frictional unemployment, and retraining to reduce structural unemployment.

Key Concepts

deflation
consumer price index
item weights
base year
cost of living
nominal income
real income
GDP deflator
nominal GDP
cost-of-living adjustment clauses
fully indexed incomes
partially indexed incomes
fixed incomes
nominal interest rate
real interest rate
inflation premium

labour force population
labour force
participation rate
underemployment
discouraged workers
frictional unemployment
structural unemployment
cyclical unemployment
seasonal unemployment
full employment
natural unemployment rate
potential output

Fill in the Blank and True False Questions

1. A general decrease in prices is known as _____.

2. An individual's real income in 2002 is \$20 000 when expressed in 1996 dollars. In this case, 1996 represents the _____year. . If the value of the CPI in 2002 is 125, then the individual's nominal income must have been \$_____.

3. **T F** When inflation is higher than expected, borrowers gain and lenders are harmed.

4. The _____ _____ is a measure of inflation that focuses on price changes for all products in the economy.

5. When the GDP deflator has a value _____ 100, nominal GDP is deflated to find real GDP; when the GDP deflator has a value _____ 100, nominal GDP is inflated to find real GDP; and when the GDP deflator has a value _____ 100, nominal GDP and real GDP are the same.

Place the following terms in the correct order in the blanks above.

less than   equal to   greater than

6. If an economy has 8 million in its labour force population, 6.4 million in its labour force, and 500 000 members of the labour force who are unemployed, its participation rate is _____ percent, and its unemployment rate is _____ percent.

7. **T F** Because of underemployment, the official unemployment rate can overstate the actual level of unemployment.

8. **T F** If more Canadians give up looking for work, the official unemployment rate rises.

9. The unemployment rate associated with full employment is known as the _____ unemployment rate. The real output associated with this unemployment rate is known as the _____ output level.

10. According to most economists, Canada's natural unemployment rate is now between __ and __ percent.

11. **T F** According to Okun's Law, for every 2.5 percentage points that the unemployment rate exceeds the natural unemployment rate, the gap between potential output and actual output is 1 percent.

12. Order the following where 1 = the oldest generation and 3 = the youngest generation.

baby-bust generation   baby-boom echo generation   baby-boom generation

1. _____
2. _____
3. _____

Multiple Choice Questions

1. A consumer price index includes only tacos and pizzas. During the base year, an average consumer buys 20 tacos and 5 pizzas. By the next year the price of tacos has risen from $2 to $2.05 and the price of pizzas from $12 to $12.40. The value of the index is therefore:
    A. 100
    B. 97
    C. 102
    D. 103
    E. 98

2. A household's annual nominal income is $65 000 at a time when the value of the consumer price index is 130. Therefore the household's annual real income is:
   A. $50 000
   B. $84 500
   C. $5 million
   D. $8.45 million
   E. $6.5 million

3. If the consumer price index has a value of 140 and a household's daily nominal income is $105, then the household's daily real income is:
   A. $71
   B. $93
   C. $75
   D. $0.93
   E. $133

4. A country's consumer price index has a value of 120 at the end of one year and a value of 126 at the end of the next year. Inflation during the year has been:
   A. 1.6 percent
   B. 5.0 percent
   C. 4.8 percent
   D. 4.6 percent
   E. 6.0 percent

5. Which of the following is not a limitation of the consumer price index?
   A. The buying patterns of individual consumers may differ markedly from the basket of products found in the consumer price index.
   B. Some consumer products undergo quality changes that are not reflected by changes in price.
   C. The CPI does not include the effects of changes in input prices.
   D. Consumers' spending habits change over time as prices change.
   E. New consumer products are introduced that are not taken into account in the index.

Figure 1   Use this table to answer question 6.

	Output of Calculators	Current Price
2001	10 000	$ 8
2002	15 000	$10

6. In the accompanying table, output levels and prices are shown in two years for an economy that produces only one good, calculators. Using 2001 as the base year, the GDP deflator in 2002 has a value of:
   A. 110
   B. 125
   C. 150
   D. 120
   E. 80

7. A one-year loan is made at a time when its lender desires a real interest rate of 4 percent and when the inflation premium is 3 percent. If the actual inflation rate during the year is 2 percent, the actual real interest rate on this loan will be:
   A. 4 percent
   B. 3 percent
   C. 7 percent
   D. 5 percent
   E. 2 percent

8. Which of the following groups is part of Canada's labour force population?
   A. prisoners
   B. part-time workers
   C. residents of native reservations
   D. those below 15 years of age
   E. those employed in Canada's armed forces

9. Which of the following groups is part of Canada's officially unemployed?
   A. part-time workers who would prefer to have full-time work
   B. discouraged workers
   C. involuntarily unemployed members of the labour force
   D. part-time workers who would not prefer to have full-time work
   E. full-time workers

10. Which of the following statements is true?
    A. A recent graduate looking for his first job is an example of structural unemployment.
    B. A sales clerk who quits one retail job and is looking for another in the same industry is an example of frictional unemployment.
    C. A former fisherman who moves from Newfoundland to Calgary to seek work is an example of frictional unemployment.
    D. An autoworker who loses her job during an economic downturn is an example of seasonal unemployment.
    E. A forestry work laid off during the winter months is an example of cyclical unemployment.

11. Full employment in Canada occurs:
    A. when every Canadian who wants a job has one
    B. when there is no frictional unemployment
    C. when the unemployment rate is between 2 and 4 percent
    D. when there is no structural unemployment
    E. when there is no cyclical unemployment

12. Which of the following trends is a probable reason for increases in Canada's natural unemployment rate over the last few decades?
    A. an accelerating pace of structural change in the Canadian economy
    B. the increasing importance of part-time jobs in Canadian labour markets
    C. falling participation rates for young people
    D. decreases in minimum wages in most Canadian provinces
    E. an increased frequency of recessions in the past few decades

13. Based on Okun's Law, if Canada's unemployment rate is 0.4 percent higher than the country's natural unemployment rate, then real output could have been:
    A. higher by 10 percent.
    B. lower by 10 percent.
    C. higher by 1 percent.
    D. lower by 1 percent.
    E. lower by 2.5 percent.

14. According to David Foot, which of the following statements is true?
    A. The oldest members of the baby-boom generation had a harder time entering the labour force than the youngest members of this generation had.
    B. The baby-bust generation was born after 1995.
    C. Generation X was born from 1980 to 1995.
    D. The baby-boom echo generation was born from 1947 to 1966.
    E. The baby-bust generation has been a favoured group because of its small numbers.

15. According to David Foot, the group that has had (or will have) the most difficulty entering the labour force is:
    A. the baby-boom echo generation
    B. the baby-boom generation
    C. Generation X
    D. the baby-bust generation
    E. the millennium generation

Short Answer Questions

1. a. A pensioner's monthly income automatically increases from $1200 in year 1 to $1224 in year 2 at a time when CPI-based inflation is 3 percent. Does this pensioner win or lose from inflation during this period? By how much has the pensioner's real income changed between year 1 and year 2, if year 1 is the base year?

   b. An amount of $1000 is lent out at a nominal interest rate of 5 percent. If the lender's inflation premium is 1 percent and inflation during the year is 3 percent, then what is the anticipated real interest rate? the actual real interest rate? Does the lender or the borrower gain from inflation, and by how much?

   c. An economy's real GDP in a given year is $220 billion, and the value of the GDP deflator is 50. What must the economy's nominal GDP be?

Figure 2 Use this table to answer question 2.

| | Prices | | Quantities | |
	(2002)	(2003)	(2002)	(2003)
Hamburgers	$2.00	$2.50	2	1
Hour of internet access	0.75	0.50	3	5

2. Data for Consumer X's weekly purchases during 2002 and 2003 are shown in Figure 2.
   a. What is the value of consumer X's 2002 shopping basket using 2002 prices? using 2003 prices?

    b.   If 2002 is the base year, what is the value of the CPI in 2002? in 2003?

    c.   What is the value of consumer X's 2003 shopping basket using 2003 prices? using 2002 prices?

    d.   If 2003 is the base year, what is the value of the CPI in 2003? in 2002?

    e.   What is the annual inflation rate found using 2002 as the base year? using 2003?

    f.   Why do your two answers in part e differ?

Figure 3   Use this table to answer question 3.

Participation rate	62 percent
Unemployed in the labour force	500 000
Part-time workers who are looking for full-time employment	350 000
Discouraged workers	650 000
Full-time workers	7 million
Part-time workers who are not looking for full-time employment	1.5 million

3.   Employment data for a hypothetical economy are shown in Figure 3.

    a.   What is this economy's labour force?

    b.   What is this economy's official unemployment rate?

    c.   What is this economy's labour force population?

    d.   If discouraged workers were included in the labour force, and both underemployed workers and discouraged workers were included in the official unemployment rate, what would this rate be?

4.   In the late 1990s and early 2000s, there are indications that the natural unemployment rate in Canada has begun to decrease, after its long gradual climb since the 1970s. Can you think of any reason(s) for this change?

Solutions to Questions for Chapter 10

Fill in the Blank and True False Questions

1.   **deflation** This is different than disinflation, which is a state of gradually falling inflation.

2.   **base, 25 000** The base year used by Statistics Canada periodically changes. Nominal income is found by multiplying real income by the CPI expressed in hundredths [=(20 000 x 1.25)].

3.   **T** Borrowers gain at the expense of lenders because the nominal interest rate they pay includes an inflation premium set lower than the actual inflation rate, so the real interest rate they expected to pay is higher than the actual interest rate.

4.   **GDP deflator** Products are weighted as they appear in the current year's GDP.

5.   **greater than, less than, equal to** With a GDP deflator exceeding 100, nominal GDP is diminished when it is transformed into real GDP. With a GDP deflator less than 100, nominal GDP is expanded when transformed into real GDP. When the GDP deflator equals 100, nominal GDP and real GDP are the same.

6.   **80, 7.8** The participation rate is found by dividing the labour force of 6.4 million by the labour force population of 8 million, then multiplying the result by 100. The unemployment rate is found by dividing the 500 000 unemployed in the labour force by the total force of 6.4 million, then multiplying the result by 100.

7.   **F** Underemployment can cause the official rate to understate unemployment, because the presence of part-time workers who would prefer to work full-time is not being captured by the official rate.

8.   **F** With more discouraged workers, the official unemployment rate falls because there are fewer unemployed in the labour force.

9. **natural, potential** The natural unemployment rate represents the highest reasonable expectation of employment for the economy as a whole, and is associated with potential output.
10. **6, 7** Definitions of Canada's natural unemployment rate vary, though most current estimates are in this range.
11. **F** According to this law, for every percentage point the unemployment rate exceeds the natural unemployment rate, the gap between potential output and actual output is 2.5 percent.
12. **baby-boom generation, baby-bust generation, baby-boom echo generation.** The baby-boom generation were born between 1947 and 1966, the baby-bust generation between 1967 and 1979, and the baby-boom echo generation between 1980 and 1995.

Multiple Choice Questions

1. **D** The value of the index is found by multiplying base-year quantities by current-year prices, then adding the result ((20 x $2.05) + (5 x $12.40)), dividing this number by the sum of base-year quantities multiplied by base-year prices ((20 x $2) + (5 x $12)), then multiplying by 100.
2. **A** This is found by dividing nominal income ($65 000) by the CPI value expressed as a decimal (1.30).
3. **C** A nominal income of $105 divided by a consumer price index of 1.40 (expressed as a decimal) gives the real income of $75.
4. **B** This is the difference between 120 and 126 divided by 120, then multiplied by 100.
5. **C** The CPI is not meant to be a direct measure of changes in input prices.
6. **B** This is found by multiplying the current-year quantity by the current-year price (15 000 x $10), dividing this number by the current-year quantity by the base-year price (15 000 x $8), then multiplying by 100.
7. **D** This is found by subtracting the actual inflation rate of 2 percent from the nominal interest rate of 7 percent (the 4 percent desired real interest rate plus the 3 percent expectation of inflation).
8. **B** Since part-time workers are employed, they are part of the labour force population.
9. **C** The official unemployment rate includes involuntarily unemployed members of the labour force.
10. **B** The sales clerk is an example of frictional unemployment, since this situation is the sort of unemployment that commonly occurs in the job market regardless of a person's skills or the state of the economy.
11. **E** Full employment is defined in terms of the natural unemployment, which includes frictional and structural unemployment, but not cyclical unemployment.
12. **A** The accelerating pace of structural change has likely caused an increase in structural unemployment, and hence in the natural unemployment rate as well.
13. **C** According to Okun's Law, real output could have exceeded its actual value by 1 percent if the economy had been at full employment. This is the difference between the actual and natural unemployment rates (0.4 percent) multiplied by 2.5.
14. **E** The baby-bust generation has had a relatively easy time because its small numbers have meant a lower supply of new entrants in the labour market.
15. **C** This is because Generation X came at the tail end of a large intake of young people into the labour force.

Short Answer Questions

1   a. The pensioner's nominal income has increased by 2 percent [= (1224 - 1200)/1200], which is less than the 3 percent inflation rate. Because prices are rising faster than the pensioner's nominal income, the pensioner is losing from inflation. In year 1, the pensioner's real income is $1200 [=(1200/1.00)], which is the same as nominal income, since year 1 is the base year. In year 2, the pensioner's real income is $1188.35 [=(1224/1.03)], so it has declined by $11.65 in base-year dollars.

    b. The anticipated real interest rate is 4 percent [= (5% - 1%)], while the actual real interest rate is 2 percent [= (5% - 3%)]. Because the actual real interest rate is 2 percent lower than the anticipated interest rate, the lender receives $20 less (= .02 x $1000) than she thought she would. Therefore, this is the amount she loses from unanticipated inflation.

c. A nominal GDP of $110 billion, when divided by a GDP deflator of 50 (expressed in hundredths) results in a real GDP of $220 billion. (See the discussion of deriving nominal GDP in the helpful hints above.)

2. a. Using 2002 prices, the value of X's 2002 shopping basket is $6.25 [= ($2.00 x 2) + ($0.75 x 3))]. Using 2003 prices, this same basket costs $6.50 [= ($2.50 x 2) + ($0.50 x 3)].

b. Because 2002 is the base year, the 2002 value of the CPI is 100. In 2003, the value of the CPI is 104 [= ($6.50/$6.25) x 100].

c. Using 2003 prices, the value of X's shopping basket is $5.00 [= ($2.50 x 1) + ($0.50 x 5)]. Using 2002 prices, this same basket costs $5.75 [= ($2.00 x 1) + (0.75 x 5)].

d. Because 2003 is the base year, the 2003 value of the index is 100. In 2002, the value of the index is 115 [= ($5.75/$5.00) x 100].

e. Using 2002 as the base year, the annual inflation rate is 4 percent [= ((104 - 100)/100)]. Using 2003 as the base year, the annual deflation rate is (-)13 percent [= ((100 - 115)/115)].

f. This is because of the quantity changes that have occurred between 2002 and 2003. In 2002, the product whose price has decreased (internet access) is given a low quantity weighting, while the product whose price has increased (hamburgers) is given a high quantity weighting. Therefore, the increase in hamburgers is the trend that dominates, giving inflation when this year is the base year. In 2003, internet access is given a high quantity weighting, while hamburgers are given a low quantity weighting. Therefore, the decrease in the price of internet access is the trend that dominates in 2003, giving deflation when this is the base year.

3   a. The labour force is the sum of all those working (7 million + 1.5 million+ 350 000) as well as unemployed members of the labour force (500 000), which totals to 9.35 million.

b. The official rate is the ratio of the unemployed members of the labour force and the total labour force, multiplied by 100, or 5.3 percent [= (500 000/9.35 million) x 100].

c. The labour force population is found using the participation rate (62 percent) and the labour force found in part a. Because the labour force divided by the labour force population equals the participation rate (expressed in hundredths), the labour force population must equal the labour force divided by the participation rate (expressed in hundredths), or 15.08 million [= (9.35 million/.62)].

d. If discouraged workers are included in the labour force, then the labour force rises to 10 million [= 9.35 million + 650 000]. Adding both discouraged workers and underemployed workers to those who are unemployed in the labour force means that the unemployment rate rises to 15.0 percent [= ((500 000 + 650 000 + 350 000)/10 million) x 100].

4. Reasons for this possible recent decline in Canada's natural unemployment rate include tighter restrictions on unemployment insurance and a slowdown in minimum wage increases in some provinces. Also, much of the displacement of workers caused by the removal of trade barriers has already passed.

Chapter 11

Economic Fluctuations

Learning Objectives

In this chapter you will:
- learn about aggregate demand and the factors that affect it
- analyze aggregate supply and the factors that influence it
- study the economy's equilibrium and how it differs from its potential

Chapter Highlights

- Aggregate Demand
    1. The relationship between real expenditures and the price level in the entire economy is known as aggregate demand. When graphed, this relationship results in a downsloping curve known as the aggregate demand curve.
    2. The fact that real expenditures and the price level are inversely related is dependent on the wealth effect and foreign trade effect. According to the wealth effect, a rise in the price level reduces the real value of household financial assets, causing a reduction in the consumption component of real expenditures. According to the foreign trade effect, a rise in the price level causes exports to become costlier in foreign markets, while imports become relatively cheaper in the domestic market. The result is a reduction in the net exports component of real expenditures.
    3. Aggregate demand factors cause shifts in the aggregate demand curve – either a rightward increase or a leftward decrease. Aggregate demand factors can be categorized based on which component of aggregate demand they affect.
    4. Consumption-related aggregate demand factors include households' disposable income, household wealth, consumer expectations, and interest rates. A rise in disposable income, a rise in wealth, a fall in interest rates, or more optimistic consumer expectations will raise consumption and therefore increase aggregate demand.
    5. Investment-related factors include interest rates and business expectations. A fall in interest rates or more optimistic business expectations will raise investment and therefore increase aggregate demand.
    6. Net exports-related factors include foreign incomes and exchange rates. A rise in foreign incomes or a fall in the value of the Canadian dollar in terms of the US dollar will raise net exports and therefore increase aggregate demand.

- Aggregate Supply
    1. The relationship between real output and the price level in the entire economy is known as aggregate supply. When graphed, this relationship results in an upsloping curve known as the aggregate supply curve.
    2. Real output and the price level are directly related along the aggregate supply curve because input prices are constant. If the price level for output rises, for example, businesses choose to produce more, raising the economy's real output.

3. When the economy is far below potential output, there is significant excess capacity, so a rise in the price level causes a large increase in output. The aggregate supply curve is therefore flatter in this output range. When the economy is at or above potential output, a lack of excess capacity means that a rise in the price level results in only a small increase in output. The aggregate supply curve steepens in this output range.

4. Aggregate supply factors cause shifts in the aggregate supply curve – either a rightward increase or a leftward decrease. Aggregate supply factors can be categorized based on whether they are short-run or long-run factors.

5. With short-run changes in aggregate supply, the economy's potential output does not change. These changes are caused by fluctuations in input prices, with a rise in these prices causing a short-run decrease, and a fall causing a short-run increase.

6. With long-run changes in aggregate supply, the economy's potential output adjusts in the same direction as the aggregate supply curve. These changes are caused by variations in resource supplies, labour productivity, taxes, or government regulation. A rise in resource supplies, an increase in labour productivity, lower taxes or less government regulation results in a long-run increase in aggregate supply, with the opposite movements causing a long-run decrease.

♦ Equilibrium
1. The economy's equilibrium occurs at the intersection of the aggregate demand and aggregate supply curves. The economy reaches equilibrium through unintended changes in inventories, also known as unplanned investment. Positive unplanned investment occurs when the price level exceeds its equilibrium value. With inventories unexpectedly expanding, businesses reduce prices and real output until equilibrium is reached. Conversely, negative unplanned investment is the result of a price level below its equilibrium value. Because inventories are unexpectedly falling, businesses raise prices and real output until equilibrium is reached.

2. Equilibrium can also be analyzed by looking at the economy's total injections and withdrawals. Injections are additions to the economy's income-spending stream, while withdrawals are deductions from this stream.

3. There are three pairs of linked injections and withdrawals: investment and saving, government purchases and taxes, and exports and imports. While there is no need for each of these pairs to balance, total injections (I + G + X) and total withdrawals (S + T + M) are equal in equilibrium, since total additions and deductions to the income-spending stream must balance if this stream is to circulate at a steady rate.

4. When total injections exceed total withdrawals, flows into the income-spending stream exceed outward flows, so that the stream quickens and real output expands until total withdrawals are made equal to total injections at equilibrium. In contrast, if total withdrawals exceed total injections, outward flows from the income-spending stream exceed inward flows. This slows the stream, so that real output falls until real withdrawals are in balance with total injections at equilibrium.

5. There is guarantee that equilibrium output equals its potential level. When equilibrium output is less than potential output, there is a recessionary gap equal to the discrepancy between the two output levels. If, instead, equilibrium output exceeds potential output, there is an inflationary gap equal to this discrepancy.

♦ Economic Growth and Business Cycles
1. Economic growth can be defined either as an increase in real GDP or as an increase in per capita GDP. The first definition is used when studying changes in the economy's productive capacity. The second definition is most appropriate when studying changes in living standards.

2. Between 1870 and 1914, Canadian per capita real output grew gradually, more than doubling during this period. Between 1914 and 1945, growth in per capita real output was more unstable, with upswings in the 1920s and the early 1940s countered by the Great Depression during the 1930s. Since 1945, per capita real output has more than tripled, though growth has been lower since 1973 than before this date.
3. Economic growth is closely tied to changes in labour productivity, found by dividing real output by the total hours worked in an economy.
4. There is a long-run upward trend in potential output as the economy's resources expand and technology improves, but actual real output has a less stable path. Its changes follow a pattern called the business cycle, with periods of expansion and contraction as well as peaks and troughs.
5. Expectations play a major role in the business cycle. During a contraction, decreases in aggregate demand are magnified because the pessimistic expectations of households and businesses (both domestic and foreign) reduce consumption, investment and exports. In contrast, during an expansion, increases in aggregate demand are magnified because optimistic expectations raise consumption, investment, and exports.
6. Periods of contraction that last for six months or more are known as recessions. Particularly deep and long downturns are known as depressions.

Helpful Hints

♦ Aggregate Demand
1. It is important to distinguish between the wealth effect, which is a reason for the aggregate demand's negative slope, and the possible role of wealth as an aggregate demand factor. The wealth effect applies only to the case where a change in the general price level affects the real value of household assets. For example, a rise in the price level reduces the real value of these assets and therefore decreases real expenditures, causing a movement down an aggregate demand curve. In contrast, the role of wealth as an aggregate demand factor shifts the entire aggregate demand curve. Any time the total value of household assets changes (for example, due to a change in stock prices or real estate values), the aggregate demand curve shifts to the left (in the case of a decrease in the value of households assets) or to the right (in the case of an increase the value of these assets).

♦ Aggregate Supply
1. In the Canadian economy, it is more common for the economy to be operating on the segment of the aggregate supply curve below the potential output level than above it. As a result, recessionary gaps are more likely to occur than are inflationary gaps. This means that the pattern of business cycles is not as symmetrical as shown in Figure 11.13 of the text.

♦ Equilibrium
1. Because the investment component of aggregate demand includes only planned investment, total expenditures (C + I + G + (X - M)) found using the aggregate demand curve are not exactly the same as the expenditure-based estimate of GDP discussed in Chapter 9. This is because the expenditure-based GDP estimate includes both planned and unplanned investment. Only at equilibrium, where unplanned investment is zero, are the two concepts identical.
2. Taxes have an effect on both aggregate demand and aggregate supply. Taxes are an aggregate demand factor, because they affect households' disposable income and businesses' calculations of investment profitability. This means that higher taxes reduce

both consumption and investment and cause a decrease in aggregate demand. Taxes are an aggregate supply factor because they affect current production decisions. Higher taxes reduce the incentive to work and invest, and therefore cause a long-run decrease in aggregate supply. These two shifts occur at different speeds, with the impact on aggregate demand occurring more quickly than the impact on aggregate supply. Both effects lead to a reduction in equilibrium output, though they have conflicting effects on the equilibrium price level.

3. The exchange rate has an impact on both aggregate demand and aggregate supply. A fall in the international value of the Canadian dollar, for example, raises exports and reduces imports, causing an expansion in net exports and an increase in aggregate demand. At the same time, a lower Canadian dollar means higher prices for inputs from the rest of the world, which causes a short-run decrease in aggregate supply. Both effects lead to a rise in the equilibrium price level, though they have conflicting effects on equilibrium output.

♦ Economic Growth and Business Cycles
1. The distinction between a recession and a depression is not clear-cut. As a rule, supporters of the market economy are more likely refer to downturns (even severe ones) as recessions, while critics of the market economy are more likely to refer to severe downturns as depressions.

Key Concepts

aggregate demand
real expenditures
aggregate demand schedule
aggregate demand curve
wealth effect
foreign trade effect
aggregate demand factors
injections
withdrawals
increase in aggregate demand
decrease in aggregate demand
real rate of return
investment demand
investment demand schedule
investment demand curve
exchange rate
aggregate supply
aggregate supply schedule
aggregate supply curve

long-run increase in aggregate supply
long-run decrease in aggregate supply
positive unplanned investment
negative unplanned investment
aggregate supply factors
short-run decrease in aggregate supply
short-run increase in aggregate supply
recessionary gap
inflationary gap
imports
expansion
contraction
business cycle
peak
recession
depression
trough

Fill in the Blank and True False Questions

1. **T F** If total injections are greater than total withdrawals, an economy=s real output falls, and if total withdrawals are greater than total injections, an economy=s real output rises.

Figure 1 Use this graph to answer question 2.

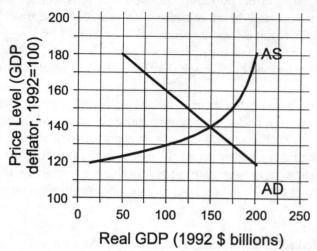

Real GDP (1992 $ billions)

2. Given the conditions shown in Figure 1, a potential output of $175 billion means this economy is facing a(n) _____ of $_____. On the other hand, if potential output level is $130 billion, the economy faces a(n) _____ of $_____.

    Place the following terms in the correct order in the blanks above.

    inflationary gap   20 billion   recessionary gap   25 billion

3. **T F** A rise in the price level increases the real value of financial assets, which leads to more consumption spending.

4. A fall in Canada's general price level causes export expenditures on Canadian products to _____ and import expenditures by Canadians to _____.

    Place the following terms in the correct order in the blanks above.

    increase   decrease

5. **T F** Canada=s exports are affected by Canadian incomes rather than by foreign incomes.

6. **T F** If the Canadian dollar goes up in value against the British pound, Canadian exports to Britain decrease.

7. A rise in interest rates causes a(n) _____ in aggregate demand, while a rise in government purchases causes a(n) _____ in aggregate demand.

    Place the following terms in the correct order in the blanks above.

    increase   decrease

8.   A rise in raw material prices causes a short-run _____ in aggregate supply, while a decrease in wages causes a short-run _____ in aggregate supply.

   Place the following terms in the correct order in the blanks above.

   increase   decrease

9.   A drop in taxes paid by households and businesses leads to a long-run _____ in aggregate supply, while a fall in labour productivity leads to a long-run _____ in aggregate supply.

   Place the following terms in the correct order in the blanks above.

   increase   decrease

10.   When equilibrium output is $625 billion and potential output is $650 billion, the difference between these two values represents a(n) _____ gap equal to $25 billion.

11.   **T F** If an economy=s unemployment rate is below the natural unemployment rate, the economy is experiencing an inflationary gap.

12.   **T F** Economic growth defined as the increase in real output per capita is the best indicator when analyzing the effects of economic growth on individuals. Economic growth defined as an increase in real output is the best indicator when analyzing the effects of economic growth on the entire economy.

13.   **T F** For Canadians, real GNP per capita in 1999 was five times as high as it was in 1870.

14.   A _____ is a decline in real output that lasts 6 months or longer, while a _____ is a particularly long and deep reduction in economic activity. A _____ is the bottom of a business cycle, and a _____ is the top of a business cycle.

   Place the following terms in the correct order in the blanks above.

   depression   trough   peak   recession

15.   **T F** According to Paul Romer, the prices of newly developed ideas should be kept high to provide an incentive for research and development.

Multiple-Choice Questions

1.   Which of the following is an aggregate demand factor?
   A.   interest rates
   B.   raw material prices
   C.   labours productivity
   D.   the supply of capital
   E.   wages

2. Which of the trends below will cause consumption spending to fall?
   A. the expectation of future price increases
   B. a rise in personal income taxes
   C. an increase in stockmarket prices
   D. a decrease in consumer debt
   E. a drop in household taxes

3. If business expectations in an economy become more optimistic at the same time as the real interest rate rises, investment will:
   A. necessarily rise
   B. necessarily fall
   C. possibly rise or fall
   D. stay the same
   E. rise, then fall

4. Which of the following components of aggregate demand fluctuates most?
   A. consumption
   B. investment
   C. government purchases
   D. exports
   E. imports

5. Which of the following is an aggregate supply factor?
   A. interest rates
   B. consumer expectations
   C. input prices
   D. foreign incomes
   E. household debt

6. In the entire economy, equilibrium is reached through changes in:
   A. consumption spending
   B. unplanned investment
   C. potential output
   D. planned investment
   E. wages

7. Which of the following statements is true?
   A. A short-run decrease in aggregate supply means a fall in output at every price level, while potential output remains the same.
   B. A short-run decrease in aggregate supply means a fall in the price level at every output, while potential output remains the same.
   C. A short-run decrease in aggregate supply means a fall in the price level at every output, while potential output declines.
   D. A short-run decrease in aggregate supply means a fall in output at every price level, while potential output declines.
   E. A short-run decrease in aggregate supply means a fall in the price level at every output, while potential output rises.

8. Which of the following statements is true?
   A. A short-run decrease in aggregate supply causes a drop in the equilibrium price level and a rise in equilibrium output.
   B. A short-run decrease in aggregate supply causes a rise in both the equilibrium price level and equilibrium output.
   C. A short-run decrease in aggregate supply causes a drop in both the price level and equilibrium output.
   D. A short-run decrease in aggregate supply causes a rise in the equilibrium price level and a fall in equilibrium output.
   E. A short-run decrease in aggregate supply causes a rise in the equilibrium price level while equilibrium output stays the same.

9. Which of the following statements is true?
   A. A long-run increase in aggregate supply means a rise in output at every price level, while potential output remains the same.
   B. A long-run increase in aggregate supply means a rise in the price level at every output, while potential output remains the same.
   C. A long-run increase in aggregate supply means a rise in the price level at every output, while potential output declines.
   D. A long-run increase in aggregate supply means a rise in output at every price level, while potential output declines.
   E. A long-run increase in aggregate supply means a rise in output at every price level, while potential output also rises.

10. Which of the following statements is true?
   A. A rise in the price level causes a small increase in output when the economy is far below potential output, and a large increase when the economy is near or above potential output.
   B. A rise in the price level causes a large decrease in output when the economy is far below potential output, and a small decrease when the economy is near or above potential output.
   C. A rise in the price level causes a small decrease in output when the economy is far below potential output, and a large decrease when the economy is near or above potential output.
   D. A rise in the price level causes a large increase in output when the economy is far below potential output, and a small increase when the economy is near or above potential output.
   E. A rise in the price level causes a small decrease in output no matter where the economy is operating relative to potential output.

Figure 2 Use this graph to answer questions 11 and 12.

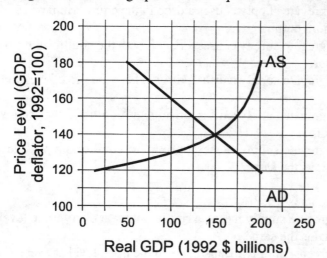

11. Given the conditions shown in Figure 2, when the price level has a value of 180:
    A. real expenditures exceed real output, meaning there is positive unplanned investment
    B. real expenditures exceed real output, meaning there is negative unplanned investment
    C. real output exceeds real expenditures, meaning there is positive unplanned investment
    D. real output exceeds real expenditures, meaning there is negative unplanned investment
    E. real output equals real expenditures, meaning the economy is at equilibrium

12. Given the conditions shown Figure 2, when the price level has a value of 120:
    A. real expenditures exceed real output, meaning there is positive unplanned investment
    B. real expenditures exceed real output, meaning there is negative unplanned investment
    C. real output exceeds real expenditures, meaning there is positive unplanned investment
    D. real output exceeds real expenditures, meaning there is negative unplanned investment
    E. real output equals real expenditures, meaning the economy is at equilibrium

13. Which of the businesses below is most affected by an economic downturn?
    A. a grocery store
    B. a restaurant
    C. a lawyer
    D. a video rental store
    E. a computer manufacturer

14. An increase in aggregate demand can be magnified into a protracted expansion through:
    A. a rise in consumption due to more optimistic consumer expectations
    B. a rise in investment due to more optimistic business expectations
    C. a rise in exports due to similar trends in other countries
    D. all of the above choices
    E. none of the above choices

15. According to Paul Romer, which of the following is the most important factor that causes economic growth?
    A. the amount of investment spending
    B. growth in the economy's labour force
    C. an expansion in the stock of ideas
    D. the discovery of natural resources
    E. international trade

Short Answer Questions

1. Outline the effects of each of the following on aggregate demand, as well as on equilibrium price and output. In each case, outline which component(s) of aggregate demand will be affected:
    a. Stockmarket prices drop significantly.
    b. Canadian interest rates fall.
    c. As a cost-saving measure, the federal government reduces its purchases of goods and services.
    d. Household incomes in the US rise.

2. Outline the effects of each of the following on aggregate supply, as well as on equilibrium price, equilibrium output, and potential output. In each case, identify whether the shift in aggregate supply is short-run or long-run.
    a. There is a reduction in the extent to which Canadians are willing to engage in entrepreneurial activity.
    b. Due to an international pact on air pollution, Canadian environment regulations are made much more stringent.
    c. Wages in the Canadian economy fall.
    d. Due to immigration, the Canadian labour force expands.

Figure 3 Use this graph to answer question 3.

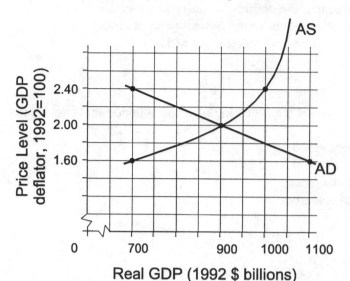

Real GDP (1992 $ billions)

3.   Figure 3 shows aggregate demand and aggregate supply curves in a hypothetical economy.
    a.   Based on this graph, what is the equilibrium price level and quantity?
    b.   What happens if the price level in this economy is at 2.40? at 1.60?
    c.   If the potential output in this economy is $1 trillion, then is there a recessionary or inflationary gap when the economy is at equilibrium? How large is this gap? Explain.

Solutions to Questions for Chapter 9

Fill in the Blank and True False Questions

1.   **F** An excess of injections over withdrawals raises real output, whereas real output is reduced by an excess of withdrawals over injections.
2.   **recessionary gap, 25 billion, inflationary gap, 20 billion**
3.   **F** A higher price level reduces the real value of financial assets, which causes a decline in consumption spending.
4.   **increase, decrease** Assuming that other variables (such as incomes and exchange rates) are constant, Canada's export sales rise because these products are now cheaper in foreign markets. In contrast, import purchases fall since these products are now more expensive in Canadian markets.
5.   **F** It is foreign incomes that have an impact on Canada's exports.
6.   **T** There will a decrease in Canada's exports to Britain because these products have been made relatively more expensive.
7.   **decrease, increase** Aggregate demand decreases with higher interest rates and it increases with higher government purchases.
8.   **decrease, increase**
9.   **increase, decrease** Aggregate supply undergoes a long-run increase with lower taxes and it undergoes a long-run decrease with a drop in labour productivity.
10.   **recessionary** Since potential output exceeds actual real output, this is a recessionary gap.
11.   **T** When the unemployment rate falls short of the natural unemployment rate, actual output exceeds potential output.
12.   **T** The growth of real output per capita is the best indicator of effects on individuals, while the growth of real output is the best indicator of effects on the economy.

13. **F** It was twelve times as high.
14. **recession, depression, trough, peak**
15. **F** Romer believes that prices of these ideas should be kept low to encourage the discovery of new ideas.

Multiple-Choice Questions

1. **A** All the other options are aggregate supply factors, not aggregate demand factors.
2. **B** All of the other possible options would cause consumption spending to rise.
3. **C** The final result depends on whether the rise in investment spending due to greater business optimism exceeds or falls short of the fall in investment spending caused by a higher real interest rate.
4. **B** Investment fluctuates widely because it depends on business expectations, which are highly volatile.
5. **C** All of the other possible options are aggregate demand factors.
6. **B** This unplanned investment represents unintended changes in inventories that occur whenever amounts demanded and supplied are unequal.
7. **A** With a short-run decrease in aggregate supply, real output falls at each price level, but potential output remains the same.
8. **D** With a leftward shift in aggregate supply, the equilibrium price level rises while equilibrium output declines.
9. **E** With a long-run increase in aggregate supply, real output rises at each price level and potential output increases as well.
10. **D** This is because the aggregate supply curve is flat at output levels far from potential output and steeper the closer the economy is operating to potential output.
11. **C** A price level above equilibrium means that real output exceeds real expenditures and that there is positive unplanned investment
12. **B** A price level below equilibrium means that real expenditures exceed real output and that there is negative unplanned investment.
13. **E** The computer manufacturer will be most affected, since purchases of durable items such as computers are postponable.
14. **D** An expansion can be magnified by a simultaneous increase in consumption, investment, and exports.
15. **C** According to Romer, new ideas are the most important determinant of economic growth.

Short Answer Problems

1. a. A significant drop in stockmarket prices causes a decline in household wealth and therefore reduces consumption. Aggregate demand decreases, reducing both the equilibrium price level and equilibrium real output.
   b. A fall in Canadian interest rates expands investment as well as consumption of durable goods. Aggregate demand increases, raising both the equilibrium price level and equilibrium output.
   c. A reduction in government purchases means that aggregate demand decreases, reducing both the equilibrium price level and equilibrium output.
   d. A rise in US household incomes expands Canadian exports and therefore net exports rise. Aggregate demand increases, raising both the equilibrium price level and equilibrium real output.
2. a. A reduction in Canadians' willingness to engage in entrepreneurial activity means that real output will be reduced at every price level, representing a long-run decrease in aggregate supply. The equilibrium price level therefore rises and equilibrium output falls. Because this is a long-run decrease in aggregate supply, potential output falls as well.
   b. With more stringent environmental regulations, real output is reduced at every price level, which means a long-run decrease in aggregate supply. The equilibrium price level rises and equilibrium output falls. Because this is a long-run decrease in aggregate supply, potential output falls as well.
   c. A fall in wages for Canadian workers reduces production costs, causing a short-run increase in aggregate supply. The equilibrium price level falls and equilibrium output rises. Because this is a short-run change in aggregate supply, potential output does not change.
   d. With an expansion in the Canadian labour force, real output is raised at every price level, representing a long-run increase in aggregate supply. The equilibrium price level therefore falls and

equilibrium output rises. Because this is a long-run increase in aggregate supply, potential output rises as well.

3. a. The equilibrium price level is 2.00 and equilibrium output is $900 billion.

   b. With a 2.40 price level, real output is $1 trillion and real expenditures are $700 billion, which means there is positive unplanned investment equal to $300 billion. As a result, prices fall until the equilibrium price level of 2.00 is achieved. In contrast, with a 1.60 price level, real output is $700 billion and real expenditures are $1.1 trillion, which means there is negative unplanned investment equal to $400 billion. As a result, prices rise until the equilibrium price level of 2.00 is achieved.

   c. With a $1 trillion potential output, and an equilibrium output of $900 billion, there is a recessionary gap of $100 billion, since equilibrium output falls short of its potential level.

Chapter 12

Fiscal Policy

Learning Objectives

In this chapter you will:
♦ learn about expansionary and contractionary fiscal policies, which are used by governments seeking economic stability
♦ analyze the multiplier effect of fiscal policy, as determined by the marginal propensities to consume and withdraw
♦ consider budget surpluses and deficits and their impact on public debt and public debt charges

Chapter Highlights

♦ Fiscal Policy
1. Governments use stabilization policy to reduce the impact of the business cycle. Expansionary policies are used to reduce unemployment and raise output. Contractionary policies are used to stabilize prices and reduce output.
2. Stabilization policies are either fiscal or monetary. Fiscal policy uses the annual budgets of governments, through changes in taxes or government purchases. Monetary policy involves changing interest rates and the money supply.
3. Expansionary fiscal policy means raising government purchases, reducing taxes, or both in order to increase aggregate demand and output. The intention is to eradicate a recessionary gap. Contractionary fiscal policy means reducing government purchases, raising taxes, or both in order to decrease aggregate demand and stabilize prices. The intention is to eradicate an inflationary gap.
4. With any fiscal policy, the balance of total injections and total withdrawals is affected. An expansionary fiscal policy raises injections (by increasing government purchases) and/or reduces total withdrawals (by decreasing taxes). With total injections now higher than total withdrawals, the income-spending stream adjusts to a greater equilibrium output. A contractionary fiscal policy reduces injections (by decreasing government purchases) and/or raises total withdrawals (by increasing taxes). With total withdrawals higher than total injections, the income-spending stream adjusts to a lower equilibrium output.
5. Because fiscal policy necessitates discretionary action, it is known as discretionary policy. In contrast, automatic stabilizers are programs such as Employment Insurance, which automatically adjust to stabilize the economy. During a economic downturn, these programs reduce net tax revenues, increasing aggregate demand. During an economic upturn, these programs raise net tax revenues, decreasing aggregate demand.

♦   The Spending Multiplier
1. The multiplier effect represents the magnified impact of any spending change on aggregate demand. For example, a rise in government purchases has not only a direct effect on output and income, but also an indirect effect, as households who receive the added funds from government spend a portion of their increased income on domestic items.
2. The marginal propensity to consume (MPC) is found by dividing a change in consumption on domestic items by the related change in income. The marginal propensity to withdraw (MPW) is found by dividing a change in withdrawals by the related change in income. Because all income is either spent on domestic items or withdrawn, MPC and MPW sum to one.
3. According to the spending multiplier formula, the total shift in aggregate demand resulting from a spending change is this initial spending change times the spending multiplier, which is the reciprocal of MPW.
4. In the case of a tax change, the spending multiplier formula is expressed to take account of the fact that the change in spending occurs indirectly through adjustments in disposable income. The shift in the aggregate demand equals the marginal propensity to consume times the tax change (this whole expression preceded by a minus sign) multiplied by the spending multiplier.
5. The spending multiplier shows the shift in aggregate demand caused by an initial change in spending; the resulting change in equilibrium output depends on the slope of the aggregate supply curve. If this curve is relatively flat, then the output change is almost as large as the shift in aggregate demand. In contrast, if aggregate supply is steep, then most of the spending change translates into a higher price level rather than an output change.

♦   Impact of Fiscal Policy
1. Discretionary fiscal policy and automatic stabilizers both have an impact on government budgets, which include both government revenues and expenditures. When a government's revenues and expenditures are equal, there is a balanced budget. In contrast, revenues in excess of expenditures mean there is a budget surplus. Finally, expenditures in excess of revenues mean there is a budget deficit.
2. Government debt is the accumulation of budget deficits over time, minus any budget surpluses.
3. The first possible principle to guide fiscal policy is one of annually balanced budgets, which means government revenues and expenditures are made equal in each fiscal year. This principle is often criticized because governments must adjust their budgets in a way that worsens the business cycle. For example, during an economic downturn, when government revenues decrease, governments must reduce their expenditures as well, which has a contractionary impact just when an expansionary policy is needed.
4. The second possible guiding principle is one of cyclically balanced budgets, which means that budget deficits and surpluses should balance over the entire business cycle. This has become the dominant principle in recent years for Canadian governments.
5. The third possible guiding principle is functional finance. This states that governments should focus on the yearly needs of the economy rather than be concerned with their debt. This was the dominant principle for many Canadian governments in past decades.

Helpful Hints

◆ Fiscal Policy

1. The decision on how much the government should change its purchases or taxes in order to eradicate any recessionary or inflationary gap is not an easy one. Fiscal policy-makers must not just estimate the size of the spending multiplier, in order to forecast how much a policy will shift the aggregate demand curve, they must also estimate the slope of the aggregate supply curve, to predict how much of any spending change will translate into an adjustment in prices and how much will translate into a variation in output.

2. It is important to understand the way that automatic stabilizers operate to stabilize the economy. Canada's Employment Insurance scheme is an example. During a downturn, this program undergoes two trends. First, because there are fewer people working, program contributions from workers and employers decrease. Second, because more people are unemployed, program payments increase. Both trends cause net tax revenues to fall, increasing aggregate demand and stimulating the economy during the downturn. In contrast, during an upturn, there are more program contributions from workers and employers, while program payments decrease due to a lower level of unemployment. Both trends lead to a rise in net tax revenues, which decreases aggregate demand and restrains spending and prices in the economy.

◆ The Spending Multiplier

1. Because MPC and MPW are related, it is possible to re-express the spending multiplier formula in terms of MPC rather than MPW. Since the spending multiplier equals (1/MPW) and MPW equals (1 – MPC), then the spending multiplier formula becomes:

$$\text{spending multiplier} = 1/(1 - \text{MPC})$$

◆ Impact of Fiscal Policy

1. Budget deficits are sometimes confused with public debt charges, but they are quite different concepts. A budget deficit is the amount that a government's expenditures exceed its revenues in an given fiscal year, and is added to the government's debt at the end of the previous year to find the new level of the government's debt. In contrast, public debt charges are the amount of interest the government must pay on its outstanding debt. The public debt charges for any given fiscal year are found by multiplying the government's debt at the end of the previous year by the prevailing interest rate (expressed as a decimal). The two concepts are related: if public debt charges rise due to a higher outstanding government debt, or higher interest rates, then the budget deficit will increase as well, since this raises the government's expenditures without raising its revenues.

2. In Canada, public debt and government debt have different meanings. Public debt refers only to the federal government's debt, while total government debt includes the debts of provincial and territorial governments.

Key Concepts

stabilization policy
expansionary policies
contractionary policies
fiscal policy
fiscal year
monetary policy
expansionary fiscal policy
contractionary fiscal policy
discretionary policy
automatic stabilizers
net tax revenues
multiplier effect
marginal propensity to consume
marginal propensity to withdraw

public debt charges
balanced budget
budget surplus
budget deficit
spending multiplier
recognition lag
decision lag
impact lag
public debt
annually balanced budget
cyclically balanced budget
functional finance

Fill in the Blank and True False Questions

1. Government initiatives to reduce fluctuation in the business cycle are known as _____ policy

2. **T F** Government policies designed to reduce unemployment are known as expansionary policies, and those designed to reduce inflation are called contractionary policies.

3. A tax cut is an example of a _____ policy, while a rise in interest rates is an example of a _____ policy.

    Place the following terms in the correct order in the blanks above.

    fiscal   monetary

4. When the government wishes to decrease real output, it can do so by _____ taxes or _____ its purchases.

    Place the following terms in the correct order in the blanks above.

    reducing   raising

5. **T F** A change in personal income taxes has a more direct impact on aggregate demand than a change in government purchases.

6. Stabilization policies that are intentionally initiated by governments to adjust the economy are known as _____ policy.

7. **T F** When real output increases, automatic stabilizers operate to reduce net tax revenues, which decreases real output.

8. When Dana's income increases by $500, she spends $200 extra on Canadian products and uses the rest for saving, imports and taxes. Therefore her marginal propensity to withdraw is _____.

9. **T F** An increase in government purchases represents an immediate rise in withdrawals which is matched by a gradual increase in injections during successive rounds of new spending.

Figure 1   Use this graph to answer question 10

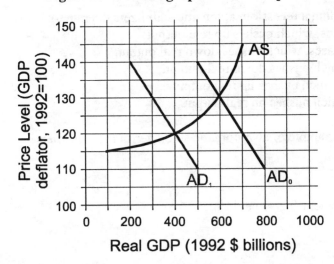

10. **T F** If the shift from AD_0 to AD_1 in Figure 1 occurred because of a $150 billion change in government purchases, then the economy's spending multiplier must equal 1.33.

11. The amount owed by the federal government due to its past borrowing is known as the _____ _____.

12. If Canada's public debt is $500 billion and the average interest rate on this debt is 6 percent, public debt charges are $____ billion.

13. If a government's expenditures are $124 billion and its revenues are $136 billion, it has a _____ of _____. If instead the government's revenues are $137 billion and its expenditures are $154 billion, it has a _____ of _____.

   Place the following terms in the correct order in the blanks above.

   budget deficit   budget surplus $12 billion $17 billion

14. A government=s _____ is measured over a period of time, while a government=s _____ is measured at a given point in time.

   Place the following terms in the correct order in the blanks above.

   deficit   debt

15. **T F** The multiplier effect of any change in spending is largest when real output in an economy is far below its potential output.

16. **T F** Based on various empirical studies, the average estimated value of Canada's spending multiplier is 2.5.

Multiple-Choice Questions

1. When the economy is undergoing a recession, automatic stabilizers operate to:
    A. raise government purchases, which pushes up real output.
    B. reduce government purchases, which pushes down real output.
    C. raise net tax revenues, which pushes down real output.
    D. reduce net tax revenues, which pushes up real output.
    E. raise net tax revenues, which pushes up real output.

2. Which of the following is an example of an automatic stabilizer in the Canadian economy?
    A. health expenditures
    B. military expenditures
    C. government spending on scientific research
    D. welfare payments
    E. education expenditures

3. Which of the following statements is correct?
    A. The time period during which a tax cut is introduced and passed in Parliament is an example of the impact lag.
    B. The time period it takes policy-makers to realize that the economy is experiencing a recessionary gap is an example of the decision lag.
    C. The time period during which a tax cut raises aggregate demand and creates new jobs is an example of the recognition lag.
    D. The time period during which a tax cut raises aggregate demand and creates new jobs is an example of the impact lag.
    E. The time period during which a tax cut is introduced and passed in Parliament is an example of the recognition lag.

4. An economy=s marginal propensity to consume is 0.33. What is the value of the economy's spending multiplier?
    A. 0.67
    B. 1.5
    C. 0.33
    D. 3
    E. 3.33

Figure 2   Use this graph to answer question 3

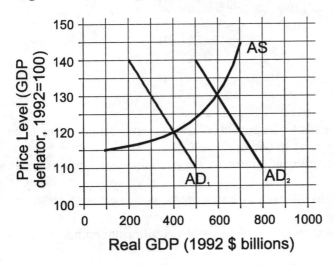

Real GDP (1992 $ billions)

5.   In Figure 2, the shift in aggregate demand from AD_0 to AD_1 could be caused by:
A. a contractionary fiscal policy in the form of a drop in government purchases
B. a contractionary fiscal policy in the form of a rise in government purchases
C. an expansionary fiscal policy in the form of a drop in government purchases
D. an expansionary fiscal policy in the form of a rise in government purchases
E. an expansionary fiscal policy in the form of a rise in taxes

6.   A government increases its purchases by $1 million in an economy with a marginal propensity to consume of 0.4. As a result, the overall increase in aggregate demand will be:
A. $400 000
B. $1 666 667
C. $4 000 000
D. $2 500 000
E. $40 000 000

7.   A $20 billion tax cut causes an initial $8 billion increase in consumption spending on domestic items. The marginal propensity to consume in this economy is therefore:
A. 0.4
B. 0.8
C. 0.6
D. 0.2
E. 1.6

8.   A tax cut causes an initial $1 billion increase in consumption spending on domestic items in an economy with a marginal propensity to withdraw of 0.57. As a result, the overall shift in aggregate demand will be:
A. $2.33 billion
B. $1.75 billion
C. $1.57 billion
D. $0.57 billion
E. $1 billion

9. A $1 billion tax increase occurs in an economy with a marginal propensity to withdraw of 0.6. As a result, the overall shift in aggregate demand will be:
    A. -$0.67 billion
    B. $0.67 billion
    C. -$1.67 billion
    D. $1.67 billion
    E. -$1 billion

10. Which of the following cases leads to the greatest change in equilibrium output in an economy with a marginal propensity to withdraw of .67?
    A. a $2 billion decrease in government purchases when equilibrium output is above its potential level
    B. a $2 billion decrease in taxes when equilibrium output is far below its potential level
    C. a $2 billion increase in government purchases when equilibrium output is far below its potential level
    D. a $2 billion decrease in taxes when equilibrium output is above its potential level billion
    E. a $2 billion increase in taxes when equilibrium output and potential output are the same

11. One benefit of fiscal policy as a tool of stabilization policy is:
    A. the fact that it can be focused on particular regions
    B. its high visibility as a political tool
    C. its close association with changes in government debt
    D. the short delays in implementing changes in government purchases and taxes
    E. its low visibility as a political tool

12. A political party suggests that the government should continue to increase transfer payments until the unemployment rate has fallen to 6 percent. This party subscribes to which principle of fiscal policy?
    A. annually balanced budget
    B. cyclically balanced budget
    C. functional finance
    D. debt-minimization budget
    E. cost-minimization budget

13. According to Say's Law:
    A. demand automatically creates its own supply.
    B. an economy's equilibrium output is not necessarily the same as its potential output
    C. supply automatically creates its own demand
    D. workers suffer from money illusion
    E. nominal wages exhibit downward stickiness

14. John Maynard Keynes= creation of a new theory of macroeconomics was prompted by which historical situation?
    A. the low unemployment in industrial countries during World War II
    B. the chronically high unemployment suffered by many countries during the Great Depression
    C. the recession that followed World War I
    D. the boom experienced in Great Britain during the 1920s
    E. the gradual rise in per capita incomes before World War I

15. An expansionary policy operates through:
    A. an increase in either total injections or total withdrawals
    B. an increase total injections or a decrease in total withdrawals
    C. a decrease in either total injections or total withdrawals
    D. an increase in total injections, but not through a change in total withdrawals
    E. an increase in total withdrawals, but not through a change in total injections

Short Answer Questions

1. In each of the following cases, calculate the values of MPC, MPW, and the spending multiplier.
   a. A $300 000 decrease in income results in a $200 000 drop in withdrawals.
   b. A $10 million increase in consumption on domestic items is caused by a $25 million rise in income.
   c. Withdrawals decrease by $2 million at the same time consumption on domestic items falls by $1.5 million.

2. An initial increase in government purchases of $4 billion causes a $6 billion shift in aggregate demand.
   a. What is the size of the spending multiplier in this economy?
   b. What is the size of this economy's MPW? MPC?
   c. Will the overall change in equilibrium output be greater than or less than $6 billion? Explain.
   d. Would your answers to the above questions have been the same if, instead of a $4 billion change in government purchases, the initial spending change was a $4 billion change in consumption or net exports?

3. A government starts its fiscal year with a debt of $700 billion when the interest rate is 4 percent.
   a. If the governments expenditures (excluding public debt charges) are $210 billion and its revenues are $230 billion then what is the size of its budget deficit or surplus? What is the government's debt at the end of the year?
   b. Recalculate your answer to part a based on the assumption that the interest rate is 3 percent rather than 4 percent.

Solutions to Questions for Chapter 12

Fill in the Blank and True False Questions
1. **stabilization** This policy can be in the form of either fiscal policy or monetary policy.
2. **T** Expansionary policies are so called because they expand the economy, while contractionary policies contract the economy.
3. **fiscal, monetary**
4. **raising, reducing**
5. **F** Changes in personal income taxes have a more indirect impact since they affect consumption spending and aggregate demand only after an initial effect on disposable income.
6. **discretionary** These policies should be distinguished from automatic stabilizers, which operate automatically
7. **F** In this case, automatic stabilizers raise net tax revenues. Because a tax increase acts as a contractionary policy, this pushes down output.
8. **0.6** To find the MPC, the change in domestic consumption ($200) is divided by the change in income ($500), while the MPW is found by deducting the MPC from 1.
9. **F** It is injections which undergo an immediate rise and withdrawals that increase gradually. The gradual rise in withdrawals occurs because accompanying each new round of spending is a new round of withdrawals.
10. **F** The spending multiplier is 2, since the shift in aggregate demand ($300 billion) is twice the initial $150 billion change in spending.
11. **public debt**
12. **30** The correct answer of $30 billion is found by multiplying public debt ($500 billion) by the average interest rate, expressed as a decimal (0.06).
13. **budget surplus, $12 billion, budget deficit, $17 billion**
14. **deficit, debt** A deficit is usually measured over a fiscal year, while debt is usually measured at the beginning and end of a fiscal year.
15. **T** In this case, a shift in aggregate demand affects primarily output rather than the price level.
16. **F** The average estimate is in the range of 1.5.

Multiple-Choice Questions
1. **D** In this case, automatic stabilizers reduce net tax revenues. This tax decrease acts as an expansionary policy, which pushes up real output.
2. **D** Welfare payments are an automatic stabilizer, because they expand and decrease in a way that reduces the severity of the business cycle.
3. **D** The impact lag is the time period it takes a policy to have its intended effect on the economy.
4. **B** The marginal propensity to withdraw is found by deducting the marginal propensity to consume (0.33) from 1. The spending multiplier is then found by taking the reciprocal of 0.67 (1/0.67).
5. **A** A leftward shift in aggregate demand is caused by a contractionary policy, such as a reduction in government purchases.
6. **B** This is found by multiplying the $1 million change in government purchases by the spending multiplier of 1.67 (1/0.6).
7. **A** This is because MPC is the initial increase in consumption on domestic items ($8 billion) as a proportion of the tax cut ($20 billion).
8. **B** This is found by multiplying the initial spending change ($1 billion) by the spending multiplier of 1.75 (1/0.57).
9. **A** Aggregate demand shifts leftward by -$0.67 billion. This answer is found by multiplying the $1 billion increase in taxes by the MPC of 0.4 (which is MPW minus 1), then placing a minus sign in front of this expression and multiplying by the spending multiplier of 1.67 (1/0.6).
10. **C** This is because a change in government purchases has a larger effect on aggregate demand than a tax change, and because a change in aggregate demand far below potential output has a greater effect on equilibrium output than a change in aggregate demand above or at potential output.
11. **A** Unlike monetary policy, fiscal policy can be focused on particular regions.

12. **C** The party subscribes to the view that government budgets should be geared to yearly needs of the economy
13. **C** According to Jean-Baptiste Say (after whom Say's Law is named), supply creates its own demand.
14. **B** It was the high unemployment of the Great Depression that prompted Keynes to create his new theory.)
15. **B** An expansionary policy involves either an increase in total injections, or a decrease in total withdrawals.

Short Answer Problems

1. a. The MPW is 0.67 (-$200 000/-$300 000), the MPC is 0.33 (1 - 0.67), and the spending multiplier is 1.5 (1/0.67).

    b. The MPC is 0.4 ($10 million/$25 million), the MPW is 0.6 (1 - 0.4), and the spending multiplier is 1.67 (1/0.6).

    c. The total decrease in income is -$3.5 million (-$2 million - $1.5 million), the MPW is 0.57 (-$2 million/$3.5 million) and the MPC is 0.43 (1 – 0.57). Therefore, the spending multiplier is 1.75 (1/0.57).

2. a. The spending multiplier has a value of 1.5, found by dividing the $6 billion shift in aggregate demand by the $4 billion initial change in spending.

    b. The MPW is 0.67, found by taking the reciprocal of the spending multiplier. The MPC is 0.33, found by subtracting MPW from 1.

    c. Equilibrium output increases by less than $6 billion because part of the spending change translates into higher prices.

    d. The answer would be the same. As long as the initial spending change is $4 billion, it does not matter whether it is a change in government purchases, consumption or net exports.

3. a. With an interest rate of 4 percent, public debt charges during the year are $28 billion ($700 billion x 0.04). If other expenditures are $210 billion, then total expenditures are $238 billion ($28 billion + $210 billion). The budget deficit is therefore (-)$8 billion ($230 billion - $238 billion).

    b. With an interest rate of 3 percent, public debt charges during the year are $21 billion ($700 billion x 0.03). Total expenditures are therefore $231 billion, and the budget deficit is (-)$1 billion ($230 billion - $231 billion).

Chapter 13

Money

Learning Objectives

In this chapter you will:
+ examine the functions of money, its components, and the various definitions of money
+ learn about the demand for and supply of money and about equilibrium in the money market
+ see how money is created and consider the money multiplier

Chapter Highlights

+ Money and its Uses
  1. Money has three functions. First, it serves as a means of exchange, by overcoming the need for a double coincidence of wants, which applies if barter is used instead. Second, it acts as a store of purchasing power, providing the benefit of liquidity, though sacrificing the income from holding wealth in some other form. Third, it serves as a measure of value, providing a single unit of account for all prices, which contrasts with the multitude of relative values in a barter economy.
  2. The money supply is closely associated with the financial system, in particular deposit-takers. These are businesses that take deposit funds from savers and lend them to borrowers, while holding a portion of their assets in the form of cash reserves. The main type of deposit-takers are chartered banks. In Canada, chartered banks hold most of the deposits of the public.
  3. Other deposits of the Canadian public are held by near banks (in particular, trust companies, mortgage loan companies, credit unions and caisses populaires), whose services are more specialized than those provided by chartered banks. Canada's financial system also includes insurance companies and investment dealers.
  4. Canada's supply of money includes currency, demand deposits, notice deposits, term deposits, and foreign currency deposits held by Canadian residents. The M1 definition includes currency outside chartered banks and publicly held demand deposits at chartered banks. M2 includes M1 as well as notice deposits and personal term deposits at chartered banks. M3 includes M2 as well as nonpersonal term deposits and foreign-currency deposits held by Canadian residents. M2+ includes M2 as well as corresponding deposits at near banks and some other liquid assets.
  5. With the increased use of credit cards and debit cards, M2 and M2+ are becoming more accurate measures of the money supply, as nonchequable notice deposits gain in popularity.

+ The Money Market
  1. The demand for money has two components. The transactions demand is related to money's function as a means of exchange, and varies directly with the price level and real output. The asset demand for money is related to money's function as a store of

purchasing power. At low nominal interest rates, money becomes relatively more attractive as an asset, while at high interest rates, it becomes relatively less attractive. Therefore the asset demand for money is inversely related to the nominal interest rate.

2. Money demand is the combination of the transactions demand and asset demand. Due to the asset demand, the money demand curve has a negative slope relative to the interest rate. Due to transactions demand, the money demand curve shifts either right or left if the price level or real output rise or fall.

3. Given a vertical money supply curve, reflecting the money supply set by the central bank, the equilibrium interest rate occurs at the intersection of money demand and money supply.

4. If the interest rate is above its equilibrium level, a surplus of money causes the nominal interest to fall. This is because people purchase high-earning bonds, raising the price of bonds and reducing the nominal interest rate. In contrast, an interest rate below its equilibrium level means there is a shortage of money, which causes the nominal interest rate to rise. This occurs because people sell low-earning bonds, reducing the price of bonds and raising the nominal interest rate.

♦ Money Creation
1. Deposit-takers hold part of their assets in desired reserves to cover expected withdrawals. The amount they hold in this way depends on the reserve ratio, which is the ratio of desired reserves to total deposits.

2. Actual reserves held over and above desired reserves are known as excess reserves.

3. Deposit-takers create money whenever they lend out excess reserves. Presuming the public holds all its money in one form of deposit at a single type of deposit-taker, the amount of money that can be created in this way is found by multiplying the change in excess reserves by the money multiplier. This multiplier is the reciprocal of the reserve ratio.

4. In reality, the amount of money created by deposit-takers is less than the amount derived using the money multiplier formula, because the public holds some of its money in currency rather than deposits, and not all deposits necessarily appear in the relevant definition of the money supply.

Helpful Hints

♦ Money and Its Uses
1. Remember that not all deposit-takers are chartered banks, and not all financial institutions are deposit-takers. Deposit-takers include not just chartered banks but also near banks, since these institutions take in deposit funds and lend out the funds to generate revenue, just as chartered banks do. Other types of financial institutions, such as insurance companies, mutual fund companies or investment dealers, are not deposit-takers.

2. Not all money supply definitions are cumulative. In particular, M3 and M2+ are based on additions to M2, but are not based on each other. In the year 2000, M2+ was larger than M3, as shown in Figure 13.2. But a gradual shift is occurring in the relative sizes of these two definitions, because chartered banks are become increasingly more important in the Canadian financial system, at the expense of near banks, and so are their deposits.

- ◆ The Money Market
  1. The reason that the demand for money is defined relative to the nominal interest rate rather than the real interest rate is that, even if the real interest rate were zero, there would still be an opportunity cost of holding money, equal to the inflation rate.
  2. The analysis in the text of how the money market reaches equilibrium is based on a simplifying assumption: that the only ways of holding wealth are bonds and money. Given this assumption, movements in the bond market play a vital role in driving the nominal interest rate towards its equilibrium value. At an interest rate below equilibrium, there is a shortage (excess demand) of money, which translates into an excess supply for bonds, pushing bond prices down and the interest rate up, since bond prices and interest rates are always inversely related. In contrast, at an interest rate above equilibrium, a surplus (excess supply) of money exists. This translates into an excess demand for bonds, pushing bond prices up and the interest rate down.

- ◆ Money Creation
  1. The money creation process outlined in the text starts with Saver A's initial deposit of currency in a bank, as shown in Figure 13.6. This currency is not newly issued by the central bank. Instead, it is currency that was previously out of circulation. That is why Saver A's original receipt of this currency is not included as part of the money creation process.

Key Concepts

barter
coincidence of wants
liquidity
unit of account
deposit-takers
cash reserves
chartered banks
credit card
debit card
near banks
currency
demand deposits
notice deposits
term deposits
foreign currency deposits
M1
transactions demand

M2
M3
M2+
near money
asset demand
money demand
money demand schedule
money demand curve
money supply
money supply schedule
money supply curve
desired reserves
reserve ratio
excess reserves
money multiplier

Fill in the Blank and True False Questions

1. **T F** Transactions made with money are possible only if there is a coincidence of wants between the buyer and the seller.

2.   Money has the advantage of _____, which means that money can easily be turned into a means of payment.

3.   **T F** The main disadvantage of holding money for long periods is the income that could have been earned by holding wealth in another form.

4.   Deposit-takers can increase their profits by charging a _____ interest rate on loans and paying a _____ interest rate on deposits.

  Place the following terms in the correct order in the blanks above.

            lower   higher

5.   Order the following definitions of the money supply in the Canadian economy, where 1 = greatest dollar value, 4 = least dollar value.

            M2   M3   M1   M2+

  1. _____
  2. _____
  3. _____
  4. _____

6.   **T F** M1 does not include publicly held currency.

7.   While some _____ deposits are included in M3, some _____ deposits are included in M2+.

  Place the following terms in the correct order in the blanks above.

            foreign currency   near bank

Figure 1 Use this graph to answer questions 8 to 13.

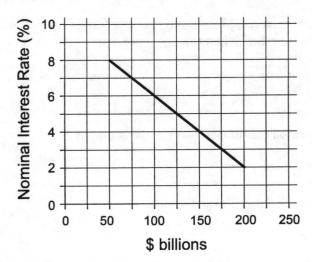

8. The line in Figure 1 represents the _____ _____curve.

9. If the price level rises, the line in Figure 1 shifts to the _____, while if real output falls, the line shifts to the _____.

Place the following terms in the correct order in the blanks above.

left   right

10. In the money market shown in Figure 1, the money supply is $150 billion. The equilibrium interest rate is therefore ___ percent.

11. In the money market shown in Figure 1, the money supply is $150 billion. At an interest rate of 8 percent, the demand for high-earning assets such as bonds _____, and the interest rate _____.

Place the following terms in the correct order in the blanks above.

falls   rises

12. In the money market shown in Figure 1, the money supply is $150 billion. At an interest rate of 2 percent, the demand for high-earning assets such as bonds _____, and the nominal interest rate _____.

Place the following terms in the correct order in the blanks above.

falls   rises

13. In the money market shown in Figure 1, the money supply falls to $100 billion. The equilibrium interest rate therefore becomes ___ percent.

14. The minimum cash reserves held by deposit-takers for potential withdrawals are known as _____ reserves.

15. Caribou Bank has $500 000 in actual reserves, $10 million in outstanding deposits, and no excess reserves. The bank=s reserve ratio is therefore ____ percent.

Multiple-Choice Questions

1. Which of the following is not a function that money plays in the economy?
    A. a store of purchasing power
    B. a means of exchange
    C. a unit of account
    D. a way to overcome the need for specialization and trade
    E. none of the above

2. Canada's chartered banks together form a(n):
    A. monopoly
    B. oligopoly
    C. monopolistically competitive industry
    D. perfectly competitive industry
    E. none of the above

3. Which of the following financial institutions is a near bank?
    A. a small chartered bank
    B. a mortgage-loan company
    C. an insurance company
    D. an investment dealer
    E. a mutual fund company

Figure 2 Use this table to answer questions 4 to 7.

Currency outside chartered banks	$45 billion
Notice & personal term deposits at chartered banks	$467 billion
Publicly held demand deposits at chartered banks	$61 billion
Notice & personal term deposits at near banks	$173 billion
Other liquid assets in M2+	$36 billion
Nonpersonal term & foreign currency deposits at chartered banks	$51 billion

4. Given the information for a hypothetical country Plutonia in Figure 2, the value of M1 in Plutonia is:
    A. $45 billion
    B. $61 billion
    C. $106 billion
    D. $157 billion
    E. $279 billion

5. Given the information for a hypothetical country Plutonia in Figure 2, the value of M2 in Plutonia is:
    A. $157 billion
    B. $279 billion
    C. $573 billion
    D. $106 billion
    E. $609 billion

6. Given the information for a hypothetical country Plutonia in Figure 2, the value of M3 in Plutonia is:
    A. $624 billion
    B. $609 billion
    C. $573 billion
    D. $106 billion
    E. $746 billion

7. Given the information for a hypothetical country Plutonia in Figure 2, the value of M2+ in Plutonia is:
   A. $624 billion
   B. $746 billion
   C. $782 billion
   D. $573 billion
   E. $279 billion

8. The use of debit and credit cards:
   A. is making M1 a more accurate definition of the money supply.
   B. is making M3 a more accurate definition of the money supply.
   C. is increasing because traditional currency is being phased out of use in Canada.
   D. is falling as chartered banks are losing their importance in the Canadian financial system.
   E. is making M2 and M2+ more accurate definitions of the money supply

9. Which of the following statements is true?
   A. A rise in the economy's real output increases the asset demand for money.
   B. A fall in the economy's price level increases the transactions demand for money.
   C. A rise in the nominal interest rate increases the transactions demand for money.
   D. A rise in the nominal interest rate decreases the asset demand for money.
   E. A rise in the economy's real output decreases the transactions demand for money.

10. You buy a $20 000 bond with an interest rate originally specified at 5 percent. If the prevailing interest rate rises to 10 percent, the price of this bond will change to:
    A. $40 000
    B. $10 000
    C. $19 000
    D. $5000
    E. $21 000

11. Maple Leaf Bank has a reserve ratio of 4 percent and initially has no excess reserves. If $10 000 is deposited in the bank, its excess reserves are now:
    A. $400
    B. $10 000
    C. $9600
    D. $4000
    E. $10 400

12. If $100 000 in currency is deposited in a chartered bank, the maximum amount the banking system can increase the money supply, given an average reserve ratio of 5 percent, is:
    A. $2 000 000
    B. $1 900 000
    C. $100 000
    D. $95 000
    E. $1 000 000

13. Because the public holds some money in cash, and because not all deposits are necessarily part of the money supply:
    A. the money multiplier overestimates the money-creating potential of the banking system.
    B. desired reserves are less than actual reserves.
    C. actual reserves are less than desired reserves.
    D. the reserve ratio is usually close to 100 percent
    E. the money multiplier underestimates the money-creating potential of the banking system.

14. If excess reserves in the Canadian banking system are $4 500, then the maximum amount the banking system can increase the money supply, given a reserve ratio of 2.5 percent:
    A. $180 000
    B. $200 000
    C. $11 250
    D. $1800
    E. $4500

15. Which of the following statements concerning Harold Innis's staples theory is incorrect?
    A. Wheat was the main staple in the Canadian economy during two decades before World War I.
    B. Minerals were the main staple in the Canadian economy in the decades after World War I.
    C. Lumber was the main staple in the Canadian economy from the early 1800s to the 1860s.
    D. Furs were the main staple in the Canadian economy from the 1600s to early 1800s.
    E. Fish were the main staple in the Canadian economy between World War I and World War II.

Short Answer Questions

1. Identify which of the following functions of money is illustrated by the following events.
    a. A department store customer uses a debit card to purchase a piece of clothing.
    b. A consumer uses the internet to compare prices for a certain book from online sellers.
    c. A stockholder checks through the prices of her shares to measure the weekly change in her net worth.
    d. A traveler increases the balance in his bank account so that he will have sufficient funds while he is traveling out of the country.

2. A bond has an initial price of $10 000 when it is issued, at a time when the prevailing interest rate is 3 percent.
    a. What happens to this bond's price if the prevailing interest rate rises to 5 percent?
    b. What happens to the bond's price if, instead, the prevailing interest rate falls to 2 percent?

3. Frobisher Bank has $150 million in outstanding deposits and $7.5 million in desired reserves.
   a. What is the reserve ratio for this bank?
   b. If the bank's excess reserves are $4.5 million, what are its actual reserves?
   c. What happens to this bank's actual reserves if it receives a new $10 million deposit? What has happened to its excess reserves?

Solutions to Questions for Chapter 9

Fill in the Blank and True False Questions
1. **F** This is a condition of barter transactions, not those made with money.
2. **liquidity**
3. **T** This income that could have been earned represents money's main opportunity cost.
4. **higher, lower**
5. **M2+, M3, M2, M1**
6. **F** M1 includes publicly held currency, but does not include currency held by chartered banks.
7. **foreign currency, near bank**
8. **money demand** The downward-sloping curve relating the interest rate with the quantity of money is the money demand curve.
9. **right left** The transactions demand for money is pushed up by higher prices and reduced by lower real output.
10. **4** This is the point where the money demand and money supply curves intersect.
11. **rises, falls** At an 8 percent interest rate, there is an excess supply of money equalling $100 billion ($150 billion - $50 billion). As wealthholders try to use this money to purchase high-earning assets such as bonds, the price of bonds rises and the interest rate falls.
12. **falls, rises** At a 2 percent interest rate, there is an excess demand for money equalling $50 billion ($200 billion - $150 billion). As wealthholders try to turn high-earning assets such as bonds into money, the price of bonds falls and the interest rate rises.
13. **6** This is the point where the new money supply curve intersects the money demand curve.
14. **desired** They have this name because deposit-takers can hold whatever minimum amount of cash reserves they desire.
15. **5** Because the bank has no excess reserves, the reserve ratio is the ratio between the $500 000 in reserves and the $10 million in outstanding deposits.

Multiple-Choice Questions
1. **D** Overcoming the need for specialization and trade is not a function that money plays in the economy.
2. **B** Canada's chartered banks form an oligopoly, since there are only a few major businesses in this market.
3. **B** Mortgage-loan companies are near banks.
4. **C** This is found by adding currency outside banks ($45 billion) and publicly held demand deposits at chartered banks ($61 billion)
5. **C** This is found by adding notice and personal term deposits at chartered banks ($467 billion) to M1 ($106 billion).
6. **A** This is found by adding nonpersonal term and foreign currency deposits at chartered banks ($51 billion) to M2 ($573 billion).
7. **C** This is found by adding notice and personal term deposits at near banks ($173 billion) and other liquid assets in M2+ ($36 billion) to M2 ($573 billion).
8. **E** This is because a wide range of nonchequable notice deposits are now easier to use for transactions purposes.
9. **D** This is because the asset demand for money is inversely related to the nominal interest rate.

10. **B** This bond provides an annual interest payment of $1000 (0.05 x $20 000). Because newly issued $20 000 bonds now provide twice this amount – $2 000 (0.10 x $20 000) – this bond's price will fall by half to $10 000.

11. **C** This because reserves and deposits have both risen by $10 000. Since desired reserves have increased by $400 (0.04 x $10 000), the remaining $9600 represents excess reserves.

12. **B** Reserves and deposits have both risen by $100 000, with desired reserves increasing by $5000 (0.05 x $10 000), and excess reserves by $95 000. The maximum change in the money supply is found by multiplying $95 000 by the money multiplier, which is the reciprocal of the reserve ratio – 1/0.05, or 20.

13. **A** This is because not all available cash is used to create deposits that are included in the money supply.

14. **A** This is found by multiplying the $4500 in excess reserves by the money multiplier, which is the reciprocal of the reserve ratio – 1/.025, or 40.

15. **E** Fish were the main staple in the Canadian economy in the early years of European settlement.

Short Answer Problems

1. a. means of exchange
   b. unit of account
   c. unit of account
   d. store of purchasing power

2. a. This bond provides an annual interest payment of $300 (0.03 x $10 000). Because newly issued $10 000 bonds now provide five-thirds as much in annual interest – $500 (0.05 x $10 000) – as this bond does, the bond's price will fall by three-fifths to $6000.
   b. Because newly issued $10 000 now provide two-thirds as much in annual interest interest – $200 (0.02 x $10 000) – as this bond does, the bond's price will rise by three-halves to $15 000.

3. a. The reserve ratio is 5 percent, found by dividing the $7.5 million in desired reserves by the $150 million in outstanding deposits.
   b. Actual reserves are $12 million, found by summing desired reserves of $7.5 million and excess reserves of $4.5 million.
   c. With a new $10 million deposit, actual reserves increase by $10 million to $22 million. Meanwhile, outstanding deposits have now risen by $10 million to $160 million, which means that desired reserves are now $8 million (0.05 x $160 million). Excess reserves rise to $14 million ($22 million - $8 million).

Chapter 14

Monetary Policy

Learning Objectives

In this chapter you will:
- learn about the Bank of Canada and its functions
- analyze the tools the Bank of Canada uses to conduct monetary policy
- examine the tradeoff between inflation and unemployment

Chapter Highlights

- The Bank of Canada
  1. As Canada's central bank, the Bank of Canada conducts monetary policy by managing the Canadian money supply, holds deposits of Canadian Payments Association (CPA) direct clearers and provides them with advances when necessary, manages the federal government's bank deposits, clears the federal government cheques, and handles the financing of federal debt. It also helps ensure the stability of financial markets, in conjunction with other government agencies.
  2. The Bank of Canada conducts monetary policy through changing the money supply and the nominal interest rate. Expansionary monetary policy is used when there is a recessionary gap. This policy involves a rise in the money supply and a reduction in the nominal interest rate, which expands both investment and consumption of durable items. The result is an increase in aggregate demand and a rise in real output towards its potential level. Contractionary monetary policy is used with an inflationary gap. A fall in the money supply and a rise in the nominal interest rate reduces both investment and consumption of durable items. This leads to a decrease in aggregate demand and a decline in real output towards its potential level.
  3. For either expansionary or contractionary monetary policy, the impact of a change in investment and consumption spending on aggregate demand is found using the spending multiplier.

- Monetary Policy
  1. When the economy is experiencing a recessionary gap, the Bank of Canada uses expansionary monetary policy to raise the money supply and reduce interest rates. This increases investment and consumer spending on durable items, which then raises aggregate demand, expands equilibrium output, and brings down unemployment. The goal is to reach the economy's potential output where unemployment is at its natural rate.
  2. If the economy is experiencing an inflationary gap, a contractionary monetary policy is used by the Bank of Canada to reduce the money supply and raise interest rates. This decreases investment and consumer spending on durable items, thereby reducing aggregate demand as well as equilibrium output, and putting downward pressure on the

price level. The goal is to reach the economy's potential output where inflationary pressures are under control.

- ◆ Tools of Monetary Policy
    1. To conduct monetary policy, the Bank of Canada can use open market operations, switch government deposits, and (as a signaling device) change the bank rate.
    2. When the Bank of Canada sells a $1000 bond to a bondholder, the bondholder's bank deposit declines by $1000, which automatically reduces the money supply by the same amount. Assuming the reserve ratio is 0.10, there is a further $9000 reduction in the money supply, found by multiplying the initial $900 fall in excess reserves by the money multiplier of 10 (= 1/.10). Likewise, a purchase of a $1000 bond by the Bank of Canada leads to an immediate $1000 increase in the money supply, followed by a further $9000 rise, found by multiplying the initial $900 increase in excess reserves by the money multiplier of 10.
    3. When the Bank of Canada moves a $1000 government deposit to a CPA member, assuming a reserve ratio of 0.10, there is no immediate change in the money supply, because government deposits are not considered to be money. But because of the $900 increase in excess reserves, the money supply rises by $9000, found by multiplying the change in excess reserves by the money multiplier of 10. Likewise, the movement of a $1000 government deposit to the Bank of Canada does not cause an immediate change in the money supply, but does lead to a $9000 reduction in the money supply, found by multiplying the $900 decrease in excess reserves by the money multiplier of 10.
    4. The bank rate is the interest rate paid by CPA members when they borrow Bank of Canada advances. This rate is at the ceiling of the 50-basis-point target band that the Bank of Canada sets for the overnight rate, which is the interest rate on overnight loans between chartered banks and other financial institutions. Whenever the Bank of Canada changes this target range, the bank rate is also adjusted, which provides a signal to financial markets of the Bank's intentions concerning monetary policy.
    5. Monetary policy has two major benefits: its separation from day-to-day politics, and its short decision lag. However, monetary policy has two major drawbacks: it is relatively weak as an expansionary tool (since there is no guarantee that deposit-takers will lend out excess reserves during an economic downturn) and its impact cannot be focused on particular regions, as can fiscal policy.

- ◆ Inflation and Unemployment
    1. Demand-pull inflation occurs when an increase in aggregate demand raises the general price level. Because this type of inflation is associated with higher output, it is inversely related to unemployment, with demand-pull inflation associated with a fall in the unemployment rate.
    2. The Phillips curve represents the inverse relationship between unemployment and inflation, based on a demand-pull view of inflation. It assumes a fixed and predictable relationship between these two variables.
    3. In the past the Phillips curve was treated as a 'policy menu', with governments choosing fiscal and monetary policies to reach different points on the curve. However, during the 1970s and early 1980s the Phillips curve in most industrialized countries shifted outward as a result of stagflation, which is the combination of rising inflation with constant or expanding unemployment. Stagflation can result from cost-push inflation, which arises when aggregate supply decreases due to increased costs.

4. In the 1970s and early 1980s, one reason for decreases in aggregate supply was higher oil prices, because of the activity of OPEC, the oil cartel. Another reason was the economy's own self-stabilizing process. This process depends on how equilibrium output compares with potential output. When output exceeds its potential level, unemployment is below its natural rate. Over time, this discrepancy raises nominal wages, causing aggregate supply to decrease until equilibrium output has fallen to its potential level. Likewise, when output is less than its potential level, unemployment is above its natural rate. Over time, this discrepancy reduces nominal wages, which means that aggregate supply increases until equilibrium output has risen to its potential level. As a result of this self-stabilizing process, the long-run aggregate supply curve is a vertical line at the potential output level.

Helpful Hints

- The Bank of Canada
  1. The fact that the Bank of Canada can adjust both supply and its own demand in the weekly auction of federal treasury bills means that it can affect the nominal interest rate on treasury bills. For example, by reducing its weekly supply or increasing the size of its own weekly demand, the Bank of Canada can raise the average price of treasury bills sold, which reduces their nominal interest rate. Likewise, by raising its weekly supply or decreasing the size of its weekly demand, the Bank can reduce the average price of treasury bills, which raises their nominal interest rate.
  2. Because Canada Savings Bonds cannot be bought and sold after they are first issued, but must rather be cashed in with the Bank of Canada, they are particularly safe investments. Unlike ordinary bonds, their value does not fall when general interest rates rise, since the price at which they can be cashed remains constant. Moreover, during a period of rising interest rates, the Bank of Canada will often be forced to retroactively raise the interest payments on outstanding Canada Savings Bonds to stop savers from cashing them to acquire newly issued bonds. This security feature does not apply to ordinary bonds.

- Monetary Policy
  1. The fact that the Bank of Canada has direct control over nominal interest rates, and not real interest rates, makes their task in conducting monetary policy a more difficult one. The Bank's policy-makers must be continually aware of the relationship between the inflation rate and nominal interest rates to ensure that the real interest rate is moving in the direction they intend. For example, during periods of rising inflation, raising the nominal interest rate may not be sufficient if the Bank wishes to increase the real interest rate, since inflationary expectations during such a period will be rising as well.

- Inflation and Unemployment
  1. The fact that the economy's self-stabilizing tendency gradually pushes real output towards its potential level does not negate the relevance of government stabilization policies. These policies are still necessary if the self-stabilizing tendency associated with the long-run aggregate supply curve is a very slow one.

Key Concepts

bank rate
Canada Savings Bonds
treasury bills
expansionary monetary policy
contractionary monetary policy
open market operations
overnight rate

prime rate
demand-pull inflation
Phillips curve
stagflation
cost-push inflation
long-run aggregate supply curve

Fill in the Blank and True False Questions

1. If a chartered bank, or some other CPA member, borrows from the Bank of Canada, it is charged the _____ rate.

2. **T F** Some deposit-takers, known as direct clearers, have accounts at the Bank of Canada that are part of their cash reserves.

3. **T F** The federal government has deposits both at the Bank of Canada and at private banks, and these deposits are held wherever the government can receive the highest interest rate.

4. Long-term bonds issued by the federal government, known as _____, have values that do not vary with interest rates, since they must be cashed in with the government. Short-term bonds issued by the federal government, known as _____, provide no interest payments, but instead are sold at a marked down price.

   Place the following terms in the correct order in the blanks above.

   Canada Savings Bonds   treasury bills

5. Interest rates go up with a(n) _____ monetary policy and they go down with a(n) _____ monetary policy.

   Place the following terms in the correct order in the blanks above.

   expansionary   contractionary

6. The Bank of Canada has a 50-basis-point target range for the _____. The ceiling on this range is where the _____ is set, which in turn helps determine the _____.

   Place the following terms in the correct order in the blanks above.

   bank rate   overnight rate   prime rate

7. Inflation that is caused by a rise in spending is known as _____-_____ inflation.

Figure 1 Use this graph to answer questions 8 and 9

8. The curve shown in Figure 1 is known as a _____ curve.

9. A movement southeast along the curve shown in Figure 1 could be caused by a(n) _____ policy, while a movement northwest along the curve could be caused by a(n) _____ policy.

Place the following terms in the correct order in the blanks above.

expansionary   contractionary

10. **T F** Stagflation is usually caused by demand-pull inflation.

11. Inflation that results from increasing production costs is known as _____-_____ inflation.

12. **T F** Between 1973 and 1982, the Canadian Phillips curve shifted significantly to the left.

13. In monetarist theory, the _____ of money is the number of times, on average, that money is spent on final goods and services during a given year.

14. **T F** In the monetarist quantity theory of money, the money supply and the price level are assumed to be constant.

Multiple-Choice Questions

1. Which of the following is the most important role of the Bank of Canada?
    A. acting as a bank for members of the Canadian Payments Association
    B. managing the money supply
    C. acting as a fiscal agent for the federal government
    D. ensuring the stability of financial markets
    E. issuing paper currency

2. A one-year $1 million treasury bill is originally purchased at a price of $975 000. The nominal rate of interest on this bill is therefore:
    A. 1.03 percent
    B. 2.56 percent
    C. 2.50 percent
    D. 9.75 percent
    E. 10.26 percent

Figure 2 Use this graph to answer question 3.

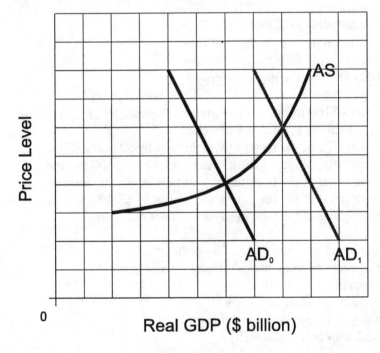

3. In Figure 2, a shift in aggregate demand from AD_0 to AD_1 could:
    A. be caused by a contractionary monetary policy through lower investment and consumption of durable goods.
    B. be caused by a contractionary monetary policy through higher investment and consumption of durable goods.
    C. be caused by an expansionary monetary policy through lower investment and consumption of durable goods.
    D. be caused by an expansionary monetary policy through higher investment and consumption of durable goods.
    E. not be caused by monetary policy.

4. If the Bank of Canada sells a $10 million bond to a member of the public and the reserve ratio in the banking system is 5 percent:
    A. the money supply immediately rises by $10 million.
    B. the money supply immediately falls by $10 million.
    C. the money supply immediately rises by $9.5 million.
    D. the money supply immediately falls by $9.5 million.
    E. no immediate effect on the money supply.

5. If the Bank of Canada sells a $10 million bond to a member of the public, and the reserve ratio in the banking system is 5 percent:
    A. the total change in the money supply is a fall of $190 million.
    B. the total change in the money supply is a rise of $200 million.
    C. the total change in the money supply is a fall of $200 million.
    D. the total change in the money supply is a rise of $190 million.
    E. the total change in the money supply is a rise of $10 million.

6. If the Bank of Canada moves $100 million in government deposits to CPA members, and the reserve ratio in the banking system is 4 percent:
    A. the money supply immediately rises by $100 million.
    B. the money supply immediately falls by $100 million.
    C. the money supply immediately rises by $96 million.
    D. the money supply immediately falls by $96 million.
    E. there is no immediate effect on the money supply.

7. If the Bank of Canada moves $100 million in government deposits to CPA members, and the reserve ratio in the banking system is 4 percent:
    A. the money-creating potential of the banking system falls by $2 400 million.
    B. the money-creating potential of the banking system rises by $2 500 million.
    C. the money-creating potential of the banking system falls by $2 500 million.
    D. the money-creating potential of the banking system rises by $2 400 million.
    E. the money-creating potential of the banking system is not changed.

8. Which of the following is an advantage of monetary policy?
    A. it effectiveness during an economic downturn is relatively assured
    B. it can be focused on particular regions
    C. its impact on the economy is relatively quick
    D. it is separated from day-to-day political influence
    E. it is closely connected with political activity

9. Which of the following is a drawback of monetary policy?
    A. it is relatively weak as an expansionary tool
    B. it is relatively weak as a contractionary tool
    C. it affects various regions of the country in different ways
    D. it takes a long time to make decisions about monetary policy
    E. it is closely connected with political activity

10. An outward shift of the Phillips curve could be caused by:
   A. a rise in raw-material prices
   B. falling wages
   C. demand-pull inflation
   D. contractionary stabilization policy
   E. lower unemployment

11. Stagflation is defined as a combination of:
   A. constant or falling unemployment and rising inflation
   B. constant or expanding unemployment and falling inflation
   C. constant or falling unemployment and falling inflation
   D. constant or expanding unemployment and rising inflation
   E. constant or falling unemployment and deflation

Figure 3 Use this graph to answer questions 12 and 13.

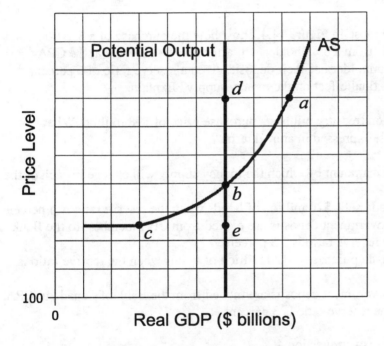

12. If the economy in Figure 3 is at point *a*, there will be a gradual move to:
   A. point *b* because of a decrease in AD.
   B. point *b* because of a decrease in AS.
   C. point *d* because of a decrease in AS.
   D. point *d* because of a decrease in AD.
   E. point *e* because of an increase in AS.

13. If the economy in Figure 3 is at point *c*, there will be a gradual move to:
   A. point *b* because of an increase in AS.
   B. point *b* because of an increase in AD.
   C. point *e* because of an increase in AD.
   D. point *e* because of an increase in AS.
   E. point *d* because of an increase in AS.

14. The basic equation of monetarism is:
    A. $V = P \times Q$.
    B. $P = Q \times M$.
    C. $P \times V = M \times Q$.
    D. $M \times V = P \times Q$.
    E. $Q = M \times V$.

15. According to monetarist thinking:
    A.   equilibrium output often diverges significantly from its potential level.
    B.   central banks should operate on the basis of a set monetary rule.
    C.   the velocity of money fluctuates widely.
    D   governments have a major role to play in stabilizing the economy.
    E.   inflation is primarily caused by higher prices of raw materials, such as oil.

Short Answer Questions

1. Using T-accounts like those in Figure 14.4, show how the purchase of a $50 000 bond by the Bank of Canada from a bondholder will affect excess reserves at the CPA member where the bondholder has their deposit, given a reserve ratio of 6 percent. What is the maximum final effect on the money supply? Explain.

2. A one-year $100 million treasury bill has a purchase price of $98 million. What is its nominal rate of interest expressed in annual terms?

3. Calculate the maximum amount by which the money supply will change in each of the following cases:
    a.   The Bank of Canada sells $20 million of bonds when the reserve ratio is 4 percent.
    b. $100 million in government deposits are moved from CPA members to the Bank of Canada when the reserve ratio is 2.5 percent.
    c.   The Bank of Canada purchases $120 million of bonds when the reserve ratio is 2 percent.
    d. $300 million in government deposits are moved from the Bank of Canada to CPA members when the reserve ratio is 3 percent.

Figure 4 Use this table to answer question 4.

Year	Inflation Rate	Unemployment Rate
2000	4	6
2001	2	10
2002	6	5

4. a.   Draw a Phillips curve based on the information in the above table.
   b.   Suppose that, in the year 2003, the inflation rate is 3 percent and the unemployment rate is 6 percent. What has happened to the Phillips curve? What could be a possible reason for this change?

Solutions to Questions for Chapter 14

Fill in the Blank and True False Questions

1. **bank** This rate acts as a signal of the Bank of Canada's monetary policy intentions.
2. **T** These direct clearers are the chartered banks and large near banks.
3. **F** While the federal government's deposits reside at both the Bank of Canada and at private banks, it is the Bank of Canada which decides where these deposits are held as a tool of monetary policy.
4. **Canada Savings Bonds, treasury bills**
5. **contractionary, expansionary** A lower money supply (a contractionary policy) raises interest rates and a higher money supply (an expansionary policy) reduces them.
6. **overnight rate, bank rate, prime rate**
7. **demand-pull** This is called demand-pull inflation, since rising aggregate demand tends to pull up prices.
8. **Phillips**
9. **contractionary, expansionary** A contractionary policy causes a southeast movement because it leads to a simultaneous reduction in inflation and rise in unemployment. In contrast, an expansionary policy causes a northwest movement because it results in a simultaneous increase in inflation and decrease in unemployment.
10. **F** Stagflation tends to be the result of cost-push inflation, which causes prices to rise and real output to fall simultaneously.
11. **cost-push** This term refers to the fact that cost increases push up prices.
12. **F** During this period, the curve shifted significantly to the right, due to cost-push inflation.
13. **velocity**
14. **F** In the quantity theory, it is the velocity of money and the level of real output that are assumed to be constant.

Multiple-Choice Questions

1. **B** Managing the money supply (which is more wide-ranging than simply issuing paper currency) is the Bank's main role.
2. **B** This is found by dividing the difference between its price and its face value ($25 000) by its price ($975 000), then multiplying the result by 100.
3. **D** With an expansionary monetary policy and a drop in interest rates, investment and consumption rise, which causes an increase in aggregate demand.
4. **B** This is due to the loss of the deposit previously held by the new bondholder.
5. **C** This is results both from the immediate $10 million decrease in the money supply and the decrease in the money-creating potential of the banking system, which is found by multiplying the change in excess reserves of $9.5 million ($10 million - (.05 x $10 million)) by the money multiplier of 20 (1/.05).
6. **E** There is no immediate effect on the money supply, since the federal government's deposits are not included in the definition of money.
7. **D** This move increases excess reserves in the banking system by $96 million ($100 million – (.04 x $100 million)). The overall change in the banking system's money-creating potential is found by multiplying this number by the money multiplier of 25 (1/.04).
8. **D** Unlike fiscal policy, monetary policy is separated from day-to-day political influence.
9. **A** Its potential weakness as an expansionary tool is related to the difficulty in assuring that banks will lend out additional cash reserves during an economic downturn.
10. **A** A rise in raw material prices leads to cost-push inflation, which is causes an outward shift in the Phillips curve.
11. **D** Stagflation combines high inflation and high unemployment.
12. **C** This decrease in AS occurs because of rising wages that gradually result from unemployment being below its natural rate.
13. **D** This increase in AS occurs because of falling wages that gradually result from unemployment being above its natural rate.

14. **D** This is known as the equation of exchange.
15. **B** According to monetarists, monetary policy is too powerful an instrument to be used in a discretionary way. So it is necessary to have a monetary rule governing the operation of central banks.

Short Answer Problems

1. *Bank of Canada's T-Account:* On the assets side, bonds rise by $50 000. On the liabilities side, the CPA member's deposit rises by $50 000.

CPA member's T-Account: On assets side, the reserves at the Bank of Canada rise by $50 000. On the liabilities side, the bondholder's deposit rises by $50 000.

Changes in Reserves and the Money Supply: This $50 000 purchase of bonds leads to an immediate $50 000 increase in the money supply due to the rise in the bondholder's deposit at the CPA member. The CPA member's actual reserves have risen by $50 000, while its desired reserves have risen by $3000 (.06 x $50 000 in new deposits). Therefore the CPA member's excess reserves have risen by $47 000. Meanwhile, the increase in the money-creating potential of the banking system is $783 333, found by multiplying the initial change in excess reserves ($47 000) by the money multiplier, which is the reciprocal of the reserve ratio expressed as a decimal (1/.06 = 16.67). Therefore the maximum final effect on the money supply is an increase of $833 333, found by adding the initial $50 000 increase in the money supply to the $783 333 change in the money-creating potential of the banking system.

2. If a one-year treasury bill has a purchase price of $98 million, its nominal rate of interest is 2.04 percent, which is found by dividing the difference between the face value and the purchase price ($100 million - $98 million = $2 million) by the purchase price ($98 million), then multiplying by 100.

3a. A $20 million sale of bonds by the Bank of Canada leads to an immediate $20 million decrease in the money supply as the buyers of the bonds pay the Bank of Canada from their accounts at CPA members. Given a reserve ratio of 4 percent, the actual reserves of CPA members have fallen by $20 million while their desired reserves have dropped by $800 000 (.04 x -$20 million in lost deposits). Therefore, CPA members' excess reserves have fallen by $19.2 million. Through the multiple contraction of lending, the maximum amount by which the money supply can fall further is $480 million (-$19.2 million x (1/.04)). Therefore, the maximum amount by which the money supply can decrease is $500 million ((-$20 million) + (-$480 million)).

b. A movement of $100 million in government deposits from CPA members to the Bank of Canada has no immediate effect on the money supply, since the deposits lost by CPA members were not part of the money supply. Given a reserve ratio of 2.5 percent, the actual reserves of CPA members have decreased by $100 million while their desired reserves have declined by $2.5 million (.025 x -$100 million in lost deposits). Therefore CPA members' excess reserves have fallen by $97.5 million. Through the process of multiple declines in lending, the maximum amount by which the money supply can fall is $3900 million (-$97.5 million x (1/.025)).

c. A $120 million purchase of bonds by the Bank of Canada leads to an immediate $120 million increase in the money supply as the Bank of Canada deposits funds in the bondholders' accounts at CPA members. Given a reserve ratio of 2 percent, the actual reserves of CPA members have risen by $120 billion while their desired reserves have risen by $2.4 million (.02 x $120 million). Therefore, CPA members excess reserves have increased by $117.6 million. Through the process of multiple lending, there is an additional potential increase in the money supply of $5.88 billion ($117.6 million x (1/.02)). Therefore, the maximum amount by which the money supply can increase is $6 billion ($120 million + $5.88 billion).

d. The movement of $300 million in government deposits from the Bank of Canada to CPA members has no immediate effect on the money supply, since deposits gained by CPA members are not part of the money supply. Given a reserve ratio of 3 percent, the actual reserves of CPA members increase by $300 million while their desired reserves increase by $9 billion (.03 x $300 million). Therefore, CPA members' excess reserves have risen by $291 billion. Through the process of multiple lending, the money supply increases by a maximum of $9.7 billion ($291 million x (1/.03)).

4a.

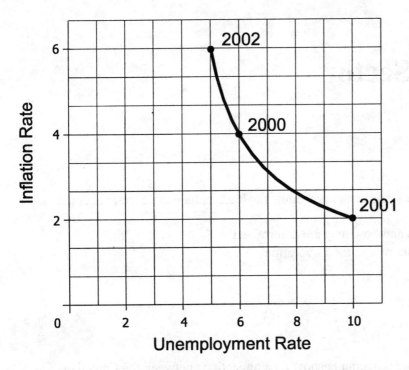

b. Because this point is southwest of original Phillips curve, the Phillips curve must have shifted to the left. This shift could have been caused by an increase in the aggregate supply curve, caused by higher labour productivity or lower raw material prices.

Chapter 15

The Foreign Sector

Learning Objectives

In this chapter you will:
- be introduced to the balance-of-payments accounts, which include the current account and the capital account
- learn about exchange rates and how they are determined
- examine exchange rate systems and their evolution

Chapter Highlights

- The Balance of Payments
  1. The balance-of-payments accounts show the connections between the Canadian economy and the rest of the world. In these account, monetary inflows to Canada are classified as positive receipts, while monetary outflows are classified as negative payments. Inflows are associated with foreign purchases of Canadian exports and Canadian financial assets, whereas outflows are related to Canadian purchases of foreign imports and foreign financial assets.
  2. The current account summarizes all international transactions tied to current economic activity in Canada. This includes trade in merchandise and services, flows of investment income, and transfers. Canada typically has a large surplus on its merchandise trade account and a large deficit on its investment income account. In the past, Canada's current account showed an overall deficit, but in recent years this is no longer always the case.
  3. The capital account summarizes all international transactions of financial assets involving Canadian dollars. The account includes portfolio investment, direct investment, and other capital flows. All three of these flows fluctuate widely. In the past, Canada's capital account usually showed a surplus, but this is no longer always the case.
  4. When the current and capital accounts (including the statistical discrepancy) sum to a negative number, the result is a balance-of-payments deficit. This means the Bank of Canada is buying Canadian dollars and selling foreign currency, which leads to a positive value for the change in official reserves account. When added to the balance-of-payments deficit, this account ensures the balance-of-payments accounts sum to zero. Likewise, when the current and capital accounts (including the statistical discrepancy) sum to a positive number, the result is a balance-of-payments surplus. This means the Bank of Canada is selling Canadian dollars and buying foreign currency, which results in a negative value for the change in official reserves account. Again, when added to the balance-of-payments surplus, this account ensures the balance-of-payments accounts sum to zero.

♦ Exchange Rates

1. Currencies are bought and sold in a global foreign exchange market. In this market, any price can be expressed in two ways. For example, the Canadian dollar can be valued in terms of the US dollar, or the US dollar can be valued in terms of the Canadian dollar.

2. The demand for Canadian dollars in any particular foreign exchange market represents the purchase of Canadian currency by foreigners for the purpose of acquiring Canadian exports or Canadian financial assets. It incorporates an inverse relationship between the price of the Canadian dollar and the number of Canadian dollars demanded. This is because a higher Canadian dollar leads to higher prices for Canadian exports and therefore a smaller quantity demanded of Canadian dollars by foreigners.

3. The supply of Canadian dollars in any foreign exchange market represents the sale of Canadian currency by Canadians for the purpose of acquiring foreign imports or foreign financial assets. It incorporates a direct relationship between the price of the Canadian dollar and the number of Canadian dollars supplied. This is because a higher Canadian dollar leads to lower prices for imports into Canada and therefore a larger quantity supplied of Canadian dollars by Canadians.

4. With a flexible exchange rate, equilibrium in any foreign exchange market occurs at the intersection of demand and supply. So changes in equilibrium occur whenever the demand and supply curves shift.

5. The first factor that affects equilibrium is price differences. For example, if Canada's price level increases more quickly than in the US, Canadian products become more expensive in both countries. The result is a leftward shift in the demand for Canadian dollars, as Canada's exports become less attractive to US consumers, and a rightward shift in the supply of Canadian dollars, as imports become more attractive to Canadian consumers. Both trends cause the equilibrium value of the Canadian dollar to fall.

6. The second factor that affects equilibrium in foreign exchange markets is product demand. For example, if the quality of Canada's products improves, demand for these products increases both in Canada and in other countries such as the US. The result is a rightward shift in the demand for Canadian dollars as more Canadian exports are sold in the US market, and a leftward shift in the supply of Canadian dollars as fewer US imports are sold in Canada. Both trends cause the equilibrium value of the Canadian dollar to rise.

7. The third factor that affects equilibrium in foreign exchange markets is interest rates. For example, a fall in Canadian interest rates makes Canadian bonds less attractive both to Canadians and to foreign wealthholders. The result is a leftward shift in the demand for Canadian dollars as fewer Canadian bonds are sold to US wealthholders, and a rightward shift in the supply of Canadian dollars as more foreign bonds are sold to Canadians. Both trends cause the equilibrium value of the Canadian dollar to fall.

8. The fourth factor that affects equilibrium in foreign exchange markets is speculation. For example, if Canadian and foreign speculators believe that the value of the Canadian dollar will soon rise against the US dollar, they immediately enter foreign exchange markets to buy Canadian dollars and sell US dollars. The result is a rightward shift in the demand for Canadian dollars and a leftward shift in the supply of Canadian dollars. Both trends cause an immediate rise in the value of the Canadian dollars.

♦ Exchange Rate Systems

1. With a system of flexible exchange rates (also known as floating rates), a government allows the international value of its currency to vary freely. While a flexible exchange rate provides a benefit by quickly eliminating currency shortages and surpluses on

foreign exchange markets, it also has a cost given the risks it creates for businesses which export or import. With a system of fixed exchange rates, a government intervenes to ensure the international price of its currency stays constant. This reduces risks for businesses that export or import, but can lead to significant shortages or surpluses of the currency.

2. A fixed exchange rate below equilibrium results in an excess demand for the currency. Because the central bank must meet the excess demand by selling its own currency and buying foreign currency, there is a balance of payments surplus equal to the excess demand. In contrast, a fixed rate above equilibrium leads to an excess supply of the currency. The central bank must meet this excess supply by buying its own currency and selling foreign currency, which means there is a balance of payments deficit equal to the excess supply.

3. A target rate for a currency below its equilibrium value suggests that the government is attempting to boost exports and reduce imports as an expansionary strategy to promote economic growth. But this strategy runs the risk of creating inflation through high import prices. Also, a country's trading partners might react by doing the same thing, which would negate the strategy's effect.

4. A target rate for a currency above its equilibrium value suggests the government is reducing import prices and raising export prices to dampen inflation as well as output and employment. However, this is only a temporary strategy, since the official reserves of foreign currency, which are needed to maintain this policy, will gradually be exhausted.

5. Central banks can use monetary policy to affect exchange rates, since a rise in a country's interest rates pushes up the exchange rate of the country's currency, and a reduction in interest rates pushes down the exchange rate.

6. Over the past hundred years there have been three major exchange rate systems: the gold standard (1879 to 1934), the Bretton Woods System (1945 to 1971) and the system of a managed float (1971 to the present). With the gold standard, countries set values for their currency in terms of a certain amount of gold. The Bretton Woods system was based on adjustable fixed exchange rates. Today's managed float system means that currency values are allowed to vary over time, but short-term fluctuations are sometimes stabilized by government intervention.

Helpful Hints

◆ The Balance of Payments
1. It is useful to distinguish between the balance of merchandise trade and the balance of trade. While the balance of merchandise trade includes only merchandise (ie. tangible goods) , the balance of trade includes not just merchandise but also services. The main reason it is so easy to confuse these two balances is that media commentators often refer to the balance of trade when in fact they are talking about the balance of merchandise trade.
2. It may seem strange that flows of investment income are included in the current account rather than in the capital account, where the purchases and sales of the financial assets that cause these income flows are recorded. The reason is that the flows of dividends and interest payments that make up investment income are part of current activity in the Canadian economy, in the same way as are exports, imports, and transfers.

◆ Exchange Rates
1. The demand for Canadian dollars in foreign exchange markets is from foreigners, to buy Canadian exports and Canadian financial assets. But it is only the purchases related to Canadian exports that give this demand curve a negative slope, with a rise in the Canadian dollar reducing the quantity demanded of Canadian dollars, as Canadian exports become more expensive in foreign markets. Purchases of financial assets do not follow the same pattern, since buyers of these assets are not so much concerned with the current value of the Canadian dollar as they are with expected changes in this value over the period of their investment. Such expected changes in exchange rates have their own separate causes.
2. A similar comment applies to the supply of Canadian dollars in foreign exchange markets. This supply is from Canadians, to buy foreign imports and foreign financial assets. It is only the purchases related to foreign imports that give this supply curve a positive slope, with a rise in the Canadian dollar raising the quantity supplied of Canadian dollars, as foreign imports become cheaper in the Canadian market. Purchases of financial assets do not follow the same pattern, again because buyer of these assets are concerned not so much with the current value of the Canadian dollar as with expected changes in this value.

◆ Exchange Rate Systems
1. Note, in Figure 15.6 of the text, that a balance-of-payments deficit is associated with a *surplus* of Canadian dollars, while a balance-of-payments surplus is associated with a *shortage* of Canadian dollars. It is best to think of balance-of-payments deficits and surpluses in terms of Canada's official reserves of foreign currency rather the demand and supply of Canadian dollars. A balance-of-payments deficit means the Bank of Canada is selling foreign currency and therefore depleting its official reserves, while a balance-of-payments surplus means the Bank is buying foreign currency and therefore adding to its official reserves.

Key Concepts

current account
merchandise balance of trade
current account deficit
current account surplus
balance of trade
capital account
portfolio investment
direct investment
capital account surplus
capital account deficit
balance-of-payments surplus
balance-of-payments deficit

change in official reserves
foreign exchange market
demand for Canadian dollars
supply of Canadian dollars
appreciate
depreciate
speculation
flexible exchange rates
fixed exchange rates
devaluation
revaluation
managed float

Fill in the Blank and True False Questions

1. In Canada's balance-of-payments accounts, a purchase of Canadian dollars using a foreign currency is classified as a _____ and given a _____ sign, while a sale of Canadian dollars to buy foreign currency is classified as a _____ and given a _____ sign.

   Place the following terms in the correct order in the blanks above.

   payment   receipt   minus   plus

2. The purchase of a Japanese TV by a Canadian appears in Canada's _____ account and is classified as a _____. In contrast, the purchase of a Canadian bond by an Australian appears in Canada's _____ account and is classified as a _____.

   Place the following terms in the correct order in the blanks above.

   capital   payment   receipt   current

3. The deposit of funds by a Canadian in a US-dollar bank account appears in Canada's _____ account and is classified as a _____. In contrast, the payment of dividends by a Polish company to a Canadian shareholder appears in Canada's _____ account and is classified as a _____.

   Place the following terms in the correct order in the blanks above.

   capital   payment   receipt   current

4. **T F** Canada's merchandise trade balance usually shows a surplus.

5. In the past, Canada typically had a current account _____ and a capital account _____.

   Place the following terms in the correct order in the blanks above.

   surplus   deficit

6. **T F** If a country has a balance of trade deficit, then the country's current account necessarily shows a deficit.

7. **T F** Sales and purchases of corporate bonds are always classified as portfolio investment.

8. **T F** Sales and purchases of corporate shares are always classified as direct investment.

9. If an American car has a price of $10 000 in US dollars and a US dollar can be exchanged for $1.25 Canadian, the Canadian price of this good is _____.

10. With a system of _____ exchange rates, there is no need for intervention by central banks in foreign-currency markets. With a system of _____ exchange rates, such intervention occurs on a continual basis.

11. A government that raises the adjustable fixed exchange rate for its currency is engaging in a _____.

Multiple-Choice Questions

Figure 1 Use this graph to answer questions 1 to 4.

Xanadu's Balance of Payments Accounts

Direct Investment	+$4 million
Merchandise Trade	+$5 million
Portfolio Investment	-$1 million
Investment Income	-$6 million
Other Capital Flows	-$2 million
Trade in Services	+$1 million
Transfers	-$1 million
Statistical Discrepancy	+$1 million
Change in Official Reserves	not given

1. Given the information in Figure 1, Xanadu's current account balance is:
    A. +$1 million.
    B. -$1 million.
    C. +$2 million.
    D. -$2 million.
    E. +$3 million.

2. Given the information in Figure 1, Xanadu's capital account balance is:
    A. +$1 million.
    B. -$1 million.
    C. +$2 million.
    D. -$2 million.
    E. $0.

3. Given the information in Figure 1, Xanadu has
    A. a balance-of-payments deficit of -$1 billion.
    B. a balance-of-payments surplus of +$1 billion.
    C. a balance-of-payments surplus of +$2 billion.
    D. a balance-of-payments deficit of -$2 billion.
    E. neither a balance-of-payments deficit nor a balance-of-payments surplus.

4. Given the information in Figure 1, Xanadu's change in official reserves account must have a value of:
    A. +$1 million.
    B. -$3 million.
    C. +$2 million.
    D. -$2 million.
    E. -$1 million.

5. If in any given year the financial investments made by foreigners in Canada exceed the financial investments made by Canadians in foreign countries, then Canada has a:
    A. capital account deficit.
    B. capital account surplus.
    C. balance-of-payments surplus.
    D. balance-of-payments deficit.
    E. current account deficit.

6. If Canada's change in official reserves in a given year is negative, then Canada has a:
    A. capital account deficit.
    B. capital account surplus.
    C. balance-of-payments surplus.
    D. balance-of-payments deficit.
    E. current account deficit.

7. If Canada's change in official reserves in a given year is positive, then:
    A. the Bank of Canada bought Canadian dollars and sold foreign currency.
    B. the Canadian dollar is being kept a target value below its equilibrium.
    C. the Bank of Canada sold Canadian dollars and bought foreign currency.
    D. the Canadian government wishes to boost the amount of Canadian exports and reduce the amount of imports.
    E. Canada has a balance-of-payments surplus.

8. If it costs $1.33 in Canadian currency to buy one US dollar, then one Canadian dollar is worth:
    A. $1.25 in US dollars.
    B. $1.33 in US dollars.
    C. $0.67 in US dollars.
    D. $0.75 in US dollars.
    E. $0.33 in US dollars.

9. If a Canadian good has a price of $4 in Canadian dollars and US dollar can be exchanged for $1.20 Canadian, then the American price of this good is:
    A. $4.80.
    B. $4.83.
    C. $3.80.
    D. $5.20.
    E. $3.33.

10. When the Canadian dollar rises against its American counterpart, the quantity of Canadian dollars demanded in exchange for US dollars:
    A. rises because Canadian products have higher American prices.
    B. rises because Canadian products have lower American prices.
    C. falls because Canadian products have higher American prices.
    D. falls because Canadian products have lower American prices.
    E. stays the same because a change in the Canadian dollar does not affect the American prices of Canadian products.

11. When the Canadian dollar rises against its American counterpart, the quantity of Canadian dollars supplied in exchange for US dollars:
    A. rises because American products have higher Canadian prices.
    B. rises because American products have lower Canadian prices.
    C. falls because American products have higher Canadian prices.
    D. falls because American products have lower Canadian prices.
    E. stays the same because a change in the Canadian dollar does not affect the Canadian prices of American products.

Figure 2 Use this graph to answer questions 12 and 13.

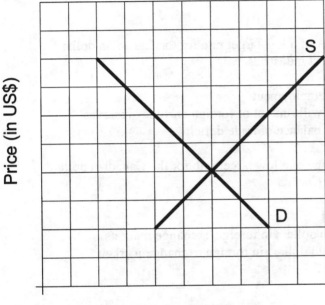

Quantity C$ (billions)

12. In the market shown in Figure 2, sudden worries over Canadian national unity will cause:
    A. the Canadian dollar to appreciate because of an increase in both the demand and supply for Canadian dollars.
    B. the Canadian dollar to appreciate because of an increase in the demand for Canadian dollars and a decrease in the supply of Canadian dollars.
    C. the Canadian dollar to depreciate because of a decrease in both the demand and supply for Canadian dollars.
    D. the Canadian dollar to depreciate because of a decrease in the demand for Canadian dollars and an increase in the supply of Canadian dollars.
    E. no change in the value of the Canadian dollar, since Canada's imports and exports are unaffected.

13. In the market shown in Figure 2, a sudden increase in American inflation relative to Canadian inflation causes:
    A. the Canadian dollar to appreciate because of an increase in both the demand and supply for Canadian dollars.
    B. the Canadian dollar to appreciate because of an increase in the demand for Canadian dollars and a decrease in the supply of Canadian dollars.
    C. the Canadian dollar to depreciate because of a decrease in both the demand and supply for Canadian dollars.
    D. the Canadian dollar to depreciate because of a decrease in the demand for Canadian dollars and an increase in the supply of Canadian dollars.
    E. no change in the value of the Canadian dollar, because Canadian inflation has not been affected.

14. Which of the following is a drawback of a low target rate for the Canadian dollar?
    A. the harm it causes Canada's export industries
    B. its potential to cause inflation
    C. its potential to cause a rise in unemployment
    D. the risk that the Bank of Canada will run out of foreign currency reserves
    E. its potential to cause a Canadian balance of trade deficit

15. Which of the following is an advantage of a low target rate for the Canadian dollar?
    A. it raises the level of imports into Canada
    B. it can help reduce inflation
    C. it can help reduce unemployment
    D. it reduces the supply of Canadian dollars in foreign exchange markets
    E. it adds to the demand for Canadian dollars in foreign exchange markets

Short Answer Questions

1. For each of the following events, identify where it appears in Canada's balance-of-payments accounts, and whether it is a receipt or a payment.
    a. A Canadian manufacturer purchases Japanese freight and shipping services.
    b. A Mexican wealthholder buys 100 shares in a large Canadian corporation.
    c. A Canadian cellular phone is sold to a business in India.
    d. A recent Canadian immigrant transfers funds back to her family in Brazil.
    e. A German wine is bought by a Canadian consumer.
    f. A Canadian bondholder receives an interest payment on a bond issued by a company in the United States
    g. A Canadian retail company is purchased by a British corporation.

Figure 3 Use this table to answer question 2.

Carpathia's Balance of Payments (Carpathia $ millions)

	Receipts	Payments	Balance
Current Account			
Merchandise trade	34.7	_(i)_	+11.3
Trade in services	_(ii)_	23.2	-5.6
Investment income	6.7	8.4	_(iii)_
Transfers	3.5	_(iv)_	+2.4
Capital Account			
Portfolio investment	_(v)_	12.5	+3.5
Direct investment	15.9	_(vi)_	-4.6
Other capital flows	23.4	24.9	_(vii)_

2   a.   Copy and fill out the above table.

      b.   What is Carpathia's balance of trade?

      c.   Calculate the surplus or deficit on Carpathia's current account and the surplus or deficit on Carpathia's capital account.

      d.   If the statistical discrepancy for Carpathia's balance of payments is -$1.7 million, is Carpathia running a balance of payments surplus or deficit? Explain.

      e.   What is the value of Carpathia's "change in official reserves" account? Explain

3.   Assume that one Canadian dollar exchanges for US $0.68.

      a.   What does a US dollar exchange for in terms of Canadian dollars?

      b.   If an item costs $17.48 in Vancouver and $12.35 in Seattle, where would you get a better buy? Explain.

      c.   If one Canadian dollar instead exchanges for US 0.72, would your answer to part b change?

Figure 4 Use this graph to answer question 4.

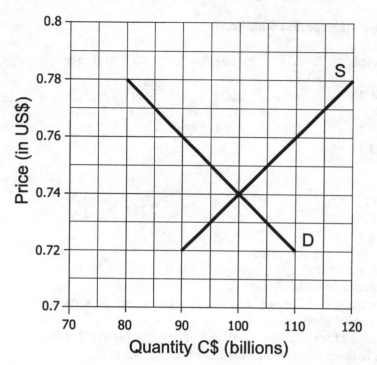

4. Figure 4 shows the foreign exchange market for Canadian dollars.
    a. What is the equilibrium value for the Canadian dollar in terms of US dollars?
    b. If the Canadian government has a target exchange rate for the Canadian dollar of 78 American cents, will Canada have a balance-of-payments surplus or deficit? Why might the Canadian government choose have a target exchange rate above its equilibrium level?
    c. If instead the Canadian government has a target exchange rate for the Canadian dollar of 72 American cents, will Canada have a balance-of-payments surplus or deficit? Why might the Canadian government choose to have a target exchange rate below its equilibrium level?

Solutions to Questions for Chapter 15

Fill in the Blank and True False Questions
1. **receipt, plus, payment, minus**
2. **current, payment, capital, receipt**
3. **capital, payment, current, receipt**
4. **T** Canada usually exports more goods than it imports.
5. **deficit, surplus**
6. **F** It is possible for surplus on other elements in the current account (such as investment income) to offset a balance of trade deficit.
7. **T** This is because corporate bonds do not give the holder a claim of ownership in the corporation issuing the bond.
8. **F** Transactions involving corporate shares are classified as direct investment only if the shares are part of a controlling interest in the corporation.
9. **$12 500** This is found by multiplying the US dollar price by US dollar's value in terms of Canadian dollars ($10 000 x 1.25)

10. **flexible, fixed** Flexible exchange rates allow central banks to let foreign-exchange markets operate freely, while fixed exchange rate necessitate central bank intervention.
11. **revaluation**

Multiple-Choice Questions

1. **B** This is found by adding merchandise trade (+$5 million), trade in services (+$1 million), transfers (-$1 million), and investment income (-$6 million).
2. **A** This is found by adding direct investment (+$4 million), portfolio investment (-$1 million), and other capital flows (-$2 million).
3. **B** This is found by summing the current account balance (-$1 billion), the capital account balance (+$1 billion), and the statistical discrepancy (+$1 billion).
4. **E** This is the amount needed to offset the +$1 billion balance-of-payments surplus to provide an overall zero balance on the accounts.
5. **B** A capital account surplus occurs when foreign financial investments in Canada exceed Canadian financial investment in other countries in any given year.
6. **C** This balance-of-payments surplus offsets the negative change in official reserves to ensure an overall zero balance on the accounts.
7. **A** This is because the change in official reserves represents the effect of the Bank of Canada's transactions on the flow of Canadian dollars.
8. **D** A Canadian dollar is worth 75 US cents, which is found by taking the reciprocal of $1.33.
9. **E** The American price of $3.33 is found by multiplying the $4 Canadian-dollar price by the reciprocal of the US dollar's value in terms of Canadian dollars (1/1.2).
10. **C** A rise in the Canadian dollar makes Canadian exports more expensive, and therefore reduces the quantity demanded of Canadian dollars for US dollars.
11. **B** A rise in the Canadian dollar makes foreign imports cheaper, and therefore increases the quantity supplied of Canadian dollars for US dollars.
12. **D** The expectation of future political turmoil means that both foreign and Canadian wealthholders are less likely to purchase Canadian financial assets and more likely to purchase foreign financial assets, decreasing the demand for Canadian dollars and increasing the supply of Canadian dollars.
13. **B** With Canadian products becoming cheaper relative to American products in both Canada and the US, there is an increase in the demand for Canadian dollars by foreign purchasers of Canadian goods and a decrease in the supply of Canadian dollars by Canadian purchasers of American goods.
14. **B** A low target rate pushes up the prices of imports in Canadian markets.
15. **C** A low Canadian dollar can help reduce unemployment by raising the amount that Canadians export.

Short Answer Problems

1a. trade in services, current account, payment
b. portfolio investment, capital account, receipt
c. merchandise trade, current account, receipt
d. transfers, current account, payment
e. merchandise trade, current account, payment
f. investment income, current account, receipt
g. direct investment, capital account, receipt
2a. i. 23.4 ii. 17.6, iii. -1.7, iv. 1.1, v. 16.0, vi. 20.5, vii. -1.5.
b. Carpathia's balance of trade is +$5.7 million ($11.3 million + (-5.6 million))
c. Given an investment income deficit of -$1.7 million, Carpathia has a current account surplus of +$6.4 million ($11.3 m. - $5.6 m. - $1.7 m. + $2.4 m.). Given a deficit on other capital flows of -$1.5 million, Carpathia has a capital account deficit of -$2.6 million ($3.5 m. - $4.6 m. - $1.5 m.).
d. Given a statistical discrepancy of -$1.7 million, Carpathia has a balance of payments surplus of +$2.1 million ($6.4 m. - $2.6 m. - $1.7 m.), which is the sum of the capital and current accounts as well as the statistical discrepancy.
e. Carpathia's "change in official reserves" account has a value of -$2.1 million, which matches the (+)$2.1 million balance-of-payments surplus, so that Delphi's balance-of-payments accounts sum to zero.
3a. The US dollar exchanges for $1.47 (= 1/0.68) Canadian dollars.

b. The Seattle price of this item in Canadian dollars is $18.16. Since this is higher than the $17.48 Canadian-dollar price in Vancouver, the item is a better buy in Vancouver.

c. The Seattle price of this item in Canadian dollars is $17.15. Since this is lower than the $17.48 Canadian-dollar price in Vancouver, the item is now a better buy in Seattle.

4a. The Canadian dollar's equilibrium value is 74 US cents, which occurs at the intersection of the demand and supply curves.

b. At a price for the Canadian dollar of 78 US cents, Canada will have a balance-of- payments deficit of $40 billion, which is the excess supply of Canadian dollars that the Bank of Canada will have to buy up each period to keep the exchange rate at this high level. The Canadian government may choose this policy to help dampen inflation

c. At a price for the Canadian dollar of 72 US cents, Canada will have a balance-of-payments surplus of $20 billion, which is the excess demand of Canadian dollars that the Bank of Canada will have to meet by selling Canadian dollars each period to keep the exchange rate at this low level. The Canadian government may choose this policy to help stimulate net exports and the rate of economic growth.

Chapter 16

Foreign Trade

Learning Objectives

In this chapter you will:
♦ learn about Canada's foreign trade, trade relationships, and trading patterns
♦ analyze the case for trade, based on absolute and comparative advantage
♦ examine the impact of trade protection and the arguments for and against it
♦ learn about Canada's trade policies from its beginning as a country and recent international trade agreements

Chapter Highlights

♦ Canada's Foreign Trade
1. Globalization is the rapid growth in the importance of trade and investment flows, as well as the spread of international businesses and markets. It has been spurred by a fall in transportation and communication costs, as well as by trade liberalization.
2. Canada's exports, at over 40 percent of its GDP, are relatively high by international standards. Most of Canada's merchandise trade (just under three-quarters of imports and well over three-quarters of exports) is with the US. Overall, about half of Canada's merchandise exports are raw and processed natural resources, and the other half are manufactured goods. About a third of Canada's merchandise imports are raw and processed resources and the other two-thirds are manufactured.
3. Canada's trade in services has not grown as quickly as Canada's merchandise trade. This is because services are usually bought and sold within national borders. Trade in services also often escapes detection, especially when services are bundled with goods.
4. What products a country trades is determined by the country's endowment of resources, the size of the national market, and climate.

♦ The Case for Trade
1. Gains from trade include increased product variety, greater competition, and the added output that comes from specialization. Of these three gains, the last is most important.
2. There are two situations in which specialization and trade can take place between individuals or countries. In the case of absolute advantage, a producer supplies an item more efficiently than other producers do. If two countries have an absolute advantage, each in a different product, it makes sense for the two to specialize and trade, since total output will rise as a result. In the case of comparative advantage, one country is better in producing both items that are being traded. But trade can still be beneficial, if each country follows the law of comparative advantage, and supplies the product it can provide at a lower opportunity cost than can other countries.
3. The benefits of specialization and trade are distributed through the terms of trade, which represent the international price of one item in terms of another. The limits of the

terms of trade are the opportunity costs in each country, with the actual terms of trade set by the international demand for both items.

♦   The Impact of Trade Protection
   1.   A tariff can be imposed in a perfectly competitive market when the world price of a product is less than the domestic price that would exist in the absence of trade. When compared with the free trade case, the tariff results in a higher price, greater domestic production, and a lower level of imports. Consumers are harmed by the higher price, which means they purchase fewer units. Domestic producers gain because they receive a higher price and sell more units. Society as a whole is harmed, because resources are being devoted to an industry in which the country does not have a comparative advantage. However, the government does earn tariff revenue. Finally, foreign producers are harmed because they sell fewer units than before,
   2.   The impact of an import quota is similar to a tariff. When compared with the free trade case, price is higher, domestic production is greater, and imports are less. Consumers are harmed because they pay a higher price and purchase fewer units. Domestic producers gain because they receive a higher price and sell more units. Society as a whole is harmed because resources are devoted to an industry in which the country does not have a comparative advantage. In this case, government does not gain any tax revenue. Finally, there is a double impact on foreign producers. They are harmed because they are selling fewer units, but the price they receive is greater than before, which partly counteracts this loss.
   3.   Besides tariffs and import quotas, governments also use domestic regulations and export subsidies to affect trade flows.
   4.   There are five possible economic arguments in favour of trade protection. Trade barriers can encourage domestic employment, foster infant industries, improve a country's terms of trade, protect a country's environmental and safety standards, and shield domestic workers from imports produced with cheap foreign labour. There are two possible noneconomic arguments in favour of trade barriers: ensuring national security and protecting cultural sovereignty.

♦   Trade Policies
   1.   Trade policy in Canada has usually been directed towards the US. For example, the Reciprocity Treaty established favourable trade terms with the US in the years before Confederation
   2.   In 1879, John A. Macdonald established the National Policy, which set high tariffs on manufactured imports from the US to encourage the development of a domestic Canadian manufacturing sector.
   3.   After dropping in the years after World War I, tariffs rose again during the 1930s as the Great Depression led to a round of protectionism throughout the industrialized world. By reducing international trade flows, this protectionism worsened the severity of economic downturn.
   4.   In 1947, Canada was part of the multilateral trade agreement known as the General Agreement on Tariffs and Trade (GATT), which led to significant reductions in global tariff and non-tariff barriers. In 1995, this agreement was replaced by the World Trade Organization (WTO).
   5.   There are three types of trading blocs. A free trade area is a region in which trade is tariff-free, but member countries impose separate trade barriers on non-member countries. A customs union is an area in which trade is free of tariffs and has common

trade barriers with non-member countries. A common market is an area of tariff-free trade, common trade barriers with non-member countries, and the free movement of labour and capital.

6. In 1965, Canada signed the Auto Pact with the US, which established free trade in autos and auto-parts between the two countries. In 1989, the two countries signed the Canada-US Free Trade Agreement (FTA), which established a free trade area for virtually all goods and services. In 1993, this free trade area was expanded to include Mexico with the North American Free Trade Agreement (NAFTA).

Helpful Hints

♦ Canada's Foreign Trade
1. Even though the net exports component of GDP includes both goods and services, the merchandise balance of trade receives the most popular attention. This is because the merchandise trade figures are released in a timelier fashion than the corresponding service figures. Also, there are fewer difficulties in measuring merchandise trade flows than service trade, so changes in the merchandise figures are more accurate indicators of underlying trends.

♦ The Case for Trade
1. The models of absolute advantage and comparative advantage, as outlined in the text, are both based on the simplifying assumption of constant opportunity costs, with one worker producing a given amount of an item regardless of the number of units of the item being made. In terms of the production possibilities model discussed in Chapter 1, the curve is a straight line rather than concave to the origin.
2. When calculating the opportunity costs for two traded products, it is important to note that output per worker is for the production of one item rather than two items at once. For example, in Figure 16.5, one Canadian worker can produce *either* 12 tonnes of paper *or* 12 computers, but not both. Similarly, a Mexican worker can produce *either* 3 tonnes of paper *or* 9 computers.

♦ The Impact of Trade Protection
1. The analysis of the impact of tariffs and import quotas, as summarized in Figure 16.7 of the text, applies only in the case of perfectly competitive markets. In other markets, the costs of trade protection may not be as large. In these cases, it is sometimes possible to apply strategic trade policy, which depends on the possible benefits to a country if its businesses take advantage of increasing returns to scale.
2. Few people like to be seen as promoting trade protection. So arguments in favour of trade barriers are often expressed in oblique ways – such as through calls for "fair trade" rather than "free trade." It is useful when analyzing trade arguments (both for and against trade protection) to pay careful attention to the details of any proposed policies, rather than just the rhetoric of the arguments, since these details can often be crucial in determining the policy's actual effect on trade flows.

♦ Trade Policies
1. Trading blocs – especially customs unions and common markets – are not always as easily classified as they may at first appear, since they may only partially possess the necessary linkages among the various member countries. An example is the South

American trading bloc Mercosur. Though classified as a customs union, it still possesses some of the features of a free trade area, since its members have not yet been able to fully agree on a common set of trade barriers with the rest of the world. Similarly, in the past the European Union was referred to as a common market, even before free movement of labour and capital was complete.

Key Concepts

globalization
absolute advantage
comparative advantage
law of comparative advantage
terms of trade
tariff
non-tariff barriers
import quota
voluntary export restraints
export subsidies
infant industry
National Policy

General Agreement on Tariffs and Trade
World Trade Organization
trading bloc
free trade area
transactions demand
customs union
common market
European Union
Auto Pact
Free Trade Agreement
North American Free Trade Agreement

Fill in the Blank and True False Questions

1. The rapid increase in world trade and cross-border investment flows, as well as the spread of international businesses and markets, is known as _____.

2. **T F** Since 1950, world trade has grown almost as fast as world GDP.

3. Order the following countries based on the exports of each as a proportion of its GDP (largest = 1, smallest = 4)

Japan	Belgium	US	Canada

1. _____
2. _____
3. _____
4. _____

4. **T F** In 2000, 74 percent of Canada's merchandise exports went to the US, while 86 percent of Canada's merchandise imports were from the US.

5. A producer who can make a certain product more efficiently than another producer has a(n) _____ advantage in making this product.

Figure 1   Use this table to answer questions 6 to 8.

Daily Output per Worker

	Crystal Balls	Magic Lamps
Sagittarius	15	3
Capricorn	20	5

6. Based on the information in Figure 1, the opportunity cost of a crystal ball in Sagittarius is _____ magic lamps, the opportunity cost of a crystal ball in Capricorn is _____ magic lamps, the opportunity cost of a magic lamp in Sagittarius is _____ crystal balls, and the opportunity cost of a magic lamp in Capricorn is _____ crystal balls.

   Place the following terms in the correct order in the blanks above.

   4   0.20   0.25   5

7. Based on the information in Figure 1, Sagitarrius should produce _____ and Capricorn should produce _____.

   Place the following terms in the correct order in the blanks above.

   magic lamps   crystal balls

8. Based on the information in Figure 1, trade in this case is based on the principle of _____ advantage.

9. The policy of trade protection initiated by Canada's first prime minister, John A. Macdonald, was known as the _____ _____.

10. **T F** The most important cause of liberalized world trade since World War II has been the General Agreement on Tariffs and Trade (GATT).

11. NAFTA illustrates a _____, Mercosur illustrates a _____, and the European Union illustrates a _____.

    Place the following terms in the correct order in the blanks above.

    free trade area   common market   customs union

12. **T F** So far, the Canadian economy has not been significantly affected by the transformation of the Free Trade Agreement (FTA) into the North American Free Trade Agreement (NAFTA).

13. **T F** John Helliwell argues that national borders are still a significant impediment to the flow of products and capital.

14. **T F** According to John Helliwell, globalization means that small countries are finding it increasingly difficult to compete against large countries in terms of living standards as well as broader social indicators.

Multiple-Choice Questions

1. Daily transactions in global foreign exchange markets now exceed what value?
   A. US$1 billion
   B. US$10 billion
   C. US$100 billion
   D. US$1 trillion
   E. US$100 trillion

2. Which of the following statements concerning Canada's merchandise exports is true?
   A. About a quarter are related to manufacturing and the rest are raw and processed natural resources.
   B. About a third are related to manufacturing and the rest are raw and processed natural resources.
   C. About a half are related to manufacturing and the other half are raw and processed natural resources.
   D. About two-thirds are related to manufacturing and the rest are raw and processed natural resources.
   E. About three-quarters are related to manufacturing and the rest are raw and processed natural resources.

3. Which of the following statements concerning Canada's merchandise imports is true?
   A. About a quarter are related to manufacturing and the rest are raw and processed natural resources.
   B. About a third are related to manufacturing and the rest are raw and processed natural resources.
   C. About a half are related to manufacturing and the other half are raw and processed natural resources.
   D. About two-thirds are related to manufacturing and the rest are raw and processed natural resources.
   E. About three-quarters are related to manufacturing and the rest are raw and processed natural resources.

4. Which of the following is the most important economic gain from trade?
   A. Trade enhances competitiveness in product markets.
   B. Specialization allows each country to concentrate on what it does best.
   C. Trade increases product variety.
   D. Trade enhances understanding about different cultures.
   E. Trade makes it more likely that world government will come into being.

Figure 2   Use this table to answer questions 5 to 6.

Daily Output per Worker

	CD Players	**CDs**
Euphonia	1	50
Harmonia	2	20

5.   Based on the information in Figure 2:
   A.   Harmonia should supply CD players and Euphonia should supply CDs, on the basis of the absolute advantage.
   B.   Euphonia should supply CD players and Harmonia should supply CDs, on the basis of absolute advantage.
   C.   Harmonia should supply CD players and Euphonia should supply CDs, on the basis of comparative advantage.
   D.   Euphonia should supply CD players and Harmonia should supply CDs, on the basis of comparative advantage.
   E.   Both countries should supply both items, since neither has an absolute or comparative advantage in these products.

6.   Based on the information in Figure 2:
   A.   The opportunity cost of CD players is 2 CDs in Euphonia and .4 CDs in Harmonia, while the opportunity cost of CDs is .5 CD players in Euphonia and 2.5 CD players in Harmonia.
   B.   The opportunity cost of CD players is .4 CDs in Euphonia and 2 CDs in Harmonia, while the opportunity cost of CDs is 2.5 CD players in Euphonia and .5 CD players in Harmonia.
   C.   The opportunity cost of CD players is 50 CDs in Euphonia and 10 CDs in Harmonia, while the opportunity cost of CDs is .02 CD players in Euphonia and .1 CD players in Harmonia.
   D.   The opportunity cost of CD players is 10 CDs in Euphonia and 50 CDs in Harmonia, while the opportunity cost of CDs is .1 CD players in Euphonia and .02 CD players in Harmonia.
   E.   The opportunity cost of CD players is .02 CDs in Euphonia and .1 CDs in Harmonia, while the opportunity cost of CDs is 50 CD players in Euphonia and 10 CD players in Harmonia.

Figure 3 Use this graph to answer questions 7 to 11.

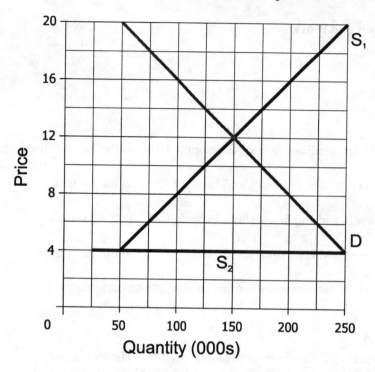

7. In Figure 3, which shows the market for electronic calculators, the equilibrium price with the domestic supply curve the supply curve, S_1, in the absence of tariffs is:
   A. $4
   B. $8
   C. $12
   D. $16
   E. $20

8. In Figure 3, the supply curve S_2 shows an unlimited supply of electronic calculators that becomes available through international trade at a price of $4. In this case, what is the total level of imports?
   A. 50 000 calculators
   B. 100 000 calculators
   C. 150 000 calculators
   D. 200 000 calculators
   E. 250 000 calculators

9. Given the information in Figure 3, if a $4 tariff is placed on imported calculators, then what will the new level of imports be?
   A. 50 000 calculators
   B. 100 000 calculators
   C. 150 000 calculators
   D. 200 000 calculators
   E. 250 000 calculators

10. Given the information in Figure 3, if a $4 tariff is placed on imported calculators, then how much tariff revenue will the government gain?
    A. $100 000
    B. $200 000
    C. $300 000
    D. $400 000
    E. $500 000

11. If, instead of a tariff, the government imposes an import quota on electronic calculators of 100 000, then given the information in Figure 3, what will be the new domestic price for this product?
    A. $4
    B. $8
    C. $12
    D. $16
    E. $20

12. Which of the following is not an argument used in Canada to defend trade protection?
    A. Trade barriers help develop new Canadian industries that otherwise would not be able to compete effectively against foreign competitors.
    B. Trade barriers help stimulate domestic employment by creating new demand for Canadian-made items.
    C. Trade barriers encourage the diversification of the Canadian economy away from a few resource-based industries.
    D. Trade barriers are needed to stop the import of products made by exploiting cheap labour in foreign countries.
    E. Trade barriers are needed to promote economies of scale and lower prices for Canadian consumers.

13. Which of the following statements is correct?
    A. A group of countries with free trade and common tariffs on outside countries is a free trade area.
    B. A group of countries with free trade, common tariffs with outside countries, and freely moving labour and capital is known as a free trade area.
    C. A group of countries with free trade but separate tariffs on outside countries is known as a common market.
    D. A group of countries with free trade, common tariffs with outside countries, and freely moving labour and capital is known as a customs union.
    E. A group of countries with free trade, common tariffs with outside countries, and freely moving labour and capital is known as a common market.

14. Which of the following statements is true?
    A. The WTO was a multilateral trade agreement first signed by 22 countries in 1947.
    B. GATT is a multilateral trade organization initiated in 1995, which includes over 120 countries.
    C. NAFTA is a bilateral trade agreement signed by Canada and the US in 1988.
    D. The FTA is a trilateral trade agreement signed by Canada, the US, and Mexico in 1993.
    E. The FTAA is a Pan-American free trade agreement currently being discussed by governments in North and South America.

15. One of the drawbacks of the Free Trade Agreement (FTA) between Canada and the United States has been:
    A. Canada has been unable to find a range of goods in which it possesses a comparative advantage relative to the US.
    B. Canadian jobs have been lost in previously protected sectors, and many of those who lost jobs have had difficulty finding new ones.
    C. Canadian merchandise exports to the United States have grown slowly since the agreement came into effect.
    D. The dispute settlement procedure put in place by the agreement has usually worked against Canada's interests.
    E. The proportion of Canada's merchandise trade with the US has fallen since the agreement came into effect.

Short Answer Questions

1. Natasha can construct a wooden cabinet in 5 hours and mow a lawn in 3 hours while Alfred can construct a wooden cabinet in 10 hours and mow a lawn in 2 hours.
   a. Who is more efficient at constructing a wooden cabinet? mowing a lawn?
   b. What are the two opportunity costs for the two activities for Natasha? for Alfred?
   c. Who should specialize in which activity? Why?

   Figure 4   Use this table to answer question 2.

   Daily Output per Worker

	TVs	VCRs
Aurora	6	9
Hesperia	12	24

2. Figure 4 shows how many TVs and VCRs can be produced daily by one worker in Aurora and Hesperia.
   a. Which country is more efficient at production TVs? VCRs?
   b. What are the opportunity costs for each product in Aurora? Hesperia?
   c. On the basis of comparative advantage, which country should specialize in the production of each item? Explain.
   d. Identify the limits of the terms of trade for the two products.
   e. Suppose there are 60 000 workers in Aurora and 25 000 workers in Hesperia, and before trade, half of each country=s labour force makes each product. Outline how specialization and trade lead to a gain in the total output of both products.

3. Suppose that in East Oceania 1 fishing boat has an opportunity cost of 10 fishing nets while in West Oceania 1 fishing boat has an opportunity cost of 20 fishing nets.
   a. Identify the limits of the terms of trade for the two products when they are traded by these two countries.
   b. What international price would be preferred by East Oceania? by West Oceania?

Solutions to Questions for Chapter 16

Fill in the Blank and True False Questions

1. **globalization**
2. **F** During this period, world trade has grown almost three times as fast as world GDP.
3. **Belgium, Canada, US, Japan**
4. **F** The numbers are reverse: 86 percent of Canada's merchandise exports went to the US, and 74 percent of Canada's merchandise imports were from the US.
5. **absolute**
6. **0.20, 0.25, 5, 4**
7. **crystal balls, magic lamps** Sagittarius should produce crystal balls, since their opportunity cost in Sagittarius (0.20 magic lamps) is less than in Capricorn (0.25 magic lamps). Meanwhile Capricorn should produce magic lamps, since their opportunity cost in Capricorn (4 crystal balls) is less than in Sagittarius (5 crystal balls).
8. **comparative** Trade cannot be based on absolute advantage, since Capricorn is more efficient than Sagittarius in the production of both goods. However, Sagittarius has a comparative advantage in the production of crystal balls, while Capricorn has a comparative advantage in the production of magic lamps.
9. **National Policy**
10. **T** Through successive rounds of GATT negotiations since World War II, average global tariff levels have been reduced by more than two-thirds.
11. **free trade area, customs union, common market**
12. **T** This is because trade with Mexico is relatively minor as a proportion of Canada's exports and imports.
13. **T** Helliwell cites empirical results showing that national borders are still important in limiting trade and capital flows.
14. **F** Helliwell argues that globalization does not threaten the economic viability of small countries.

Multiple-Choice Questions

1. **D** Transactions in global foreign exchange markets now total well over US$1 trillion a day.
2. **C** Approximately half are related to manufacturing, and the other half are resource-related.
3. **D** Approximately two-thirds are related to manufacturing, while about a third are resource-related.
4. **B** The opportunity for specialization is the major economic gain provided by trade.
5. **A** This is because, with the same resources, Harmonia can produce more CD players than Euphonia can, while Euphonia can produce more CDs than Harmonia can.
6. **C** The opportunity cost of CD players is 50 CDs (50/1) in Euphonia and 10 CDs (20/2) in Harmonia, while the opportunity cost of CDs is .02 (1/50) CD players in Euphonia and .1 CD (2/20) players in Harmonia.
7. **C** This is where the demand curve (D) and the domestic supply curve (S_1) meet.
8. **D** This is found by taking the difference between the quantity demanded (250 000) and domestic production (50 000) at a price of $4.
9. **B** This is found by taking the difference between the quantity demanded (200 000) and domestic production (100 000) at a price of $8.
10. **D** This is found by multiplying total imports (100 000) by the tariff of $4.
11. **B** This found by drawing a new supply curve (S_3) 100 000 units to the right of S_1 at every possible price, then finding where S_3 intersects the demand curve (D).
12. **E** This is an argument made by those who oppose trade protection.
13. **E** A free trade area is a group of countries with free trade but separate tariffs on outside countries, while a customs union is a group of countries with free trade and common tariffs on outside countries.
14. **E** The FTA is the bilateral agreement between Canada and the US; NAFTA is the trilateral agreement between Canada, the US, and Mexico; GATT was the multilateral agreement first signed in 1947, and the WTO is the multilateral organization initiated in 1995.
15. **B** This is especially relevant for workers in selected manufacturing industries whose Canadian operations depended on tariff protection.

Short Answer Problems

1a. Natasha is more efficient at constructing a wooden cabinet because she can do it in less time (5 hours) than it takes Alfred (10 hours). Alfred is more efficient at mowing a lawn, because he can do it in less time (2 hours) than it takes Natasha (3 hours).

b. Natasha can mow 1.67 (5/3) lawns in the 5 hours it takes her to make one cabinet. Therefore, her opportunity cost of making a cabinet is the 1.67 lawns she could have mown instead, while her opportunity cost of mowing a lawn is the .6 (3/5) cabinets he could have made instead. Alfred can mow 5 (10/2) lawns in the 10 hours it takes him to make a cabinet. Therefore, his opportunity cost of making a cabinet is the 5 lawns he could have mown instead, while his opportunity cost for mowing a lawn is the .2 (2/10) cabinets he could have made instead.

c. Based on the law of absolute advantage, each person should specialize in the activity in which they are more efficient than the other person. This means that Natasha should specialize in making cabinets, and Alfred should mow lawns. Each is also producing the item for which their opportunity cost is the lowest B since the opportunity cost of making cabinets is lower for Natasha (1.67 lawns) than for Alfred (5 lawns), and the opportunity cost of mowing lawns in lower for Alfred (.2 cabinets) than for Natasha (.6 cabinets).

2a. Hesperia is more efficient at producing TVs, since a worker's daily output of TVs is higher in Hesperia (12) than in Aurora (6). Hesperia is also more efficient at producing VCRs, since a worker's daily output of VCRs in Hesperia is higher (24) than in Aurora (9).

b. In Aurora, the opportunity cost of TVs is 1.5 VCRs (and the opportunity cost of VCRs is 0.67 TVs), since a worker in Aurora can produce one and a half times as many VCRs (9) as TVs (6) in a day. In Hesperia, the opportunity cost of TVs is 2 VCRs (and the opportunity cost of VCRs is 0.50 TVs), since a worker in Hesperia can produce two times as many VCRs (24) as TVs (12) in a day.

c. On the basis of comparative advantage, each country should specialize in the good whose opportunity cost is lower than in the other country. This means that Aurora should specialize in TVs, because this product's opportunity cost is lower in Aurora (1.5 VCRs) than in Hesperia (2 VCRs). Meanwhile, Hesperia should specialize in VCRs, because this product's opportunity cost is lower in Hesperia (0.50 TVs) than in Aurora (0.67 TVs)

d. The terms of trade must be somewhere between 1 TV traded for 2 VCRs (Hesperia), and 1 TV for 1.5 VCRs (Aurora)

e. Before specialization and trade, daily output in Aurora is 180 000 TVs (30 000 workers x 6 TVs per worker) and 270 000 VCRs (30 000 workers x 9 VCRs per worker). In Hesperia, daily output is 150 000 TVs (12 500 workers x 12 TVs per worker) and 300 000 jeans (12 500 workers x 24 VCRs per worker). Therefore, total output in the two countries before specialization and trade is 330 000 (180 000 + 150 000) TVs and 570 000 (270 000 + 300 000) VCRs. After specialization and trade, daily output in Aurora is 360 000 TVs (60 000 x 6 TVs per worker) and daily output in Hesperia is 600 000 VCRs (25 000 workers x 24 VCRs per worker). The result is a gain in the two countries' output of both products – 30 000 (360 000 - 330 000) more TVs and 30 000 (600 000 - 570 000) more VCRs.

3a. The terms of trade must be somewhere between 1 fishing boat traded for 10 fishing nets (East Oceania) and 1 fishing boat traded for 20 fishing nets (West Oceania). The factors that determine the exact international price of fishing boats in terms of fishing nets are the levels of demand for each product internationally. A higher international demand for either product pushes up the product's international price in terms of the other product.

b. Because the opportunity cost of fishing boats is lower in East Oceania (10 fishing nets) than in West Oceania (20 fishing nets), East Oceania exports fishing boats. Meanwhile, the opportunity cost of fishing nets is lower in West Oceania (0.05 fishing boats) than in East Oceania (0.10 fishing boats) so West Oceania exports fishing nets. Given that East Oceanians export boats, they want the highest possible price of boats in terms of nets, which occurs when 1 boat has its maximum value of 20 nets. Because West Oceanians export nets, they want the lowest possible price of boats in terms of nets, which occurs when 1 boat has its minimum value of 10 nets.

Chapter 17

Economic Growth

Learning Objectives

In this chapter you will:
- learn about economic growth, its sources, and its impact
- examine economic development, its dynamics, the vicious circle of poverty, and the strategies used to break the circle

Chapter Highlights

- Economic Growth
    1. Economic growth is caused by a long-run increase in aggregate supply (which is associated with a rise in potential output), or short-run increases in either aggregate demand or aggregate supply.
    2. Using the production possibilities model, economic growth is shown either by an outward shift in the curve, or a movement towards the curve when the economy has unemployed resources or is not using its resources to full capacity.
    3. The production possibilities model reveals how economic growth depends on investment. If two countries begin with the same production possibilities curve, the country that devotes a larger proportion of its output to capital products rather than to consumption will see the quickest expansion in it production possibilities. Therefore, by sacrificing current consumption, future living standards can be increased.
    4. The benefits of high economic growth are magnified over time because growth builds on itself in an exponential way. This is shown by the rule of 72, which states that the approximate number of years it takes a variable to double is found by dividing 72 by the variable's annual percentage growth rate. Small differences in annual growth rates have a considerable effect on long-term growth paths.
    5. Between 1979 and 1997, 35 percent of the growth in Canada's real GDP was due to increases in the quantity of labour. When defining growth in terms of per capita GDP, the main determinant has been the increase in labour productivity. The growth in labour productivity depends, in turn, on the quantity of capital, technological progress, the quality of labour, efficiency in production, the quantity of natural resources, and social and political factors. A country's quantity of capital is determined by investment. Technological progress is closely tied to research and development expenditures. The quality of labour is associated with education levels. Efficiency in production is related to such factors as the scale of production and the allocation of resources among different sectors. The quantity of natural resources is a less important growth determinant in modern industrial economies than it was in the past, but social and political factors are still crucial.
    6. In the debate over economic growth, supporters highlight its effect on living standards, the opportunities it provides for social improvements, and its psychological benefits.

Opponents point to the opportunity cost of growth due to lower consumption in the current period, as well as the environmental and social costs associated with growth.

♦ Economic Development
1. The World Bank classifies countries into high-income, middle-income and low-income groups based on per capita GNP expressed in US dollars. High-income countries have a per capita GNP of US$9266 or more; middle-income countries have a per capita GNP of US$756 to US$9265; low-income countries have a per capita GNP of $755 or less.
2. Low-income countries have little capital and use labour-intensive production techniques, with primary industries (especially agriculture) being important in their economies.
3. Other terms used to describe groups of nations include industrially advanced countries or IACs (used to describe those nations that have a high degree of industrialization) , newly industrializing countries or NICs (used to describe those nations that have only recently industrialized), and less developed countries or LDCs (used to describe countries with traditional mixed economies and low per capita incomes).
4. It is possible to compare living standards, not just on the basis of per capita income, but also health and social indicators, and other variables such as energy consumption. The gap between rich and poor countries, when analyzed in terms of per capita income, has grown in dollar terms since 1950, even though percentage growth rates in poorer countries have exceeded those in rich countries.
5. Economic development is defined as an increase in a country's per capita income accompanied by a rise in living standards for the bulk of the population. It is often blocked by a vicious cycle of poverty, in which low per capita incomes mean low investment in capital and human resources (given the need to spend most earnings on consumption) coupled by high population growth (since low incomes often result in large families). These trends perpetuate labour-intensive production, which dampens productivity growth and stifles growth in per capita incomes.
6. Domestic strategies that can overcome the vicious cycle of poverty include ensuring a stable political and economic system, investment in economic resources such as human capital, and control of population growth. High-income countries can contribute to development through trade liberalization and foreign aid.

Helpful Hints

♦ Economic Growth
1. While expansionary fiscal and monetary policies can contribute to economic growth by helping an economy move from below its production possibilities curve to a point on this curve, over any significant period economic growth results from long-run increases in aggregate supply – especially increases related to productivity growth. Those aggregate supply factors that impact on labour productivity are therefore vital in determining long-run living standards.
2. The rule of 72 is only an approximate law, but is highly useful, not just in economic applications, but in a wide range of other contexts as well. These include applications in financial theory (such as calculating the future value of a financial investment) and demographic theory (such as calculating the future size of a country's population).

♦ Economic Development

1. There is a difference between economic growth and economic development. While economic growth occurs whenever there is an increase in per capita real output, economic development occurs only when this increase is accompanied by a general rise in living standards.

2. The term "developing country" has several possible meanings. Sometimes the term is used to describe just low-income countries; more often it is used to describe both low-income and middle-income countries (including former members of the Soviet bloc).

Key Concepts

exponential growth
rule of 72
technological progress
research and development expenditures
World Bank
high-income countries
middle-income countries

low-income countries
industrially advanced countries
newly industrializing countries
less-developed countries
economic development
vicious circle of poverty

Fill in the Blank and True False Questions

1. **T F** The only way economic growth can occur is through an outward shift in the production possibilities curve.

2. If the average annual growth of real output in a country is 3 percent, the economy will double in size every _____ years.

3. **T F** Canada's research and development expenditures are high as a percentage of GDP when compared with other industrial countries.

4. **T F** According to some recent studies, countries with a more equal distribution of income have achieved higher rates of economic growth.

5. **T F** Per capita incomes in low-income countries are catching up to those in high-income countries, since the same absolute increase in real output has a greater effect in poor countries than in rich countries.

6. **T F** Economic development occurs whenever per capita real incomes in a country rise.

7. According to the vicious cycle of poverty, _____ results in _____ in capital and human resources, and _____. This leads to _____, which in turn causes _____ and keeps per capita incomes low.

Place the following terms in the correct order in the blanks above.

labour-intensive production   low investment
rapid population growth   low productivity growth   low per capita income

8. **T F** Less-developed countries with political freedom and democracy tend to have higher rates of economic growth than those that are autocratically governed.

9. **T F** Foreign aid is most successful in developing countries with policies geared towards low inflation, small budget deficits, open trade, and the rule of law.

10. In Nuala Beck's model, a strategic industry in the commodity-processing era was _____, during the mass-manufacturing era was _____, and during the technology era is _____.

Place the following terms in the correct order in the blanks above.

the health and medical industry   auto manufacturing   the textile industry

Multiple-Choice Questions

1. Economic growth can be defined in two ways, as:
   A. a rise in nominal GDP, or a rise in real GDP.
   B. a rise in per capita GDP, or a rise in nominal GDP.
   C. a rise in per capita real GDP, or a rise in per capita GDP.
   D. a rise in real GDP, or a rise in per capita real GDP.
   E. a rise per capital GDP, or a rise in real GDP.

2. Economic growth can be caused by:
   A. long-run increases in aggregate supply, but no short-run changes in either aggregate supply or aggregate demand.
   B. short-run increases in aggregate demand or aggregate supply.
   C. long-run increases in aggregate supply, as well as by short-run increases in either aggregate supply or aggregate demand.
   D. short-run decreases in aggregate demand or aggregate supply.
   E. short-run or long-run increases in aggregate supply, as well as by short-run decreases in aggregate demand.

Figure 1 Use this graph to answer questions 3 to 5.

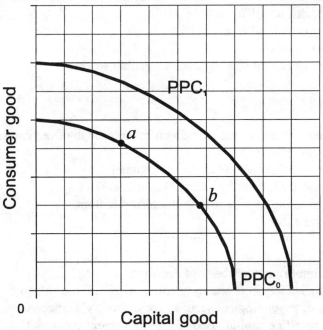

3. In Figure 1, the shift from PPC$_0$ to PPC$_1$:
   A. could be caused by a reduction in unemployment.
   B. could be caused by technological change that raises resource productivity.
   C. cannot occur unless the economy's stock of resources increases.
   D. is the result of using the economy's existing stock of resources more effectively.
   E. none of the above

4. In Figure 1, the movement from point *a* to point *b* along PPC$_0$:
   A. could be caused by a reduction in unemployment.
   B. could be caused by technological change that raises resource productivity.
   C. cannot occur unless the economy's stock of resources increases.
   D. is the result of using the economy's existing stock of resources more effectively.
   E. none of the above

5. In Figure 1, the movement from point *a* to point *b* along PPC$_0$:
   A. will cause lower rates of economic growth in the future.
   B. means that more consumption goods and fewer capital goods are produced.
   C. raises real GDP but not per capita real GDP.
   D. will cause higher rates of economic growth in the future.
   E. raises per capita real GDP but not real GDP.

6. A country's per capita real GDP is growing at an annual rate of 2 percent. How long will it take for this country's per capital real GDP to double?
   A. 50 years
   B. 36 years
   C. 18 years
   D. 9 years
   E. 5 years

7.   Which of the following factors has not been an important factor in determining the growth in Canada's real GDP between 1979 and 1997?
     A. an increase in the quantity of natural resources
     B. an increase in the quantity of labour
     C. an increase in the quantity of capital used by each Canadian worker
     D. technological progress
     E. social and political factors

8.   Which of the following is a likely cause of the slowdown in the growth of per capita real incomes in Canada in recent decades?
     A. expansionary government policies to combat unemployment
     B. a lower level of educational attainment by young Canadians
     C. the shift of employment from the service to manufacturing sectors
     D. relatively low rates of investment
     E. the introduction of more liberalized international trade

9.   Which of the following is an important drawback of economic growth?
     A. It can be achieved only if a society chooses an unequal distribution of income.
     B. It reinforces a false sense of psychological security for a country's citizens.
     C. It requires that a country sacrifice capital goods for more current consumption.
     D. It leads to greater exploitation of natural resources.
     E. It makes it harder for governments to divert economic resources to such uses as health, education, and poverty reduction.

10. Which of the following is usually considered to be the main benefit of economic growth?
     A. It provides psychological benefits in the form of hope and optimism.
     B. It leads to higher living standards.
     C. It makes it easier for governments to divert economic resources to such uses as health, education, and poverty reduction.
     D. It lessens environmental damage.
     E. It necessarily leads to a more equal distribution of income.

11. Which of the following statements is false?
     A. Egypt is an example of a middle-income country
     B. Honduras is an example of a low-income country
     C. Japan is an example of a high-income country
     D. Taiwan is an example of a newly industrializing country (NIC).
     E. China is an example of an industrially advanced country (IAC).

12. Which of the following regions of low-income countries and middle-income countries currently has the highest rate of population growth?
     A. South Asia
     B. Europe and Central Asia
     C. Middle East and Northern Africa
     D. Sub-Saharan Africa
     E. East Asia and Pacific

13. Which of the following is an important strategy for low-income countries trying to break out of the vicious cycle of poverty?
    A. providing a stable political and economic environment
    B. family planning
    C. the global liberalization of trade
    D. investing in education
    E. all of the above

14. Which of the following is not a common drawback of government-run foreign aid programs?
    A. Donor governments often devise foreign aid programs that will provide profits for business in their own countries.
    B. Government-run projects are often ill-conceived and badly managed.
    C. Projects tend to favour small-scale projects over large-scale ones.
    D. Donors often favour manufacturing over agriculture.
    E. Programs can often be sabotaged by bureaucratic corruption or incompetence.

15. Based on the theories of Nuala Beck, which of the following statements is not correct?
    A. The commodity-processing era depended on a plentiful supply of steel
    B. The mass-manufacturing era depended on a plentiful supply of oil
    C. The technology era depends on a plentiful supply of semi-conductors.
    D. Canada is badly placed to take advantage of the opportunities provided by the technology era.
    E. Britain was the technological pace-setter during the commodity-processing era.

Short Answer Questions

Figure 2 Use this graph to answer question 1.

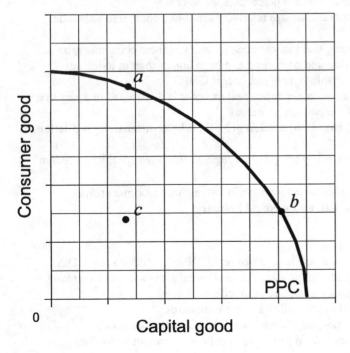

1. Figure 2 shows the production possibilities curve for Cantina, a country that produces one capital good and one consumer good.
   a. Suppose the citizens of Cantina decide to move from point *a* to point *b* on the graph. How will this affect Cantina's rate of economic growth?
   b. Would economic growth occur if there were a movement from point *c* to point *b* on the graph? Explain.
   c. Outline how a technological improvement in the production of the capital good could affect Cantina's future economic growth. Would a technological improvement in the production of the consumer good have any possible effect on Cantina's future economic growth? Explain.

2. Calculate the following with the aid of the Rule of 72.
   a. The approximate number of times a country's economy will double in size in 50 years if growth in its real GDP is 6 percent.
   b. The number of years it will take an economy's per capita real GDP to double if growth in its real GDP is 0.5 percent.
   c. The nominal interest rate if it takes a bank account 24 years to double in size.

3. Suppose a major technological innovation allows a low-income country to experience a one-time increase in per capita income. Explain how this event could be used by the country's government to help its economy escape the vicious cycle of poverty.

Solutions to Questions for Chapter 17

Fill in the Blank and True False Questions
1. **F** Economic growth can also be the result of moving towards the production possibilities curve if the economy is operating inside its feasible region.
2. **24** This is based on the rule of 72, which states that the number of years it takes a variable to double is found by dividing 72 by the variable's growth rate in percentage terms (72/3).
3. **F** Canadian research and development expenditures are relatively low when compared with other industrial countries.
4. **T** These studies go against the common view that income equality detracts from economic growth.
5. **F** Even though growth rates in many low-income countries have been higher than in industrial countries, these rates translate into lower absolute increases in real GDP.
6. **F** Economic development occurs only if a rise in per capita real incomes is distributed in a way that raises living standards for the majority of the country's citizens.
7. **low per capita income, low investment, rapid population growth, labour-intensive production, low productivity growth**
8. **T** This is because of the long-run stability usually provided by regimes that stress political freedom and democracy.
9. **T** In these countries, foreign aid leads to a sustained increase in the rate of economic growth.
10. **textile industry, auto manufacturing, health and medical industry**

Multiple-Choice Questions
1. **D** The two ways of defining economic growth are in terms of real GDP or per capita real GDP.
2. **C** Long-run increases in aggregate supply are the primary cause of growth, but short-run increases in either aggregate demand or aggregate supply can also have an effect.
3. **B** Technological change shifts the production possibilities curve rightwards.
4. **E** This results from a decision to produce more capital goods and fewer consumer goods.
5. **D** The production of more capital goods leads to higher rates of economic growth in the future.

6. **B** Based on the rule of 72, it will take 36 years (72/2) for this variable to double.
7. **A** Canada's abundant supplies of natural resources have remained relatively constant, and have not been a major determinant of recent economic growth in Canada.
8. **D** Low rates of investment in Canada are one of several likely causes of this growth slowdown.
9. **D** The depletion of natural resources is one of several important drawbacks of economic growth.
10. **B** Growth's effects on living standards is usually considered its most significant benefit.
11. **E** Though China is industrializing quickly, large portions of its economy are at a pre-industrial stage.
12. **D** Population growth in Sub-Saharan Africa is well over 2 percent annually.
13. **E** All these strategies are important.
14. **C** It is large-scale development projects that are often favoured over small-scale ones.
15. **D** According to Beck, Canada is well-placed for the technology era, partly because the country is a major supplier of some of the most important natural resources needed in the technology-driven economy.

Short Answer Problems

1a. The decision to produce more of the capital good and less of the consumer good, when moving from point *a* to point *b* contributes to any outward shift in the production possibilities curve in the future as Cantina's resources expand. This raises Cantina's future rate of economic growth.
b. Yes. A movement from *c* to *b*, which brings the economy from a point within to a point on the production possibilities curve, is associated with economic growth, since the output of both goods is being increased.
c. An improvement in the production of the capital good shifts Cantina's production possibilities curve horizontally rightwards, while the curve's vertical intercept stays the same. Because Cantina is able to produce more of both the capital good and the consumption goods (unless only the consumption good is being produced at the vertical intercept), the rate of economic growth will almost certainly increase, except in the unlikely case where the country's citizens decide that all of the new output should be in the form of the consumption good rather than capital good. Meanwhile, an improvement in the production of the consumption good shifts the production possibilities curve vertically upwards, while the curve's horizontal intercept stays the same. Again, Cantina is able to produce more of both goods (unless only the capital good is being produced at the horizontal intercept), so the rate of economic growth will almost certainly increase, unless the country's citizens decide that all of the new output should be in the form of the consumption good.
2a. Real GDP will double every 12 years (= 72/6) so the economy will double 4.2 (50/12) times in 50 years.
b. It will take 144 years (= 72/0.5) for the economy's per capita real GDP to double.
c. The nominal interest rate is 3 percent (= 72/24), found by re-expressing the Rule of 72 formula as: the annual percentage growth rate - 72/the number of years for variable to double.
3. This country's government can use some of the extra output provided by the technological innovation to raise investment in either physical or human capital and to extend population control programs. These strategies will reduce the country's dependence on labour-intensive production techniques, stimulating further productivity growth and providing the potential for a continuing rise in the country's per capita incomes.

Macroeconomics Review Test

This practice test includes multiple choice and short answer questions from Chapters 1 and 2 and Chapters 9 to 17.

Multiple Choice Questions

1. The market structure that answers most satisfactorily for society the basic economic questions of what to produce and how to produce is:
   A. monopoly
   B. monopolistic competition
   C. oligopoly with rivalry
   D. cooperative oligopoly
   E. perfect competition

2. To represent the demand curve of good A, economists place:
   A. quantity demanded on the horizontal axis and price on the vertical axis.
   B. quantity demanded on the vertical axis and price on the horizontal axis.
   C. quantity supplied on the horizontal axis and price on the vertical axis.
   D. quantity supplied on the vertical axis and price on the horizontal axis.
   E. quantity demanded of good A on the horizontal axis and good B on the vertical axis.

3. Which of the following is a component of GDP using the income approach?
   A. government purchases
   B. indirect taxes
   C. net exports
   D. investment
   E. consumption

4. The income received by Canadian households before deducting personal income taxes and other personal transfers to government is known as:
   A. Gross Domestic Product
   B. Gross National Product
   C. Net Domestic Income
   D. Personal Income
   E. Disposable Income

5. A nation's consumer price index has a value of 125 at the beginning of one year and a value of 130 at the beginning of the next year. The inflation rate during the year has been:
   A. 5 percent
   B. 4 percent
   C. 3.8 percent
   D. 3 percent
   E. 2 percent

6. Which of the following groups is not part of Canada's labour force?
    A. full-time workers
    B. part-time workers who are not looking for full-time work
    C. part-time workers who are looking for full-time work
    D. discouraged workers
    E. members of the labour force population who are unemployed and actively seeking a job

7. Which of the following will cause reductions in the equilibrium price level as well as in equilibrium output?
    A. a decrease in aggregate demand
    B. an increase in aggregate demand
    C. a short-run decrease in aggregate supply
    D. a long-run increase in aggregate supply
    E. a short-run increase in aggregate supply

8. When an economy's price level is above its equilibrium level:
    A. real expenditures exceed real output, so that there is negative unplanned investment.
    B. real output exceeds real expenditures, so that there is positive unplanned investment.
    C. real expenditures exceed real output, so that there is positive unplanned investment.
    D. real output exceeds real expenditures, so that there is negative unplanned investment.
    E. real output and real expenditures are equal, so that there is no unplanned investment.

Figure 1 Use this graph to answer questions 9 and 10.

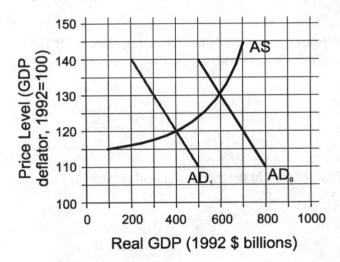

9. If the shift from AD_0 to AD_1 in Figure 1 were caused by a $100 billion decrease in investment spending, the spending multiplier in this economy has a value of:
    A. 5
    B. 4
    C. 3
    D. 2
    E. 1

10. In Figure 1, a shift in aggregate demand from AD_0 to AD_1 could be the result of:
    A. a contractionary monetary policy in the form of a decrease in the money supply and a rise in interest rates.
    B. a contractionary fiscal policy in the form of a reduction in taxes.
    C. an expansionary fiscal policy in the form of a reduction in taxes.
    D. an expansionary monetary policy in the form of an increase in the money supply and a drop in interest rates.
    E. an expansionary monetary policy in the form of a decrease in the money supply and rise in interest rates.

11. When compared with the lags associated with changes in government purchases, which of the following lags is longer for monetary policy?
    A. decision lag
    B. unemployment lag
    C. impact lag
    D. recognition lag
    E. inflation lag

12. Which of the following is not part of M2+?
    A. nonpersonal term deposits at chartered banks
    B. notice deposits at chartered banks
    C. currency outside chartered banks
    D. publicly held demand deposits at chartered banks
    E. personal term deposits at near banks

13. Mackenzie Bank has a reserve ratio of 6 percent and initially has no excess reserves. If $60 000 is deposited in the bank, Mackenzie Bank's excess reserves become:
    A. 60 000
    B. 10 000
    C. 3600
    D. 50 000
    E. 56 400

14. Which of the following will cause a rightward shift in the money demand curve?
    A. a fall in the nominal interest rate
    B. an increase in real output
    C. a rise in the nominal interest rate
    D. an increase in the money supply
    E. a drop in the price level

15. The Bank of Canada buys a $100 million bond from a member of the public when the reserve ratio in the banking system is 10 percent. As a result:
    A. the money supply immediately falls by $100 million.
    B. the money supply immediately falls by $10 million
    C. the money supply immediately rises by $10 million.
    D. the money supply immediately rises by $100 million.
    E. there is no immediate effect on the money supply.

16. If in a certain year the Bank of Canada purchases $10 billion of Canadian dollars in exchange for foreign currency, then Canada has a(n):
    A. exchange rate below its equilibrium value.
    B. $10 billion balance of trade.
    C. $10 billion merchandise balance of trade.
    D. $10 billion balance-of-payments deficit
    E. $10 billion balance-of-payments surplus

17. If Canadian interest rates fall:
    A. the Canadian dollar's value drops against the US dollar due to an increase in demand and a decrease in supply for the Canadian dollar in foreign exchange markets.
    B. the Canadian dollar's value drops against the US dollar due to a decrease in demand and an increase in supply for the Canadian dollar in foreign exchange markets.
    C. the Canadian dollar's value rises against the US dollar due to an increase in demand and a decrease in supply for the Canadian dollar in foreign exchange markets.
    D. the Canadian dollar's value rises against the US dollar due to a decrease in demand and an increase in supply for the Canadian dollar in foreign exchange markets
    E. there is no effect on the value of the Canadian dollar.

Figure 2 Use this table to answer question 18.

Daily Output per Worker

	Salmon	Trout
Pisces	15	45
Aquarius	25	50

18. Based on the information in Figure 2:
    A. the opportunity cost of salmon in Pisces is .33 trout.
    B. the opportunity cost of salmon in Aquarius is .5 trout.
    C. the opportunity cost of trout in Pisces is .33 salmon..
    D. Pisces and Aquarius cannot engage in trade because Aquarius is more efficient at producing both goods.
    E. Pisces should produce salmon and Aquarius should produce trout.

19. If the average annual inflation rate in a country is 4 percent, then how long will it take for the country's price level to double?
    A. 72 years
    B. 40 years
    C. 22 years
    D. 18 years
    E. 4 years

Short Answer Questions

1. Using the model of aggregate demand and aggregate supply, outline why a recession in the US is likely to cause a recession in Canada.

2. Calculate the spending multiplier in each of the following cases, and then find the size and direction of the shift in aggregate demand.
   a. Government purchases fall by $10 billion in an economy with an MPW of 0.7.
   b. Investment spending and consumption of durables rise by $8 billion in an economy with an MPC of 0.25.
   c. Taxes are cut by $1 billion in an economy with an MPC of 0.4.
   d. A tax rise of $5 billion causes an initial $3 billion decrease in spending on domestic items.

Figure 3 Use this graph to answer question 3.

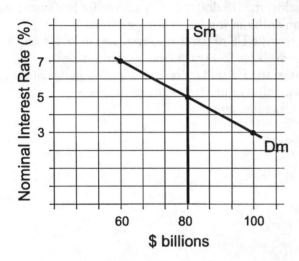

3. Figure 3 shows the demand and supply curves in a particular money market.
   a. What is the equilibrium interest rate and money supply in this market
   b. What would happen to equilibrium in this market if the money supply increased by $20 billion?
   c. What would happen to the money demand curve in the market described in part b if real output in this economy falls? In what direction would the equilibrium interest rate change? Explain.

Figure 4 Use this table to answer question 4.

Daily Output per Worker

	Digital Cameras	Scanners
Callisto	5	10
Europa	3	18

4. Figure 4 shows how many digital cameras and scanners can be made daily by one worker in Callisto and Europa.
   a. Which country is more efficient at producing digital cameras? scanners?
   b. On the basis of absolute advantage, which country should specialize in the production of digital cameras? scanners?
   c. Identify the limits of the terms of trade for these two products.

d.   Suppose there are 200 000 workers in Callisto and 250 000 in Europa. Before trade, half of each country's labour force makes each product. Outline how specialization and trade lead to a gain in the two countries' combined output of both products.

Solutions to Macroeconomics Review Test

Multiple Choice Questions

1. **E** In the long run perfect competition allows for production where price equals marginal revenue equals marginal cost equals minimum average cost, i.e., marginal-cost pricing and minimum-cost pricing are attained. Society gets the amounts of the products it wants at the lowest possible prices.

2. **A** Quantity demanded goes on the horizontal axis and price on the vertical axis.

3. **B** Indirect taxes are a component of income-based GDP.

4. **D** Income received by Canadian households before these deductions is known as personal income.

5. **B** Inflation during the year is 4 percent [= ((130 - 125)/125) x 100)].

6. **D** Discouraged workers are not considered to be part of the labour force since they are not actively seeking employment.

7. **A** A decrease in aggregate demand pushes down both the equilibrium price level and equilibrium output.

8. **B** With the price level higher than its equilibrium level, the AS curve is to the right of the AD curve. This means that real output exceeds real expenditures, and that there is positive unplanned investment.

9. **C** Given the $300 billion leftward shift in the AD curve and the initial $100 billion decrease in investment spending, the spending multiplier in this economy must have a value of 3 [= (-$300 billion/-$100 billion)].

10. **A** A fall in aggregate demand could be caused by a decrease in the money supply and rise in interest rates, which is a contractionary monetary policy.

11. **C** The impact lag is longer for monetary policy than the impact lag for changes in government purchases, because the impact of a monetary policy on the economy is indirect. It depends on the gradual effect of a change in interest rates on both investment spending and the consumption of durable items.

12. **A** Nonpersonal term deposits at chartered banks are part of M3, not M2 or M2+.

13. **C** Excess reserves become $3600, found by multiplying the 6 percent reserve ratio (expressed as a decimal) by the $60 000 deposit.

14. **B** An increase in real output raises the transactions demand for money, which leads to a rightward shift in the money demand curve.

15. **D** There is an immediate $100 million rise in the money supply, since the $100 million that the Bank of Canada deposits in the bondholder's bank account is part of the money supply.

16. **D** If the Bank of Canada is buying Canadian dollars in foreign exchange markets, it is pursuing a balance-of-payments deficit.

17. **B** The Canadian dollar's value falls because its demand decreases and its supply increases in foreign exchange markets.

18. **C** The opportunity cost of trout in Pisces is .33 [= (15/45)] salmon.

19. **D** Based on the rule of 72, it will take 18 years [= (72/4)] for the price level to double, given the 4 percent inflation rate.

Short Answer Questions

1. With a recession in the US, American incomes are falling, which reduces Canadian exports. Given that Canadian exports to the US are such a significant portion of Canadian GDP, Canadian aggregate demand will undergo a considerable decrease. This reduces both the equilibrium price level and equilibrium output, so that it is likely there will also be a recession in Canada.

2a. With an MPW of 0.7, the spending multiplier is 1.43 (1/0.7), so that the AD curve finally shifts to the left by (-)$14.3 billion (-$10 billion x 1.43).

b. Given an MPC of 0.25, MPW is 0.75 (1 - 0.25), and the spending multiplier is 1.33 (1/0.75). Therefore, the AD curve finally shifts to the right by $10.67 billion ($8 billion x 1.33).

c. With an MPC of 0.4, MPW is 0.6 (1 - 0.4) and the spending multiplier is 1.67. Therefore the AD curve finally shifts to the right by $666,667 (-($1 billion x 0.4) x 1.67).

d. The MPC is 0.6 ($3 billion/$5 billion), the MPW is 0.4 (1 – 0.6), and the spending multiplier is 2.5 (1/0.4). Therefore, the AD curve finally shifts to the left by (-)$7.5 billion (-($5 billion x 0.6) x 2.5).

3a. The equilibrium values are 5 percent and $80 billion, found at the intersection of the two curves.

b. The equilibrium interest rate would fall to 3 percent and the equilibrium money supply would rise to $100 billion.

c. If real output falls, so too does the transactions demand for money, pushing the money demand curve to the left. This would cause the equilibrium interest rate to fall, since at the initial 3 percent interest rate there would now be a surplus (or excess supply) of money, an excess demand of bonds, a rise in the price of bonds, and therefore a fall in the interest rate. This is because bond prices and the nominal interest rate are inversely related.

4a. Callisto is more efficient at producing cameras, since a worker's daily output of cameras is higher in Castillo (5) than in Europa (3). Meanwhile, Europa is more efficient at producing scanners, since a worker's daily output of scanners in Europa is higher (18) than in Callisto (10).

b. On the basis of absolute advantage, each country should specialize in the good that they are most efficient at producing. Therefore, Callisto should make cameras and Europa should make scanners.

c. In Callisto, the opportunity cost of cameras is 2 scanners, since a worker in Callisto can produce twice as many scanners (10) as radios (5) in a day. Meanwhile, in Europa the opportunity cost of cameras is 6 scanners, since a worker in Europa can produce six times as many scanners (18) as cameras (3) in a day. Therefore, the terms of trade must be somewhere between 1 camera traded for 2 scanners games in Callisto and 1 camera traded for 6 scanners in Europa.

d. Before specialization and trade, daily output in Callisto is 500 000 cameras (100 000 workers x 5 cameras per worker) and 1 million scanners (100 000 workers x 10 radios per worker). In Europa, daily output is 375 000 cameras (125 000 workers x 3 cameras per worker) and 2.25 million scanners (125 000 x 18 scanners per worker). Therefore, total output in the two countries before specialization and trade is 875 000 (500 000 + 375 000) cameras and 3.25 million (1 m. + 2.25 m.) scanners. After specialization and trade, daily output in Callisto is 1 million cameras (200 000 workers x 5 cameras per worker) and daily output in Europa is 4.5 scanners (250 000 workers x 18 scanners per worker). The result is a gain in the two countries' output of both products – 125 000 (1 million - 875 000) more cameras and 1.25 million (4.5 m. - 3.25 m.) more scanners.

Ten Basic Principles

What are the most important lessons to remember from your economics course? Here are ten basic principles you should attempt to retain after your course has ended. These principles will give you crucial insights into the way the world works – not just now but years in the future.

1. (The Definition of Cost) *The cost of something is what must be sacrificed to get it.*
2. (Comparing Costs and Benefits) *Choices depend on weighing costs and benefits.*
3. (Need for Marginal Analysis) *Economic decisions are made at the margin.*
4. (The Value of Competition) *Competitive markets are a useful way to allocate products and resources.*
5. (The Impact of Monopolies) *Monopolies may exploit their privileged position to harm consumers.*
6. (The Role of Government) *Governments must sometimes deal with problems created by market activity.*
7. (The Persistence of Inflation) *Once started, inflation is difficult to stop.*
8. (Inflation and Unemployment) *There is a short-run tradeoff between inflation and unemployment.*
9. (The Benefits of Trade) *Trade brings mutual benefits.*
10. (The Importance of Productivity) *In the long term, higher living standards can come only through increased productivity.*